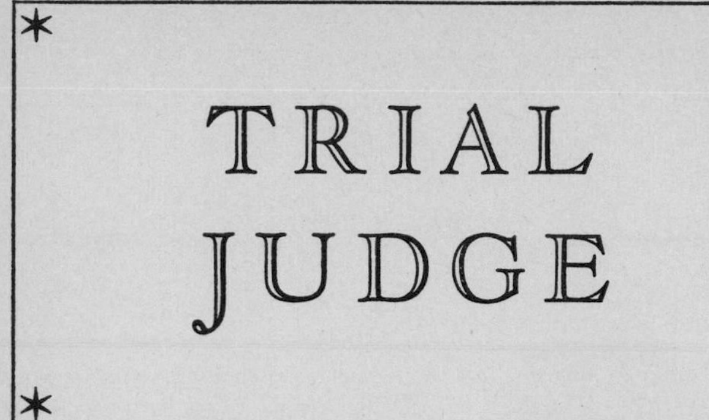

The Candid,
Behind-the-Bench Story
of

JUSTICE BERNARD BOTEIN

Simon and Schuster • New York
1952

PUBLISHED BY SIMON AND SCHUSTER, INC.
ROCKEFELLER CENTER, 630 FIFTH AVENUE,
NEW YORK 20, N. Y.

SECOND PRINTING

Acknowledgments are herewith given to the following organizations and individuals for the right to make certain quotations from previously published works:

AMERICAN INSTITUTE OF PUBLIC OPINION, and DR. GEORGE GALLUP, for statistics obtained in a 1939 poll of American voters concerning their belief in the honesty of federal, state, and local judges.
DOUBLEDAY & COMPANY, INC., for the quotation from *On the Witness Stand,* by Hugo Munsterberg. Copyright 1908, 1923, by Doubleday & Company, Inc.
G. A. JENNINGS CO., INC., for excerpts from *Modern Jury Trials,* by J. W. Donovan, 1929.
LITTLE, BROWN & COMPANY for the quotation from Volume III of the Third Edition of *Wigmore on Evidence,* by John Henry Wigmore, published by Little, Brown & Company.
THE MACMILLAN COMPANY for the quotation from *The Rise of American Civilization,* by Charles and Mary Beard. Copyright, 1933, by the Macmillan Company and used with their permission. Also, for the quotation from *Experience and Education,* by John Dewey. Copyright, 1938, by Kappa Delta Pi and used with the permission of the Macmillan Company. Also, for the quotation from *Gentlemen of the Jury,* by Francis L. Wellman. Copyright, 1924, by the Macmillan Company and used with their permission.
DR. KARL MENNINGER for his letter of September 5, 1933, which appeared in Volume III of the Third Edition of *Wigmore on Evidence,* published by Little, Brown & Company.
ELLERY QUEEN'S MYSTERY MAGAZINE for the quotation from "The Enemy," which first appeared in that magazine. Copyright, 1951, by Charlotte Armstrong and used with permission of Ellery Queen's Mystery Magazine and the author's agent, Brandt & Brandt.
VERNON LAW BOOK COMPANY for the quotation from *Judge and Jury,* by Dean Leon Green, 1930.

MANUFACTURED IN THE UNITED STATES OF AMERICA
BY H. WOLFF BOOK MFG. CO., NEW YORK

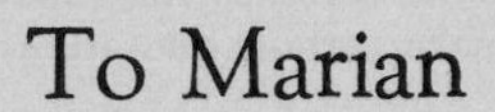

To Marian

CONTENTS

TRIAL JUDGE

* I *

Preparation

THERE IS a modern version of Lord Chancellor Lyndhurst's definition of a good judge: "First, he must be honest. Second, he must possess a reasonable amount of industry. Third, he must have courage. Fourth, he must be a gentleman. And then, if he has some knowledge of law, it will help."

As a practicing lawyer I used to smile at the observation; but I no longer discount its underlying wisdom—not since that afternoon over ten years ago, when I returned to my law offices after a long tax conference.

"Governor Lehman has been trying to reach you from Albany," the switchboard operator told me. She added that two of my law partners wished to see me before I called the Governor. A few minutes later they were in my room.

"I hear the Governor called you," Joe said. "I hope it's not another of those *pro bono publico* appointments. Every time our receptionist gets to know your face, you're off on another public-service junket. After all, you're a senior partner, woe is us, and it works hell with the office."

"Fair is fair," Fred added. "I wouldn't breathe this to a client, but surely there must be at least one other lawyer in the state the Governor can entrust with one of his jobs."

"Stop ribbing me," I said. "Let's find out first what he has in mind."

A few minutes later, the Governor was on the phone. We exchanged a few amenities, and finally he said, "As I imagine you know, Bernie, I've been holding up the appointment of a successor to Judge Church."

Now I could guess the purpose of the call. The Governor never made a judicial appointment unless the Bar Association approved the candidate's character and professional attainments. But, in addition, it was his practice to check the prospective appointee's reputation informally with a few lawyers before submitting his name to the Bar Association.

Of course, we all knew that a vacancy in the Supreme Court had been created by the resignation of Judge Church, and speculation on the subject had been buzzing around law offices for weeks. Naturally I was curious about the name of the lucky man.

The Governor went on, "I've thought a lot about this appointment. There's a letter on my desk to the Bar Association submitting your name for the vacancy. Shall I send it through?"

Somehow I blurted out my acceptance and gratitude. Somehow I told the news to my partners.

Fred shook my hand. "It's terrific," he said.

"I think you're a fool to take a job at that salary," Joe said. "You're earning much more here."

Fred was indignant. "You're crazy; you can't measure a position on the bench in money values. Think of the complete independence a judge has. This isn't just a job, it's a new way of life."

Fred had expressed it perfectly. There were mighty few lawyers, I thought, who would not forsake all other possible professional rewards for the law's crowning opportunity to render fulfilling and dedicated service. Some merely indulged the fancy, much as a boy dreams of becoming a big-league ballplayer. Others did something about it; they entered politics, communal fields, any avenue which might lead to a judgeship.

But few could succeed in this unpredictable and sometimes

heartbreaking quest. Too many factors had to mesh, along with the standard ingredients for success. A candidate, to be selected over scores of rivals, might have to be a member of the "right" party, of the "right" religious or civic group—not necessarily the dominant one—might have to live in the right district; and all of these might have to combine at the right time.

Now, when I realized that I had been selected without even the sponsorship of my political party, I felt a sense of unreality, as though my partners and I were talking about some other man. The telephone bell interrupted us.

"Mr. Warren Moscow of *The New York Times*," my secretary said.

"Put him on," I said. I had met Moscow, a well-known and astute political reporter.

"Congratulations, Judge," said Moscow. "How does it feel to be struck by lightning?"

"What do you mean?" I asked, following the instinct of public servants everywhere to admit nothing until it has been announced officially.

"I've just heard through the grapevine that the Governor is going to appoint you to the Supreme Court. He isn't going along with the party's candidate. The politicians have a phrase for that, Judge. You've been struck by lightning."

I knew Moscow well enough to give him his confirmation, off the record, and hung up.

The telephone bell rang again. This time it was Alfred A. Cook, chairman of the awesome Judiciary Committee of the Bar Association, which would report to the Governor. Cook was an old friend, but one would never have guessed it from the clipped, precise tone in which he spoke.

"The Governor's secretary has just called," he said. "We would like to sit down with you at my office, the day after tomorrow, at 10:30 A.M. Meanwhile, I'd appreciate it if you'd send me at your earliest convenience a biographical sketch, emphasizing your professional experience, trials, appeals and so forth, and copies of some briefs you have written."

I hung up. I had been brought back sharply to a cold world of comparative professional values.

"Hold everything," I said to my partners. "That stroke of lightning may still pass me by."

I was jittery during the next forty-eight hours. Although my court experience early in my career had been varied and intensive, in recent years I had conducted investigations which did not entail the trial of civil cases. As a member of a large law firm with almost departmentalized activities, I had practiced more before administrative agencies than the courts. How would the committee feel about this soft underbelly of my experience? I tried to anticipate every question that might be put to me and to muster up satisfactory answers and arguments.

Where did an aspirant for the judiciary begin in reviewing his career? With the cradle, with his admission to the bar? So many accidents had conspired to bring me to the threshold; so many temptations had been avoided, sometimes for reasons unclear to me. Would temptation overcome at one time or in one guise have prevailed at another time or in another guise?

I remembered an episode during my first year at the bar, when I had a very modest office, high hopes, and no clients. The long periods of inactivity were filled with financial anxieties and the mental stagnation of idleness. One afternoon the girl whose services I shared with three other lawyers informed me over the interoffice telephone that a Mr. Snow was in the outer office and wished to see me. I did not know a Mr. Snow.

"He says Mr. Elliott referred him to you about a case."

"Send him in," I said.

I knew Elliott only slightly. He was an older lawyer who maintained a busy, bustling office in my building. He was very successful, the envy of us younger, struggling men; I was puzzled that he should refer a case to me.

Snow was a pudgy, middle-aged man, who seated himself deliberately and ponderously. He drew the very moist end of a fat cigar from between thick lips and held it out in front of him, as though waiting for it to drip off. Then he studied me benignly, without saying a word. The cigar ashes dropped on my carpet, something which could be forgiven in a client.

Finally I said, "I understand Mr. Elliott has recommended me to you."

"Yes, he told me you were a bright young feller who needed some business."

"Well," I said with a nervous laugh, "there are mighty few lawyers who can't use more business."

"That's very true," said Snow, jabbing his cigar at me for emphasis, "but not in Jack Elliott's case. He's one lawyer who has more business than he can handle. And that's why he sent me here. Y'see, I'm an investigator."

My eagerness subsided.

"I rarely have business for an investigator," I said. "I thought you wanted to consult me about a case."

"Right you are," he said. "I never take up a man's time under false pretenses. I have an accident case that I've thoroughly investigated and it's a honey; family man, slipped on a defective step, insured building, fractured leg, good liability."

I now understood too clearly the purpose of Snow's visit. He was an "ambulance chaser," a man with sources for procuring accident cases for lawyers, and he was trying to sell me a case. A slow anger welled up in me, but so did a certain curiosity.

"Why did Elliott send you to me?" I asked.

"I told you, counselor. He's loaded up with more cases than he can handle, and he wants to lay off for a while. He said there were some nice young fellers in this office, and I'm giving you first crack."

I said nothing, but Snow was not at all discouraged.

"I gotta retainer here, all signed, calling for fifty per cent of any recovery," he went on, smoothing out a paper. "The name of the lawyer ain't filled in yet. All you gotta do is pay me five hundred bucks on account of my investigating fee and I'll write in your name. I can settle this case next week for at least five thousand bucks. That means a twenty-five-hundred-dollar fee, which we split. I give you credit for the five hundred, so you take seventeen fifty and I take seven fifty."

"I'm not interested in buying any cases," I said.

"You ain't buying any cases, counselor. We form a sort of a partnership. I take half the fee for my investigation. You take half for your legal services. You just advance me part of my share. To get started, I'll even shade the five hundred for you."

"Not interested," I repeated.

"Look," he said, "after the first case is settled, you don't have to lay out any more dough. I'll settle this case quick. I know the ropes. I'll prepare the cases, speak to the witnesses; you won't even see the plaintiff unless the case goes to trial."

"Then why do you need me?" I asked.

"Young feller, if I had your license to practice law, I wouldn't need you." He pointed his cigar at me again and again flicked ashes on the carpet.

"You'd better go," I said. "I told you I'm not interested."

"Don't get huffy, counselor. Sam Snow has made rich men of higher-class fellers than you."

"Get out!" I said, rising from my chair. He got out.

A few months later an ambulance-chasing investigation was launched in New York by the Supreme Court. Sam Snow was one of the most colorful figures under investigation. His records were seized, a number of lawyers who did business with him were publicized in the newspapers, and they became the subjects of disciplinary proceedings.

Of course, it's unethical for lawyers to solicit legal business—at least, in so direct and crude a manner as ambulance chasing. It is also unethical for a lawyer to split fees with a layman. As a young lawyer I was thoroughly indoctrinated with these canons of ethics.

I'm pretty sure these deeply rooted concepts prompted my rejection of Snow's proposition. Still, I wondered whether I shouldn't credit Sam Snow's repellent personality and cigar ashes with an assist. Was it a matter of aesthetics as well as of ethics that the precarious life line to a judgeship had not been cut?

The Judiciary Committee could not undertake to peer behind the professional façade of an applicant for judicial office. And yet, I reflected, my career and character had already been influenced by experiences seemingly far removed from a judge's job. Long before the Governor thought of appointing me to the bench, long before I ever thought of becoming a lawyer, irrevocable strengths and weaknesses, perceptions and prejudices were being locked into my personality.

Even a seemingly trivial boyhood incident had played its part, an incident stemming from a broken wrist. This calamity prevented me from playing first base for my neighborhood team in the local playground series, but gave me my first experience as an umpire.

The playground instructor, noticing the sling on my arm, drafted me for the job. There was some muttered and ineffectual opposition by our opponents. "What a break for us," one of my teammates whispered.

Everything went along smoothly until the fifth inning, when the score was tied at six to six. My team was at bat, with two out and a man on third. The hitter rapped a sharp grounder to the second baseman. He fumbled it momentarily but recovered and whipped the ball to first. Meanwhile the runner on third had crossed the plate. I had followed the play intently. I knew the man was out at first by a split second, which meant the side was out, the run didn't score, and we were still in a tied game. But the play was very close, and a decision that the batter was safe would not be considered too infamous, especially since, by sand-lot practice, a slight edge toward his own team was expected from boy umpires.

I made the mistake of appearing as indecisive as I felt—an error no experienced umpire or judge ever makes. Even when a seasoned arbiter is uncertain he will reserve decision or rule with the blandest assurance and authority.

Members of both teams swarmed onto the diamond, one group shouting, "He's safe!" the other, "He's out!" One enthusiastic supporter of the other team shrieked, "You call him safe and we'll beat your brains out."

Before I could react to the threat and establish my manhood by calling the runner safe, another voice cut through. A lean, weather-beaten man had joined us. We knew him as a spectator-coach for the opposing team who appeared at the playground for all weekend games. His son played third base for the opposition.

"Did you see the play, umpire?" he asked.

"Sure."

"Then call it as you saw it. That's what you were put in for. Whether you call him safe or out, we won't squawk. Now break it up, fellows."

In a burst of certainty I snapped, "He's out!"

Two hours later, as our team was trudging home, a badly beaten lot, one of the boys said to me, "You sure were no help."

I was unable to explain my decision to my teammates any better than I could to myself, but instinctively I avoided one major mistake. I did not moralize. They didn't pay off on righteousness in my neighborhood.

"Aw," I said, "Joe was out by a mile. I couldn't call it any other way."

"Like hell he was," said one of the rooters.

The refrain was caught up by the others, with varying ripe embellishments. Suddenly there came a reprieve.

"Drop it, fellas, I was out," Joe said unexpectedly. The United States Marines to the rescue couldn't have been more welcome.

By some alchemy this incident gave me a reputation for being a fair and yet a regular fellow. During the remainder of the baseball season I was called upon to umpire a number of times, often in games in which my team did not participate.

I learned to don that aspect of neutrality and incuriosity shared in common by umpires and judges. I made my decisions with sureness and finality, no matter how slightly the scales tipped. I never explained or discussed my decisions, beyond coldly stating that a ball had cut the outside corner or was low. When irate players sought to pursue the matter further I turned my back and studiously gazed at the sky.

Perhaps this boyhood incident should have imbued me then and there with a consuming passion for the law, and planted my feet firmly on the path to a judgeship. I could then have looked forward to facing the august members of the Judiciary Committee with the reassuring feeling that I had been called to the law. That might make an impressive story of juvenile dedication. Impressive but untrue.

Actually, seven years later, I was treading water in an arts course in the College of the City of New York, with no decision about a career beyond a vague inclination toward journalism.

During my freshman summer I worked as a copy boy on one of the large metropolitan newspapers. The chief clerk of the morgue or reference room was Dunn, an old character who had run the gamut from copy boy to publisher.

A warm friendship developed between us. Usually he snorted at journalism as a calling no sensible man would touch. But when his eyes were especially watery, his nose red and his breath strong, journalism was elevated to the ranks of a hallowed and noble profession, and we spent hours together while he related, and probably invented, anecdotes of a bygone era.

Naturally enough, I was seeing less and less of the neighborhood gang, but one Sunday I made a nostalgic visit to Frenchy's ice cream parlor and spotted an old friend. Pete Rizzutti came limping in with a cane. He told me that he had been working in the shipping room of a clothing manufacturer when one day his older brother Tony dropped in just before quitting time.

"I told Tony to wait a minute till I got my street clothes from the locker. Before I could move a step, wham! a big bolt of cloth falls from a shelf and hits the both of us. My ankle was busted but Tony was even worse. He got it in the shoulder, the neck, and the back."

Fortunately, if one could put it that way, Pete had been injured in his employer's place of business during working hours, so he was entitled to workmen's compensation payments. He would get fifteen dollars a week until he recovered, and his hospital and doctor's bills were being paid.

"How's Tony doing?" I asked.

"Tough. Ain't worked for eight weeks ever since the accident. Looks like he won't work for six months at least." What was more, Tony was married and his wife was pregnant. Everybody was after him for rent and furniture installments. Pete slipped him a few dollars now and then and the folks tried to help out but it didn't go far.

"Y'see, Tony wasn't working in his own place when he got hurt —so no compensation for him. Looks like he'll have to take charity till he's okay again."

"Hasn't he some kind of a law case?" I asked.

"Oh, sure. But he's gotta wait three years before his case will be reached."

"Three years! Can't his lawyer do something about it?"

"Nope. The lawyer's anxious enough for a quick trial. He gets half the dough."

Monday evening I found Dunn puttering about the morgue as usual, and I gave him a heated account of Tony's difficulties. Dunn was vaguely sympathetic.

"Don't you get it?" I said. "They were hit by the same roll of cloth! Why should they be treated differently?"

Dunn shrugged. Then he said suddenly, "Say, you want to be a journalist. Why don't you interview Tony and write a story showing what a rough deal he's had compared with Pete? It could run two columns. Swell counterpoint. Two brothers hurt in same accident. One comfortable, pleased, and happy with compensation payments, the other miserable, desperate, and sore at society."

"Would you help me with it?"

"Sure. You get over to Tony's house tomorrow afternoon and we'll knock out the story at night."

Next day I found Tony propped up in bed and wearing a steel brace. He readily agreed that he'd had a tough break.

"It's a damn shame you can't get compensation like Pete," I

prompted, hoping to draw out my subject like a veteran feature writer.

"Pete? He's gettin' peanuts. Who wants compensation? I'm goin' to knock my case over for ten, maybe twenty thousand bucks."

I stared at him. "But you'll have to wait so long. And suppose you lose."

"I can't lose. I gotta great lawyer. Knows all the ropes. It's got compensation beat a mile." Tony refused to let any talk of social justice mar his vision of riches.

That night, when I told Dunn about the frustrating interview, he laughed.

"You're not the first reformer to be repulsed by the object of his fervor. Look," he added, "if you're so eager to cure the ills of society there are other ways besides journalism."

"You prodding me to study law again?"

"Why not? Lawyers have probably contributed more than any other group to the molding of this country. And if you don't scale the peaks, you can still lead a useful life in your community."

This was an old argument between us. I shook my head. "It doesn't sound very exciting—spending your life with a bunch of dry, musty books. . . ."

"There wasn't anything dry and musty about Hamilton or Marshall or Webster or Lincoln." Dunn walked to the filing cabinets which lined the walls. "Go on, pick one of these files out—any one. Let's see how lawyers stack up—just how useful and romantic their lives are compared with other people's." He pulled open a drawer. "Here's one marked DA to DE. Let's begin with this."

Recalling this episode years later, I wondered about Dunn's choice of the filing cabinet drawer. Was it mere accident that it had contained the envelopes of such men as Clarence Darrow and John W. Davis?

Accident or no, here I was, a lawyer preparing personal and professional data for the Judiciary Committee. I managed somehow to worry through the next two days. At last the time set for my interview arrived.

When I entered the room there were about ten committee members present.

Cook, the chairman, introduced me. "Gentlemen, our new judge." He beamed. "You were approved unanimously ten minutes ago."

Later, at lunch with Cook in the relaxed atmosphere of a downtown club, I said, "If you'll promise me as a gentleman and a lawyer not to revoke the committee's approval, I'll make a confession."

The chairman smiled. "Go ahead. I think I can guess, though."

"You mean that I was worried? Then tell me, how did your committee come to approve a lawyer of my uneven and cockeyed experience with such a superficial inquiry?"

"Not superficial at all," Cook said. "After all, we've all known you for years. We think we know the kind of man you are. That's more important than the kind of legal technician you are." And then he quoted the definition of a good judge with which this chapter opens.

"Of course," the chairman went on, "we expect and demand professional competence, independence, and integrity, and we hope for that rare commodity, moral courage. We also expect a judge to have a decent regard for the rights and feelings of others. Nobody, not even the losing litigant or his lawyer, should ever leave the courthouse bruised in personal dignity or spirit, or feeling that his day in court has been pile-driven into minutes or seconds by an impatient judge. He goes home at night to a wife, to children, to parents, friends. He should leave the courthouse with his self-respect unimpaired." He smiled. "We don't expect miracles—but I'm confident you'll justify our faith."

Two days later a newly hatched judge paid his first visit to the courthouse. Diffidently, I entered the office of the chief clerk and asked one of the deputies for Mr. Murphy.

"What name, please?" he asked perfunctorily.

He was given the name and suddenly, with a "Yes, Judge," he jackknifed out of his chair and rushed into Murphy's room. That was the judge's first taste of his changed status.

Murphy informed me that my chambers were ready for occupancy. I was led to the private elevator for judges, which went to the sixth floor. Its very existence was a revelation. Before, I had always hurled myself into the crowded public elevators.

We stepped out of the elevator and made our way down the corridor.

Now at last I was entering the sacrosanct precincts which had always seemed so far removed. It would take me weeks merely to adapt myself to the new physical accommodations. Formerly, I made my way to the courtroom through crowded halls. Now, a personal attendant would precede me majestically through winding, private passageways, designed to shield His Honor from the public view. I had been accustomed to wait in the courtroom for the judge to appear, and to rise upon his entrance. Now the situation was reversed. A hundred little attentions would be forced upon me daily; irksome, even embarrassing at first, but taken for granted as time wore on.

As Murphy and I walked along I read the names of my associate justices on the doors leading to their chambers. Justices Wasservogel, Pecora, Rosenman, McGeehan, Collins—a great array to a neophyte judge who had practiced law for many years in that judicial district.

And then, suddenly, there it was. A door. A neatly printed card bearing the legend, "Mr. Justice Botein." I stopped in full stride; then, feeling a bit lightheaded, I walked into my chambers.

"I hope this will do for just now," Murphy apologized. "Later on you can furnish it to your own taste."

"It's fine, fine, thank you." At that moment I wouldn't have minded if the room had been furnished with egg crates. I was relieved when Murphy left me alone with my new surroundings, my new identity.

I was a judge, a real judge with my own chambers; and yet I

had not consciously planned any of the steps along the way. It was sheer accident that had propelled me into politics, into holding public office, into attracting the attention of a governor.

I went into politics because a minor politician refused to pay a tailor's bill. The tailor was one of my first clients, after I was admitted to the bar.

He had made and delivered two suits and an overcoat to a local politician, one O'Ryan, who had a job in a city department. O'Ryan had ignored all requests for payment.

On the day the case came up for trial I arrived in the courtroom twenty minutes early, answered ready for the plaintiff, and then stepped outside to telephone my client to come to court. The tailor arrived shortly, we reviewed his testimony, then entered the courtroom and found seats.

I had estimated that my case wouldn't be reached for trial for about an hour. But when the hour had passed and it was still not called I timorously approached the calendar clerk.

That harassed man snapped, "Your case was called and dismissed because no one answered for the plaintiff. Where were you, counselor?"

"But I answered ready on the general call."

"That's right, counselor. I got it marked that way. Then it was called again for trial and no one answered, so the judge dismissed it."

"But it must have been called out of turn. I wasn't gone more than fifteen minutes. Look at your calendar. Cases marked ready ahead of mine are still being held in this part."

The clerk said angrily, "What are you trying to insinuate, counselor?"

Suddenly the judge interrupted. "What's the trouble down there?"

When I explained the problem the judge said firmly, "There's nothing I can do in the absence of your adversary. You'll have to make a motion. The case stands dismissed. Step aside, young man, we have a heavy calendar today."

My spirits sank. I had practically lost the case before it started.

This was certainly no way to build up a practice in the neighborhood. I made a motion to restore the case to the calendar, the motion to be returnable the following month, when it would be heard by another judge. Everything now hinged on whether the second judge would restore the case.

The date arrived and upon the argument of the motion I again explained what had happened. Strangely, my adversary did not dispute the facts but simply argued that the default should not be opened.

To my delight, the judge said, "Surely you can't contend that the plaintiff should be deprived of his day in court on such a state of facts?"

"Well, if Your Honor feels that way," the opposing lawyer said, "you should at least give us a full bill of costs."

Since the case had been dismissed through no fault of my client, I would pay such costs out of my own pocket. I fumed at the prospect—not only because the payment would be a financial hardship, but because I felt, probably wrongly, that the calendar clerk had corruptly maneuvered the dismissal of my tailor's case.

But I could not tell this to the judge. I could not tell him that the defendant and his lawyer were active members of the local political club. How does one get to a judge, I wondered—get to him just enough to stir up his liver a bit, to stimulate him into being an active rather than a static element in the dispute? What is it that ticks behind that imposing façade, and how is that ticking translated into decisions?

When the judge asked me if I wished to oppose the imposition of costs, I answered, hotly if irrelevantly, "The defendant doesn't really need the costs. He's had various city jobs most of his life."

The judge lifted his head at this statement. The opposing lawyer blustered, "What has that to do with the merits of this motion?"

"Nothing whatsoever," agreed the judge, "but I shall grant this motion without costs."

I breathed a silent hallelujah!

At last the case came before a third judge, without a jury. The tailor testified that the defendant had been brought to his shop by an old customer; he had ordered two suits and an overcoat; he had been measured, fitted, and had expressed complete satisfaction with the garments. The agreed price was one hundred and eighty dollars.

"What did you do with these garments after you had finished them?" I asked my client.

"I send dem to O'Ryan wid my boy," the tailor answered.

"Move to strike the answer out," the opposing attorney rasped. "Hearsay, not binding on the defendant, only the boy is competent to testify to delivery."

"Motion granted. Strike it out," said the judge.

I was caught off guard. The errand boy was no longer in the employ of the tailor, and it hadn't occurred to me that we would need his testimony. After all, the defendant had admitted to the tailor that he had received the clothing; in fact, he had worn one of the suits and the overcoat when he had asked the tailor for an extension of time to pay, after the original summons had been served.

Moreover, I had not prepared the tailor to testify along these lines. And owing to language difficulties I was afraid to invade an uncharted area of questioning without a measure of indulgence from the judge.

"Did your boy bring back this receipt?" I asked the tailor.

"Sure."

"I offer it in evidence, Your Honor."

"I object, Your Honor," shouted the defendant's lawyer. "There's no proof it was signed by my client."

The judge was a little impatient. "Do you deny that this is the defendant's signature?"

"I don't know, Your Honor, and my duty to my client therefore requires me to object."

The judge snorted. "Where is your client? Isn't he going to testify?"

"No, Your Honor. He—er—had some important business to transact and I didn't think his evidence was essential to defeat this trumped-up claim."

"We'll see about that. Do you really contend your client didn't receive these clothes?"

"Your Honor, to establish his case the plaintiff must prove the clothes were delivered to my client. I have no authority to make any concessions which will help the plaintiff make out his case."

The judge turned to the tailor. "After the clothes left your shop did you see the defendant?"

"Sure. He come to my shop and wear my suit and coat."

"Did he say anything to you?"

"He say fit fine, no kick. All clothes I make fit fine. Cheap too. He say his fren' my customer suppose' to pay. I say I don' know about that."

"That's all," said the judge. "Plaintiff rests." To the defendant's lawyer, "Any defense, counselor?"

"No, Your Honor. I rest and move to dismiss on the ground the plaintiff has failed to make out a case. He . . ."

"Motion denied. Judgment directed in favor of plaintiff in the sum of one hundred and eighty dollars with interest and costs. Next case."

A few days later O'Ryan invaded my office. He was a massive, middle-aged Irishman with bright blue eyes and a ruddy complexion. "I know when I'm licked," he said and grinned. "I've come to make the best deal I can."

I was still smarting from the pushing around O'Ryan had given me, but I had to resist an impulse to grin back.

"You see," the politician went on, "I won an election bet and those suits were supposed to be paid for by the guy who lost. Then I get the bill and he takes a powder."

"That's not the fault of the little tailor. Incidentally, does your lawyer know you're here?"

"Sure. He sent me up to try and knock something off."

After O'Ryan had paid up—in full—and been handed a receipt, he showed no disposition to leave. "Say, do you belong to any political club?" he asked.

"No."

"You're making a mistake, fella. No lawyer can get far in this town unless he's got political connections. You get to know the judges, your clients have more respect for you, once in a while you get a juicy reference."

I tried not to sound stuffy as I pointed out that I'd rather stick to the law, and besides, I didn't see how I could be an asset to any club. Nevertheless, I sensed a glimmering of interest within myself. I was finding it difficult to dislike O'Ryan.

He wasn't easily discouraged. "Listen, our club's a sleeper for a bright young lawyer. We got three guys on the D.A.'s staff who should be resigning sooner or later. When they do our leader recommends the men who fill their spots. And we ain't got three lawyers in our club under sixty-five years of age."

"No, thanks, O'Ryan. I don't think I've got the taste for district politics. . . ."

"Not got the taste, huh!" O'Ryan barked. "You think you're too good for politics. You and your fancy-pants crowd—always bellyachin' about dirty politics but you'll never lift a finger to help clean it up. You gimme a pain!"

I straightened in my chair. "You know," I said slowly, "one of my college professors used to talk that way too."

"No college professor ever talked the way I do," O'Ryan said, and he grinned again.

When he finally left, his club had acquired a new member. And his advice proved fruitful.

I served several years on the district attorney's staff and then was designated by the Bar Association to investigate accident frauds. Following that, I was appointed by Governor Lehman to conduct special investigations into state printing and workmen's compensation insurance frauds.

In heading these special investigations I possessed powers greater than I had ever exercised in the district attorney's office, greater than most judges ever exercise. A special prosecutor has the authority to launch inquiry in many directions. He has the power to decide when to prosecute and when not to prosecute—and the power to prosecute is often the power to destroy. These powers carry fearful responsibilities, which weigh heavily and leave a lifetime impression upon any man charged with their fulfillment.

The workmen's compensation investigation had come about as the result of suspected collusion between many employers and the state's payroll auditors who were reporting only a fraction of actual payrolls. Since compensation insurance premiums were charged on the basis of the amount of the payrolls, the State Insurance Fund was cheated out of millions of dollars annually. A tidy windfall if the employers could get away with it—and many were getting away with it.

One of the businessmen under scrutiny was Brown, a man of good reputation who headed a well-rated firm. His books had been examined and showed a payroll differential of four hundred thousand dollars. This meant a premium shortage of thirty thousand dollars. Confronted with the discrepancy, Brown didn't bother to dispute any item. He readily, almost too readily, admitted the fraud and offered to pay the difference immediately.

One morning my assistant, Jim, came in for a hurried conference. With him was Ed, the supervising auditor on Brown's case.

"Say, chief," Jim said, "there are some entries in Brown's books that have us puzzled. Ed, you explain it."

The auditor flattened out a large accountant's work sheet. "Here it is. During the last two years Brown's books show a number of large cash withdrawals that are charged to payroll. Here's one for five thousand, one for two thousand, another for twenty-five hundred, all round figures and coming to about fifty thousand each year."

"And there's something peculiar about the items?" I said.

"Damned peculiar. They're not withdrawn on paydays and they haven't any characteristics that tie them in with payroll expenditures." He hesitated. "Chief, my bet is that they don't represent payroll at all."

Jim chimed in at this point. "Yet Brown concedes them to be payroll and he's ready to shell out the additional premiums calculated on these amounts."

I frowned. "In other words, those payments could represent

something worse than compensation fraud that Brown wants to conceal, something so bad he is ready to include them within the compensation offense, since he's hooked on that anyway."

"Right, chief."

"How do you fellows figure it?"

Jim gave me the facts. Brown did a good deal of public works contracting for the city, and they had noticed that all the checks in question were cashed within five days after he received payment from the city and that they were roughly four per cent of the city payments.

Jim summed it up. "We think they represent pay-offs to city officials."

I nodded. "Nice work. Let's get Brown in."

When Brown appeared at the investigation offices, he doggedly maintained that the cash proceeds of the checks were used for payroll purposes. He was shown entry after entry in his own books which refuted his contention and which proved conclusively that they could not be payroll expenditures. But he stuck to his story.

Finally, I had to play my trump card.

"I'm sorry, Mr. Brown," I said, "but your story just doesn't hold water. I'm going to send whatever evidence we have on this feature of the case to the district attorney."

Brown grew pale. "Why the district attorney?"

"Because we believe that these sums represent bribes to public officials or some other form of slush fund that you're trying to cover up."

Brown was quite still. The man who had parried questions so nimbly a few moments before seemed to sag. At last he spoke.

"You're all young men," he said tonelessly. "I'm middle-aged. I have a wife and children whom I love, a beautiful home, and a position of leadership in church and community affairs."

It had been bad enough pleading guilty to the compensation fraud, he went on, still in the same leaden voice, but there at least all of his colleagues had been involved, and there was no publicity. If we went into these other things, he'd never be able to stand up under it.

"I'm tired, awfully tired. Gentlemen, if you persist in hounding me, I'll have to go where you can't follow me—right out of my office window."

The man was shaking. He tried to clasp his hands in the vain hope of steadying them. I felt a little sick.

I said, "Common sense must tell you that no matter how sympathetic I may be I still have a duty to perform. I just can't drop a matter as serious as this. Why don't you go home and tell your wife everything?"

"I couldn't face her with this."

"Don't underestimate her. Go home and tell her. I'll hold everything off until tomorrow afternoon. If I haven't heard from you by then I'll proceed along the lines I've indicated."

As I watched Brown leave my uneasiness increased. This whole business was too close to playing God for comfort.

Jim said, "Chief, do you really think—?"

I tried to sound cheerful. "Don't worry," I said. "He'll live to a ripe old age." But I was whistling in the dark and we all knew it.

Jim and I took dinner in a near-by restaurant, then returned to the office for an evening's work. As we came in, the relief operator said urgently, "Chief, I've got a Mrs. Brown on the wire. She's already called three times. . . ."

My God, I thought, this is it. I grabbed a telephone.

The voice at the other end was agitated. "I just wanted you to know my husband has told me everything. We're going to see this through together. He'll be in your office tomorrow morning." Her voice shook. "Please be considerate of him." She hung up.

"What happened, chief?" asked Jim.

"Come on downstairs with me. I want to drown some butterflies in a double Scotch."

Those butterflies were an uncomfortably vivid memory as I sat, a Supreme Court Justice, in my chambers in the New York County Courthouse. In fact, they had begun to flutter again. I jumped when the telephone jangled, then slowly lifted it.

"This is the clerk of Trial Term IV, Judge," said a cheerful voice. "I heard you were in the building. You know, you're assigned to my part and I thought you'd like to look at the pleadings in your first two cases."

"What kind are they?"

"Oh, a negligence case and a work, labor, and services case."

"Fine. Would you mind bringing them up?"

"I'll be right there."

I welcomed the interruption as a call to action and an end to further retrospection. But the looking back had been good for me. I had recalled nothing which should block my development into a good judge; I might even have acquired certain immunities and strengths which could nourish that development. No lawyer ever sprang to the bench a full-grown judge—not even Brandeis, who, as Felix Frankfurter said, "came to the court with his mind dyed, as it were, in the very issues which became his chief judicial concern."

I thought ruefully of how I had worried lest the Judiciary Committee should punch holes through the thin areas of my professional background. I should have known that seasoned attorneys would not look only to the technical proficiency of the lawyer. At times lawyers appearing before brilliant judges would trade off a measure of brilliancy for some understanding and restraint. I was what I was, I concluded, and I would dedicate myself to building on that foundation.

There was a knock on the door and I called, "Come in."

The job had begun.

* II *

My First Case

MY FIRST ASSIGNMENT was to a trial term, a part of the court devoted exclusively to the trial of lawsuits. To get the "feel" of the bench, I sat alongside Judge Pecora, in his courtroom, for several hours. I soon became somewhat conditioned to the altitude from the bench—but I was seated alongside the pilot. I still had to make my solo flight.

My induction ceremony took place the following afternoon. Next morning, the pageantry was over, the laudatory speeches forgotten. I took a cold plunge into reality, in the trial term courtroom to which I was assigned. This was one of twenty courtrooms in the building, each administered by a judge. Collectively they process the endless variety of matters which surge into the court.

Before I ascended the bench that morning I had already lost an encounter. It is much more comfortable to wear the billowing silk judicial robe over shirt sleeves, and I tried to convince my personal attendant that I had spent a lifetime donning and doffing my own jacket. He gravely assured me that in twenty-five years he had never permitted a judge to perform that sacred rite for himself. It was evident that nothing would move so massive a formation of precedent and resolution, so I yielded.

A door led from the robing room directly out to the bench. As

I passed through it a court attendant "Hear ye!" 'd and everyone rose. I was about to preside over my first trial. I seated myself and soon shook off the vertigo which assailed me as I looked down upon the arena from which I had for so many years looked up.

Fortunately, I have preserved the bound volumes in which I recorded—somewhat undiscriminatingly—the evidence of those early trials. Some judges outline laboriously all of the evidence; others note only the evidence which they consider significant, using a form of judicial shorthand. I have seen one judge digest several hours of expert testimony as follows: "Dr. X; as usual, phony neurological build-up."

I have been leafing through my old notebooks. Worldly college seniors probably glance at their freshman notes with the same amused indulgence. I now realize that a few words will capture such evidence as clearly as did a closely written page when I first became a judge.

But I have not declined to the habits of Charles Dickens' Judge Stareleigh. Awakened by the silence which ensued when a barrister in the Pickwick case paused for breath, he "immediately wrote down something with a pen without any ink in it, and looked unusually profound, to impress the jury with the belief that he always thought most deeply with his eyes shut."

Still, as I scan my notes on the first case tried before me, I am grateful for the inclusion of so many entries which I no longer find it necessary to make. That was over ten years ago, and my original fresh, inquiring delight in the judicial processes is beginning to merge into certain unquestioning routines of performance. This is irrecoverable material, illuminated by my copious notes, with which to bind the matrix of my impressions of the past ten years. It was the very small beginning of a chronicle of experience and know-how which in time would make me confident of my ability to cope with almost any technical judicial problem—even though at first I might not know the answer.

Everything was brisk and businesslike on the morning of my judicial baptism. The two lawyers representing the parties in the case to be tried were pleasant enough, but this was part of their design for living—and of earning a living. Their chief concern with my maiden judicial effort, most likely, was whether in my inexperience I would commit reversible error and, if so, to whose advantage.

This first case presented no difficult legal problems, but it was based on an unusual set of facts. The plaintiff and the defendant had been friends for twenty years. The plaintiff occupied a summer cottage where the defendant was a frequent weekend guest.

One morning the friends hired a flat-bottomed rowboat and went fishing for black bass in a near-by lake. For half an hour as the boat drifted they fished, without bite or incident. Then the defendant rowed the boat to another part of the lake, to try their luck there. Suddenly, the plaintiff testified, the defendant stopped rowing, picked up his fishing pole, and "made a very bad cast."

The defendant's attorney jumped to his feet and moved to strike out the testimony. I was required to make my first ruling as a judge. Happily, it was an easy one. The answer was conclusory, i.e., it was improper for the plaintiff to characterize the cast. He could describe the manner in which it was made, but it was for the jury to decide whether it was a good or bad cast.

I granted the motion, struck the answer from the record, and huskily admonished the jury to disregard it.

Then the plaintiff's lawyer sought to elicit from him the accepted and proper methods of casting from a rowboat. The defendant's lawyer objected that this called for expert testimony, and that the plaintiff had not been qualified as an expert. This too was a simple ruling. I sustained the objection.

Thereupon the plaintiff's lawyer sought to qualify him as an expert, by asking him how long and how often he had fished for black bass from rowboats, whether he had done so in the company of other fishermen, whether he had observed their methods, and whether he had read magazine articles and books on fishing. He then asked him whether he could form an opinion with reasonable certainty as to whether an overhead cast was the proper method, and a sideways or lateral cast an improper one.

The defendant's attorney objected that on this meager experience the plaintiff could not be qualified as an expert. I overruled the objection and ruled that he had been qualified sufficiently to testify as an expert; that it was for the jury, after considering his alleged qualifications, to decide how much weight should be given to his opinion.

I recall my sense of wonder at the alchemy which now transformed my judicial impression of the law into the actual law—at least the law of this case for the duration of the trial. As a lawyer, my impression of the law had been no more than a basis for argument. I had now experienced firsthand the thesis of John Chipman Gray that the law is that which a court says is the law.

The plaintiff went on to testify that the overhead was the proper casting method. He said the defendant had slashed the hooks into his face with a horizontal cast. The defendant tried to remove the hooks, said the plaintiff, "but my face went with them." The pole was weighing the hooks down, so the defendant cut the line, and rowed the plaintiff, hooks in face, to shore for relief.

There was more testimony by the plaintiff and by the surgeon who removed the hooks. There were more objections and a motion by the defendant's attorney to dismiss the complaint at the close of the plaintiff's case. From the vantage point of ten years of experience my rulings on objections and my denial of the motion to dismiss appear somehow to have been substantially correct.

The presentation of the plaintiff's case had consumed the morning. After the luncheon recess, the attorneys approached the bench.

"Judge," began the attorney for the defendant, "my company had marked the case 'no settlement,' because it didn't want to encourage this type of claim."

"Your company?" I echoed. "What do you mean?"

"Why, I represent the Freedom Mutual Insurance Company," he replied. "We insure the defendant under a comprehensive liability policy."

This was my first inkling that the defendant was insured, and that the lawsuit was being defended on his behalf by an insurance company. The accident was certainly not one of a type covered by the more familiar forms of liability insurance.

I would now recognize the lawyer defending the suit as a member of the legal staff of the insurance company; over the years he has appeared before me often. But as a lawyer I had handled very few accident cases, and so, as a tyro judge, I could not identify him.

He went on to tell me that during the luncheon recess he had called the claims manager and told him that both parties appeared to be decent fellows, and that the plaintiff had seemingly made a good impression.

"My claims manager finally said," the lawyer went on, "that he would pay something, but nothing in the neighborhood of what such injuries would be worth in another kind of case."

"Well, we can't quarrel with that policy," I said. "I suppose insurance companies want to discourage claims brought by friend against friend."

During the morning I had noticed an unnatural amiability between the parties, unnatural in light of the fact that two former close friends were engaged in a lawsuit. Under such circumstances, one would expect great bitterness.

"We'd like to discourage them, but we can't," the lawyer replied. "We can just about imagine what happens in some cases. The injured party asks his friend, 'Are you insured?' The friend answers 'Sure.' Then the injured party says, 'I was really hurt in that accident. Do you mind if I sue you and get myself a few bucks?' It's what's known as a 'guest case' in claim circles. But jurors are pretty smart. They probably figure out there's an insurance company to pay the verdict, so they give verdicts to guests almost as readily as they do to strangers."

"Then why are you prepared to pay only a small sum in settlement?" I asked.

"Because this accident is so unusual that we don't think the jury *will* relate insurance coverage to it. Even you didn't think the defendant was insured, Judge. And then, on the merits, we believe the jury will feel there's considerable assumption of risk when two fellows undertake a sporting venture, like fishing."

I had excused the jury during this discussion, which took place in the robing room at the rear of the courtroom, and after some negotiation the case was settled.

I contributed little to this outcome, but in the next case I would sit with a little less apprehension, rule with a little more assurance, perspire a little less profusely. The very term "guest case" was unknown to me on December 2, 1941, when I started my first trial. I recall my sense of shock that an old friend should try to collect money for injuries resulting from conduct that had been neither willful nor malicious. Since then I have sat in cases in which brother sued brother and children sued parents.

I have grown accustomed to such situations, just as I have grown accustomed to the unpleasant problem presented by my second case. On the surface it was a simple one. The plaintiff, an accountant, was suing a former client for the alleged agreed price of services he had rendered. The calendar judge, putting me through my paces by easy stages, had undoubtedly assigned it to me in the belief that it was uncomplicated. He had no way of knowing that the defendant's trial counsel was one of the notorious judge-baiters of the local bar.

Encountering him in a trial was a jolting experience so early in my judicial career. Since then he has appeared before me twice, and although I had by then gained a measure of experience and assurance, I still had difficulty holding him within the bounds of decent conduct.

Almost all lawyers are courteous and respectful to the court. Occasionally, under the strain of trial pressures, an outburst will occur. It will usually be regretted and not repeated, and judges find it expedient to overlook such extemporary clashes.

This lawyer was one of a very few who were uniformly unruly. I do not believe his tactics were part of a studied pattern, nor do I profess to know whether there was a psychiatric basis for his actions. He was as close to perpetual motion as anyone I have ever seen in a courtroom, constantly bouncing out of his seat, and constantly pacing the lawyers' enclosure. When he spoke, which was almost continuously, his arms flailed violently.

From the outset, during the selection of the jury by the lawyers, he began to swarm all over his adversary. That harassed man was not permitted to finish a statement or a question. He would be interrupted by objections, arguments, and asides. Ordinarily a restrained, gentlemanly advocate, he had become so infuriated that he, too, was beginning to shout and rant. If I overruled an objection, the defendant's lawyer would continue to argue nevertheless. Finally, during the examination of the first witness, I told him I would hear no arguments; that he could make his objections, without comment, and I would rule on them. It is not an unusual device employed by judges to curb argumentative lawyers.

"Does Your Honor mean," he growled, "that you will not hear my reasons for making objections?"

"Just that," I said.

He resorted to heavy-handed sarcasm. "Most judges, some with even greater experience on the bench than Your Honor, do not take the position that they know all the law. They're willing to hear argument."

"I don't pretend to know all the law," I replied, with some asperity. "I'm limiting you this way to get the trial moving."

Despite my direction, he continued to employ the same tactics. I endured them for a while in silence. He may have been trying to goad me into losing my temper and making some outbursts from the bench. Some lawyers have the notion that scolding or rebuke by a judge casts them in the role of the underdog, and gains them, and through them their clients, jury sympathy.

As a prosecutor I had become disciplined in controlling my emotions. In criminal cases it is not uncommon for a defendant's lawyer with a weak defense to try the prosecutor instead of the case. In the examination of witnesses he will labor every scrap of testimony which might be tortured into an insinuation that the district attorney has been unfair or overzealous. In his summation he will seek to draw red herrings across the trail of the People's unanswerable evidence by charging the prosecutor with seeking to make a record over the prostrate body of his client.

When these tactics were first used in cases I had prosecuted as an assistant district attorney, I would lash back, infuriated by the aspersions upon my honor and integrity. Then I realized I was playing into the hands of opposing counsel. My heat and fury blended into the word portrait of me which he was drawing for the jury—of an ambitious young man, out to get a conviction at any cost. Comparing notes with the veteran members of the district attorney's staff, I learned that the most effective and commonly used formula for countering such conduct was passive resistance.

The approved method was to sit quietly through the tirades and personal invective, conveying an impression of deep pain but sweet forbearance. Then, upon summation, the prosecutor would quietly expose the shabby technique, and endeavor to bring the jury back to a consideration of the evidence alone. Often defense counsel's strategy backfired, for the jury sympathized with the poor tormented prosecutor who bore his cross with such patience.

But the forbearance in which I had been schooled as a prosecutor did not gain me command of my courtroom. As one of the victims of this lawyer's frenzied antics, I certainly did not want the sympathy of the jury. I was not participating in the trial in any adversary sense, and I had no wish to expose the shallow cheapness of his tactics, and thereby turn them to the disadvantage of his client.

My previous training did, however, restrain me from indulging in exchanges with this lawyer. That was most fortunate, as a furious or spluttering judge is never an edifying spectacle. If he is goaded into excoriating the lawyer in the presence of the jury, holding him in contempt or declaring a mistrial, he will most likely regret his action a little later. In view of the unevenness of the contest he will feel like something of a bully.

On the other hand, if a lawyer is not held within reasonable bounds, he can make a shambles of the courtroom. The trial will become disorderly and aimless, and the evidence presented to the jury may become distorted.

I fear that as a neophyte judge I was more concerned with piloting the case somehow to a verdict than with the quality of the evidence. I would have been content to maintain order in the courtroom, to rule correctly on objections, and finally to charge the jury properly on the law of the case.

I was unable to achieve even this limited objective in my second case. Despite my admonitions the defendant's attorney continued to shout and argue. He was so obstructive that the direct examination of the plaintiff had barely gotten beyond the preliminary stages when the time came to adjourn for lunch. I excused the jury and called the two attorneys to the bench.

"I've heard of you," I told the defendant's lawyer, "and I must say you've lived up to your reputation."

"I'm sorry if I've offended you, Judge," he said. "But my client paid me a fee and I believe in giving a client a run for his money."

I am convinced that he honestly believed in this creed.

"Starting this afternoon," I said, "I'll fine you for contempt every time you do more than merely state your objection."

When I returned from lunch I was informed that the case had been settled. I do not believe it was settled because the defendant's lawyer feared my threats of contempt holdings. He didn't scare that easily. He may have decided that instead of gaining the sympathy of the jurors he had probably alienated them because of his boorishness.

Despite the outcome of this case, I was very dissatisfied with my handling of it. I had lost control of the courtroom, and to regain it had been driven to the unpalatable recourse of threatening a member of the bar with contempt proceedings. Of course, he had been unusually offensive. Still, I have never held a lawyer in contempt; nor do I recall ever again threatening such action.

An experienced judge is seldom apprehensive about maintaining proper decorum in the courtroom. That becomes an insignificant detail, a minor preliminary to the major task of achieving a fair and just result. He will anticipate and divert potential flare-ups and outbreaks. In fact, instead of presiding repressively, he will try affirmatively to relax everyone—counsel, jurors, and witnesses.

A few years ago a case was tried before me, in which Sir Alexander Korda, the well-known movie producer, was being sued for breach of contract by his former European representative. The case was long and involved, but unusually pleasant. The attorneys were competent and gentlemanly. The parties to the lawsuit were men of stature and integrity, who merely couldn't agree on what had been the full scope of their contract.

Most of the witnesses were Europeans. The courtroom fairly exuded Old World courtesy and charm, until a point was reached in the cross-examination of Korda. He had testified that when he learned of the plaintiff's activities, which he considered a breach of their contract, he had cabled him to come to New York. Upon his arrival, the plaintiff went to Korda's hotel suite, where Sir Alexander testified he had dressed him down indignantly and at some length for his alleged breach of trust. Previously, the plaintiff had given a somewhat different version of this meeting.

The plaintiff's attorney pressed Korda as to whether his client had not made certain statements in answer to Korda's accusations. He repeated the substance of this question many times, in different forms and with an air of disbelief of Korda's reiterations of his original answer. Korda exhibited increasing asperity and temper as the questioning persisted. This was the first unpleasant note to creep into the trial.

Finally Sir Alexander vehemently snapped at his tormentor that he knew he had done all the talking because he had felt a sense of personal outrage at the plaintiff's conduct, that he had stored up his list of grievances for this showdown, that he hadn't given the plaintiff a chance to interrupt the sweeping torrent of his harangue, and that immediately upon its conclusion he had ordered him from the room.

For some time I had been looking for an opportunity to dissipate the mounting tension. Knowing that these were all theatre people, I turned toward Korda and said:

"In other words, Mr. Witness, you were not giving the plaintiff a chance to steal the scene."

Korda grinned. The cross-examiner laughed. This may have been bogus or mechanical appreciation, as lawyers are wont to laugh at the sorriest examples of judicial humor. But the important result was that he passed on to another subject and everybody's good humor was restored. So my interruption had served its purpose.

A judge presiding at a trial has one dominant concern—that the jury be afforded a full and fair presentation of the facts, and an understandable and uncomplicated exposition of the law. To the lay eye the judge may seem an elevated traffic cop, giving the stop and go signals to counsel. Actually, he is not as inanimate as he seems. He is often fighting hard, though not as a partisan, in a manner imperceptible to the jury. The judge is on the alert to fend off any extraneous proof or argument, any unfair tactics, which may confuse the issues and blur the hard outlines of the disputed lines of proof.

In this sense a trial judge is an administrator. He is engaged in so regulating the complex and often confusing machinery of a trial that an informed jury may render an informed verdict. Sometimes a judge excoriates a jury for bringing in a verdict which he regards as improper. Often, I suspect, he is not criticizing the jurors simply because he is cranky or because their combined judgment differs from his. More likely, the tirade is an inverted expression of self-reproach, because it appears to him that the jury went off at a tangent which reflects unfavorably on his conduct of the trial.

Experience will develop the assurance and deftness required to cope with distracting and explosive situations. Usually the behavior situations are so familiar and well grooved that a judge's corrective techniques are instinctive, almost in reflex. Of course, experience and deftness will avail little in deflecting rowdyism if a lawyer or lawyers are determined to bait a judge, as an important part of their trial strategy and without reckoning of consequences.

There is also the remote danger that good humor will be mistaken for weakness by someone, lawyer or witness, who will seek to take advantage. A judge must develop his own methods for coping with such offenders—methods compatible with the judge's personality.

Sometimes a judge is required hastily to improvise a makeshift procedure. I recall two behavior situations which confronted me after I had been on the bench a few years. By that time I had gained sufficient confidence in my craftsmanship to experiment with unorthodox measures. Had I encountered these problems early in my apprenticeship, I doubt that I could have handled them.

One oppressively hot June day, a few years ago, the clerk of the part approached the bench. He looked disturbed. "In the next case," he whispered to me, "Brash represents the plaintiff and Bellows the defendant." Both lawyers had appeared before me previously, although never opposed to each other, and I knew why the clerk looked disturbed. Brash was a snarling old warrior who was constantly at his adversary's throat. He knew every trick of the trade and was heedless of court admonitions, just short of the point where he could be held in contempt of court.

Bellows, his adversary, was also a blustering, bull-throated battler. But Brash had an advantage. That wily advocate simulated indignation, with an ever-wary eye to jury reaction, while Bellows would really become boiling mad and lose his head.

I decided that the usual expedients would be powerless to prevent head-on collisions between two such firebrands, especially since the case was being tried in the midst of an unseasonable heat spell.

Brash, for the plaintiff, detoured outside the proper boundaries of an opening statement outlining his case, and Bellows objected. There was a heated verbal exchange, with sparks flying, and after it had subsided I quietly sustained the objection. Brash continued. Again he went off-side and this time there was a more extended verbal altercation. I waited patiently again, then, without deigning to speak to counsel, addressed the jury as follows:

"Ladies and gentlemen of the jury, you have just been treated to a sorry spectacle of ungentlemanly and unprofessional conduct on the part of two lawyers. As a member of the legal profession, I wish to apologize for their behavior. I ask you not to judge all lawyers by the standards they have displayed here today, nor to penalize either of the parties to this lawsuit for the actions of his lawyer. I believe the oppressive heat is the reason and may be some excuse for their shortness of temper."

Brash stood silent for a minute, his head bowed in thought. He turned his back to the jury so as to shield his face from them, threw me a quizzical glance from beneath shaggy eyebrows and half grinned. I knew he would behave from then on. He resumed and quickly concluded an inoffensive opening statement. Bellows did the same. Though there was much unhappy biting of lips, there were no more outbursts. By the next day they both had endured more than human flesh could bear. They settled the case.

A party to another case tried before me, involving the sale of two popular songs, was a Broadway character. He clearly fancied himself as a wit. I suspect he would have sacrificed the verdict itself to be credited with a quip which could be quoted by the columnists or go the rounds at Lindy's.

When called to the witness stand, he leaned back in evident enjoyment, prepared to give a smash performance. After a few preliminary questions, he was asked the date of a certain transaction. Knitting his brows, he protested, "I can't think at this hour." Then turning to me, he said, "Judge, it must be unconstitutional to make theatre people get up this early in the morning."

A number of his cronies were seated in the courtroom, and there was a sympathetic titter. I granted opposing counsel's motion to strike out the answer and grimly admonished the witness to answer questions and volunteer nothing. His worried lawyer, by admonishing him and glaring at him, managed to navigate him without incident through a very short direct examination.

When his lawyer relinquished him for cross-examination, this witness evidently girded himself for a field day at the expense of the opposing counsel. He gave flip, smart answers. I cautioned him. However, I had an impression that even at the risk of his personal comfort, he would welcome the notoriety attendant upon my holding him in contempt. Fortunately for the orderly administration of my courtroom, the cross-examining lawyer was not only competent and experienced but a good psychologist.

The witness was asked to relate what had been said at a conference. He proceeded to draw word caricatures of the participants, in brisk Broadway language and tempo. His audience was convulsed.

After he had finished, the opposing lawyer turned to the court reporter and said, "Would you please read back the witness's last answer?"

The stenographer read it back, lugubriously, in flat and unpunctuated tones. Court stenographers are concerned only with syllable sounds, not with the timing of punch lines. It sounded pretty dismal. So would Mark Twain or Damon Runyon, under similar circumstances. The witness squirmed.

"Do you think that's funny?" was the next question.

The witness's lawyer sprang to his feet with an objection. The question was neither relevant nor material to the issue as to whether two song hits had been sold. The objection could have been sustained, upon strictly technical grounds.

"Objection overruled," I said. "Answer the question."

"I'll concede it's not funny," said the lawyer.

"No, let the witness answer," I ruled.

"Well," hesitated the witness, "I don't know how . . ."

"Will you repeat the witness's last answer?" I said to the court reporter.

"Oh, no, no!" hastily interjected the witness. "I don't think it's funny."

We had no further trouble with that witness.

* III *

My First Charge to a Jury

My third case consumed over three days: it was the first one which went through to a jury's verdict. A great deal of time was expended needlessly because I lacked the assurance and experience to pilot the case away from the shoals of irrelevancy and argumentation. I emerged with increased respect for the collective shrewdness of a jury—and with substantial reservations as to my own faculties for fact finding.

The plaintiff was suing a large merchandise-jobbing firm for breach of a contract of employment. He was a well-groomed, dignified, middle-aged gentleman, who had held important posts with a number of large companies.

He testified that the defendant firm's president, who lived in another city, had telephoned him, said he was in New York on business, and invited him to their office to discuss his joining its executive staff. The president had offered him a position as head of one of the firm's departments—to take entire charge of its buying and sales activities.

According to the plaintiff, the president had said to him, "This job is worth at least thirty thousand dollars a year. But the department is in bad shape. It's been badly managed and needs a shot in the arm. For that reason I'd like to take you on for a year, but on an incentive basis. I'd rather pay you a small salary and a large commission, to stimulate you to go all out. Then, after the year is up, we can discuss a long-term contract."

The plaintiff said he agreed to go to work on that basis, and that after some discussion they decided he was to receive a salary of twelve thousand dollars a year, plus one-half of one per cent of this department's sales. He testified that he had been paid his salary on that basis for three months, and then discharged, without reason. The plaintiff sued for nine thousand dollars, the remainder of the one year's salary which he claimed. He also sought one-half of one per cent of the department's sales for the year, which totaled several million dollars.

The plaintiff seemed to be a solid citizen, who testified in ponderous but unembellished fashion. He emerged unshaken from a long cross-examination.

The defendant's general manager testified that he had hired the plaintiff, pursuant to instructions from the president. He said that he had interviewed the plaintiff, informed him of his duties, and told him his instructions from the president were to pay him one thousand dollars a month, under a temporary arrangement, "until we see how things work out." He stated nothing was said about a percentage of sales. If the manager were believed, it would follow that the plaintiff had been employed at will, and could be discharged at any time, without cause, and without further payment.

The manager testified further that things did not work out and, again under instructions from the president, that the plaintiff had been discharged. He had come to work late, set a poor example for the department's employees, and was inefficient. The attorney for the defendant tried to bring out the entire conversation which the manager had had with the president, but an objection was sustained. The plaintiff was not present, and it was not binding upon him.

The president then took the stand and testified flatly that he had never interviewed the plaintiff at all, and never had any conversation with him about employment, compensation, or anything else. As previously stated by the manager, he had given instructions that the plaintiff be hired, on a monthly basis; and upon receiving certain reports, he had ordered his discharge. The president was a peppery little fellow, who testified with great heat and fervor. He was the key witness for the defense, and he did not seem to create so favorable an impression as had the restrained and dignified plaintiff.

He testified that he had directed the hiring of the plaintiff after a conversation with the latter's brother. He was asked the substance of that conversation, but upon objection I did not permit him to answer.

Upon cross-examination by the plaintiff's lawyer, the president admitted he had been in New York on the day that the plaintiff claimed to have spoken with him. He also admitted that the plaintiff's predecessor on the job had been paid twenty-five thousand dollars a year, plus a year-end bonus.

On redirect examination by the defendant's lawyer he explained that the other department managers had been employed under written contracts.

"You did not offer the plaintiff a written contract?" asked the defendant's lawyer.

"No," answered the president.

"Why not?"

"I object," shrilled the plaintiff's lawyer. "Calls for the operation of the witness's mind."

The objection was sustained. Only in rare instances may such a question be asked of one's own witness. The danger is that it could open the floodgates to a great volume of unanswerable testimony. His decision may have been influenced by gossip, erroneous information, sound or unsound reasoning, or by many other factors which could not otherwise be introduced upon the trial—and which the other side would be helpless to combat.

The lawyer asked several other questions, all calling for testimony concerning the operation of the witness's mind. Objections were sustained and he switched to another tack.

"What had you learned about the plaintiff before you hired him?" he asked.

"I object: Hearsay!" snapped his opponent.

The objection was sustained. By this time the witness was fairly spluttering with rage, which didn't help his case.

The following day the jury returned a verdict for nine thousand dollars in favor of the plaintiff. This indicated that it accepted only that part of the plaintiff's version of the employment conversation relating to salary, and rejected the alleged percentage arrangement. Or that nine thousand dollars was about the right figure and a nice round sum to award the plaintiff. Despite the plaintiff's imposing appearance, the jury had not given full faith to his testimony. Something had rung false in his case.

After the jury had been discharged the president asked if he could talk with me.

"I suppose so," I said. "The case is over."

"I'd like the lawyers to hear this. And you too, Joe," indicating the plaintiff.

They all filed after me into the robing room.

"I just wanted you to know the truth about this case, Judge," he said. "Joe's brother is one of my dearest friends and one of the most respected men in our industry. Joe is just as despised as his brother is loved. He could be a brilliant merchandising man, but he's a hopeless drunk and liar. He reached the end of his rope a couple of years ago. No one in the business would touch him with a ten-foot pole. So his brother gave him a job.

"Of course," he continued, "that wasn't good for either of them. When I was in town one day I had lunch with Joe's brother. He poured out his troubles to me and like a sap I said I had an opening and would give Joe a trial. He warned me against it but I insisted.

"I had to leave for home that afternoon, so I gave our manager instructions to take Joe on at a thousand a month and to watch him closely. Believe me, I didn't even see him on that trip. A few months later the manager reported he was ruining the department. There was nothing to do but fire him.

"This may sound childish to you, Judge, but for my nine thousand dollars I think I rate the satisfaction of telling this heel what

I think of him; and of squaring myself with you. His brother begged him to drop the lawsuit. He even offered to come here and testify against him. I wouldn't subject him to such an ordeal, although my lawyer predicted you'd exclude any testimony by me about our conversations. He then insisted on paying any judgment this chiseler recovers, and of course, I won't let him do that.

"That's all, Judge. I wanted you to know the score and I wanted Joe to know where he stands with me and every decent man in our trade. Good day, sir."

Joe said nothing.

Although I believed everything the defendant's president had said, I could not disturb the verdict. Impressive as his statement was, it was not admitted by the plaintiff, and of itself did not constitute proof.

In the years that followed I have heard scores of such posttrial confessionals, in one form or another. Is it any wonder that a judge becomes trained to examine all evidence critically and cautiously, and to subordinate his surface impressions and indignations?

At the close of every court day during this trial I repaired to the library, to study questions which had arisen, or which I had anticipated might arise. Parts of a trial judge's labors are exposed to view, and parts are concealed. The submerged portion is performed to a great extent in his chambers and in the library. There he will prepare his charge, comprising his instructions to the jury, and study questions of law which have arisen during the trial; and there he will read the endless affidavits and briefs when he is sitting in a motion part. He will often have homework; sometimes there are not enough normal business hours in the day to dispose of the work that must be done.

On the evening before the morning when I was to charge a jury for the first time, I begged off a dinner engagement and remained in the courthouse to prepare my charge. I wrote every word of it in longhand—the discussion of the facts, the "boiler plate" to be found in every charge, and the instructions on the specific rules of law governing the particular case.

In newspaper circles "boiler plate" is the term applied to the filler material, the general reading matter sold to small newspapers on electrotypes. The publisher adds local news and advertisements. Courthouse initiates have dubbed as boiler plate those general instructions which recur in all or most charges; these include instructions on the burden of proof, on the rules of damages, prejudice, bias, and contributory negligence in accident cases.

Other judges had been kind enough to lend me copies of their boiler plate, which I unashamedly appropriated and adapted to my own requirements. I now deliver these familiar portions of a charge by rote, without recourse to notes; but I laboriously read every word of my first charge.

I went through agonies of revision and rewriting in preparing that first charge. I fear that in my effort to make it intelligible to the jury I got the opposite result. I was too careful, too precise—and, I'm afraid, too legalistic. It never achieved the simplicity of a good charge, because I lacked the assurance to cleave through and even ignore some of the fringe issues, in order to come to grips with the core of the case. I'm afraid I was more concerned with its technical impregnability than its intelligibility to laymen.

I now feel there is no virtue in being legally correct at the expense of clarity. That is tantamount to not instructing a jury at all. It is very difficult to reduce the ponderous precise idiom of law to lay language. It is much easier to transmit it in the Olympian manner of textbook writers or leading case opinions. It is also much safer to use the old, tried-and-true language that has won the approval of the appellate courts.

I have heard that veteran teachers fall into two classes. One will repeat the same lessons, year after year. Such teachers make no effort to vary the basic curricular diet, to stimulate the appetite and the digestion of their students for learning. Other teachers, however, will constantly experiment, improvise, and probe in an effort to catch and hold the students' attention, and to improve their receptivity. The former is the safer and easier course, and one for which a teacher will never be hauled on the carpet. The latter is risky. An unguarded or misunderstood statement may be repeated or distorted by a student, and invoke the wrath of a parent, superintendent, or member of the school board.

In charging a jury a judge is also a teacher. He too can play it safe by parroting the timeworn instructions. Once he has attained a measure of competence and confidence, the judge too can coast along on his craftsmanship. Except to the critical eye of the expert, his services will appear satisfactory. Yet most judges constantly tinker with their charges, although they cannot check the results with jurors as readily as a teacher can with his pupils.

Without divulging his own appraisal of the evidence, a competent judge in charging a jury will marshal the facts so as to show their materiality to the issues of the case. The judge is a trained, dispassionate sifter of those facts. He will point out the conceded or undisputed facts, and the key facts in dispute which must be resolved to arrive at a verdict.

Even though a judge dares not usurp the fact-finding functions of the jury, he will pursue that illuminating spark which lights up the entire proceeding. What is the keystone of the plaintiff's case? Of the defendant's case? What are the vital contentions of each side, which if destroyed will topple its entire case? The issues in the case are fastened in the mind of the judge. They are the magnet to which material and relevant evidence clings like steel filings, while all immaterial and irrelevant evidence falls away. He will wall off from the jurors his own impressions of a witness's credibility, or of the weight to be accorded certain evidence.

Today I would never impose so formidable and turgid an exposition of the law as my first charge upon twelve hapless jurors. But today I recognize dimensions to a judge's job that I could never discern ten years ago. It calls for much more than proficiency in the application of the rules of law.

A great judge, Learned Hand, speaking of the dedicated services of the trial judge, said:

"It is by such labors that slowly the whole majestic fabric of the law has been reared; the creation of workmen—for the most part long since become anonymous—who have felt the lure of that never succeeding, yet never quite failing, pursuit. . . ."

A judge heads toward maturity when he so devotes himself to this pursuit. He must first have achieved a capacity for insights into both facts and law. With command of the facts alone he may be a practical and, therefore, a valuable dispenser of justice, even though the subtler aspects of the law may escape him. But the feel of the law will forever escape another judge who lacks an intelligent, sophisticated mastery of the facts. He will never perceive its pragmatic glints.

The law will never be entirely clear and uncomplicated to any judge, any more than any other jealous mistress is clear and uncomplicated to her suitor. Were it otherwise, each might lose something of her allure. But the wise judge, like the wise suitor, will be the master of his true love, although he may not understand her completely, and although she eludes him at times.

The dullard will accept literally and without demur whatever his beloved says. The wise man realizes that under slightly different circumstances the frown of yesterday may become the nod of today. He will study her mind and her heart, her moods and her caprices, to gain some hint of those inducing circumstances.

Similarly, the wise and experienced judge will not accept at surface value the pronouncements of his goddess of the law. He will inquire further. Why did she frown in one case and nod in another, when the manifest situations in both cases were so much alike? What were the exceptional facts which softened her frown in the one case? Were the mitigating circumstances as influential as those which tempt the judge to do likewise in the case before him? Or will he stretch the general rule to a point of deviation which will reflect upon the constancy of his goddess?

There is little difference between the emotional reactions of a judge and of a layman. A judge's capacity for indignation and compassion does not atrophy. It deepens into a disciplined passion. Judicial maturity does not bring desiccation. The judge, I assure you, sheds a furtive tear during the last scene of *Camille,* and roars with laughter at the antics of Jimmy Durante. And his notions of fairness differ little from those of a layman. Sometimes both are asked to apply a general rule of law which works a hardship in a particular case. Although he privately may regard the result as unfair and unjust, because of his training the judge will apply the law more readily and more unflinchingly than will a layman. The loudest wail of anguish a judge may permit himself, while enforcing an unpalatable rule, is that it is the province of the legislature, and not the judiciary, to change existing laws. The lawbooks are filled with such observations.

Sometimes, when he has decided upon the facts in a case or upon a motion, and the law to be applied is crystal clear, a judge may have to steel himself in order to render a decision in accordance with his conscience. I recall a discussion among a group of judges during lunch. One judge said that he usually found that he was in complete agreement with the verdict returned by a jury. A general discussion followed: Was there any substantial disagreement by judges with jury verdicts?

Finally one judge said, "Occasionally I find that I would return a different verdict from a jury's. But I must say that in most of the cases in which I disagree, the jury found the way I would like if I weren't trained to follow the law."

It is to be expected that a judge would become more impartial than a layman in deciding disputes. Impartiality, like so many other qualities, can be developed and strengthened by constant practice. In his daily work, as an integral part of it, a judge is always striving to achieve impartiality.

Seldom, on the other hand, is a layman placed in the position of judging a controversy. He may be called upon to settle an office dispute between an associate he likes and one he dislikes. He tries to exercise his judgment without regard to his likes or dislikes; but he will have to work hard and consciously at it. If he were performing this judicial function continuously, instead of at widely spaced intervals, impartiality would come closer to being a reflex reaction.

So, in his deliberations, the judge is always concentrating on eliminating prejudice, bias, favoritism, misplaced favoritism, or any other factors which might distort his decisions. Of course, he is never entirely successful; too many of the sources of prejudice or bias lie beneath the surface of consciousness. Still, when time and again conclusive evidence proves the hollowness of his initial emotions, a judge learns to keep a tight rein on them.

The judge is not more intelligent or perceptive than a juror—certainly not more than the composite of twelve jurors. He is human, and will often come to erroneous conclusions about the credibility of witnesses or the truth of evidence. Jurors are often much shrewder in sizing up a witness or in reconstructing a controverted transaction. And sometimes, in seemingly aimless and undirected fashion, they will get much closer to the truth than will a judge.

But, personality factors being equal, by virtue of his experience the judge is best qualified at least to screen, if not decide, the issues. For example, I submitted the following account of an actual case to a number of judges, lawyers, and laymen. Their group reactions were widely different.

An attractive young woman in her thirties, alone in the city, began to act strangely and was taken to a hospital. There she was kept under observation in the psychiatric division. It was discovered that, among other things, she suffered from a uterine tumor which had developed to an advanced and dangerous stage. The young woman, who was a member of a religious sect which did not believe in medicine or surgery, refused to consent to an operation. The attending physicians regarded such an operation as essential, believing that it would be only a matter of weeks or months before she might hemorrhage—possibly fatally. Despite the doctors' advice and warnings, she persisted in her refusal.

After ten days of observation in its psychiatric division, the hospital authorities submitted a petition to the Supreme Court, alleging that she suffered from schizophrenia and asking that she be committed temporarily to a state hospital for the mentally ill. The patient opposed commitment and was, therefore, accorded a hearing before a judge without a jury. Under the law, she was entitled to such a hearing in the Supreme Court. It was held before one of my colleagues, a mature, experienced judge. The hospital psychiatrist testified and recommended commitment. He had appeared often before the justices of the court and they entertained great respect for his integrity and professional ability.

In the course of the hearing my colleague also heard the testimony of the patient. In opposing commitment she spoke lucidly and quietly. The judge remarked that she had impressed him favorably, and that he was loath to commit her upon the moderate symptoms of schizophrenia described by the psychiatrist. The latter then told the judge of the patient's tumor condition, the urgent need for an operation, and her stubborn refusal.

"What bearing has this on her mental condition?" asked the judge.

"It would have some bearing if the refusal is unreasonable and irrational, Your Honor."

The judge proceeded to question the psychiatrist closely and searchingly about his diagnosis. Then, despite the testimony relating to the tumor condition, he dismissed the petition and discharged the patient.

One morning, five weeks later, she was found dead, in a small hotel bedroom. She had hemorrhaged during the night.

At the time, it was my turn to sit in the part where these incompetency hearings were held. When the news of the tragic aftermath of my colleague's decision reached the courtroom, the clerk brought me the filed record of the case. Although the case was closed, and I had no connection with it, I read the record carefully and brooded upon the trial judge's burden.

I then outlined the evidence brought out at this hearing to six different judges at six different times. Note, I did not ask these six judges how they would have decided the commitment case. I did not seek their opinions of the mental condition of the patient. It would be impossible for any judge to give such an answer upon my secondhand recital of the evidence—and without hearing and observing the patient and the psychiatrist. I did ask what significant lines of inquiry they would have pursued, had they presided at the hearing. What key question or questions would have to be answered in order to lead to the core issues of the case and inevitably shape the ultimate reasoned decision?

Four of the six judges said in substance: "The psychiatrist is not legally trained and I don't know how much weight he would attach to her legal right of freedom of person—particularly if that right were pitted against medical expediency. Uppermost in his mind, as a doctor, might be the necessity of detaining her under essential medical observation for her tumor condition. Therefore, I would first question the psychiatrist to determine whether, consciously or unconsciously, he was emphasizing or exaggerating her mental condition in order to keep her in some hospital."

The two other judges ruefully admitted that this question went to the heart of the case and they confessed they had missed it.

I posed the same outline of the evidence to six persons who were not judges. Two of them were lawyers. Not one of the six suggested that the psychology of the psychiatrist himself was a possible area of inquiry.

None of the six judges inquired about the patient's history after her discharge. To their minds this was irrelevant to the issues presented at the hearing. When I told them the outcome, they were moved as deeply as any six average men would be, but they believed it had no bearing on the soundness of the decision. However, all six of the nonjudges inquired about what had happened to the patient, and they stated, honestly enough, that her death would influence their opinions as to the fitness of the judge's decision.

The difference in viewpoint between judge and nonjudge is entirely one of training and discipline. The judge is trained, through numerous fact-finding experiences, to aim for the heart of an issue; and he becomes disciplined, for example, to respect the religious scruples of a person like the patient in this case. No matter how strange or foolish he might think her beliefs to be, he would uphold them on her behalf, and not rationalize a decision which would do them violence.

The court process as a fact-finding technique is a highly sophisticated and disciplined enterprise. It involves the reconstruction of specific factual incidents or situations, generally through the medium of words, in a given forum and within a fixed period of time. Procedural rules, as applied by the trial judge, are intended to minimize the distortion caused by the lens through which the past is thus projected into the present. This job of fact reconstruction is ordinarily accomplished through the narration of persons who may have witnessed the original event. But the ultimate fact-finding decision, whether by judge or jury, is made by persons who did not observe the matter under reconstruction.

In one of his dialogues, Plato remarked upon this phenomenon: "When, therefore, judges are justly persuaded about matters which you can know only by seeing them, and not in any other way, and when thus judging of them from report they attain a true opinion about them, they judge without knowledge, and yet are rightly persuaded, if they have judged well."

Involved in the modern trial and allied procedures is not the remembering or recalling of some relevant experience by the trier of the facts. It is instead a process whereby he learns about the facts—not unlike the manner in which a historian reconstructs past events. As a process of learning, rather than remembering, the trial, as well as all other court proceedings requiring a verdict or decision, presents endless vistas of epistemological and metaphysical problems. Do the judge and jury reconstruct a fact situation inductively, deductively, by intuition, pursuant to the principles of Gestaltism, or by all of these processes? This question is as unanswered as it is unanswerable.

At times a problem will yield to conscious and demonstrable analysis. At other times it will defy such sensible procedure.

Sometimes almost effortlessly, sometimes after the sternest pursuit, I gain a sudden insight into a contentious jangle which brings the dissonances into harmonious agreement. As a judge I am always startled by the vaulting of so many layers of reasoning to an answer which could withstand the most reasoned analysis. At first I would plunge into the flashing wake of these insights, groping for their point or place of beginning. I soon found this as fruitless as diving down a well after a firefly.

Call it the "feel" of a case, "trained intuition," or the "judicial hunch"—all judges have experienced it. Many seasoned judges half expect, half depend upon it, when the orthodox, conscious methods of reasoning have proved futile. What a thrill when it emerges! And what an uneasy sense of frustration when it eludes one; when a judge must fall back on the burden of proof or a presumption to render the necessary decision.

The law does not prescribe the type of mental processes which a judge or juror must use in reconstructing an event, so long as the decision of the fact finder is based upon evidence. However, it is fair to say that while the modern trial is a rational process for proving facts, it also accommodates the accurate perceptions we all experience as the result of sudden, sharp, intuitive insights. Intent, motive, good faith, when in issue, are seldom the subject of direct proof; they often require the trier of the facts to base his finding upon informed intuition.

A judge first searches the facts, then searches the law, and lastly searches his soul. If all three inquiries lead in the same direction, his task will be easy, but if they diverge, he cannot straddle for any appreciable distance.

Laws are not made to be broken by judges, but in sensitive hands, they have a certain tensile tolerance for yielding to meet an individual situation. The law will snap back when pressed too far by an insensitive judge who lays violent hands upon it. It can be twisted out of shape by an impetuous judge.

The judge who has come of age will shape the law within the range of its tolerance, to fit the contours of the particular case. The precise, meticulous judge will miss the contours through the unyielding severity of his plumb line. Dean Pound has said: "Yet the significant thing is not the fixed rule but the margin of discretion involved in the standard and its regard for the circumstances of the individual case."

A trial judge cannot solve his problems as one solves a crossword puzzle. He may not enter his findings of facts across, and his conclusions of law down, and call the result his decision. Too often they may be blended only by a knowing heart and a disciplined mind—often accompanied by much anguish of spirit.

Decision-making involves a good deal more than an intellectual exercise.

I'm sure the attachés of my court will not approve this admission of a judge's uncertainties and soul searchings. They unite in presenting to the public an unwavering façade of judicial infallibility.

My first encounter with this attitude occurred on the morning I was to deliver my first charge to a jury. I suddenly thought of a possible request to charge that one of the attorneys might make, and I hurried to the library to read some pertinent cases. I became so immersed in them that I did not arrive in the robing room until 10:15 A.M. I had adjourned court the preceding afternoon until 10 A.M.

"I'm pretty late," I said, as I was being helped into my robe. "I'll apologize to the jurors and counsel for keeping them waiting."

"Judge," said the clerk, "I hope you won't think I'm speaking out of turn. But when you've been here as long as I have, you'll know that no matter what time the judge enters the courtroom, it's ten o'clock."

Among themselves, the court personnel undoubtedly have the weaknesses and foibles of the judges pegged with pitiless accuracy. But to the outside world—the judge can do no wrong.

* IV *

Things Not Taught in Law School

The Supreme Court of the State of New York is primarily a trial court. It is a court of unlimited jurisdiction. This simply means that, unlike other courts, it is not restricted to a particular class of litigation, such as criminal cases, nor is there any limitation upon the amount of damages it can award.

It has entered judgments for six cents and for millions of dollars, for conviction and for acquittal. It has dissolved marriages and giant corporations, restrained picketing as well as lockouts, condemned real estate and lowered real estate taxes, rescinded contracts or ordered their performance.

The court is largely occupied with the trial of lawsuits and the myriad preliminary legal moves—called motions—relating to those trials. But each year it also churns out a great volume of work unrelated to the trial of cases.

Therefore, at times, the decisions or rulings which a judge must make do not emerge from the comfortably familiar bounds of a trial or from a conventional set of motion papers. He may be required to function in a fashion far removed from the traditional concepts of a judge's conduct. He may be confronted with a situation which does not fit neatly into any pattern described in the lawbooks. Early in my judicial career I was placed in such a position. Paradoxically, my inexperience and a heaping measure of beginner's luck stood me in good stead.

In the frenzied 1920's hundreds of millions of dollars of mortgage bonds were floated and sold to the public on the security of New York City real estate. In the 1930's these real estate values collapsed, the prices of the mortgage bonds plummeted, and the mortgages owned by tens of thousands of bondholders were foreclosed. There was no governmental agency charged with the responsibility of protecting the widely dispersed and financially illiterate bondholders. Amidst such chaos and absence of regulation, the reorganization of these bond issues provided a happy hunting ground for freebooters.

So scandalous had these activities become that the legislature entrusted the reorganization of these distressed bond issues to the Supreme Court. A special term of the court was set up with exclusive jurisdiction of their reorganization, liquidation, and incidental judicial supervision. Shortly after my appointment to the bench, I was placed in charge of this special term, which I handled in addition to my normal full calendar of trial and motion parts.

At this time a bond issue of $8,000,000 covering five business buildings, a hotel, and the Ziegfeld Theatre, all in mid-Manhattan, was in the process of reorganization. One morning an order was presented for my signature, providing for the approval of the sale of the Ziegfeld Theatre to the famous theatrical producer, Billy Rose, for $400,000, all cash. The affidavits submitted with the order indicated that the referee in reorganization had held several open hearings in connection with the proposed sale. The original offer by Rose had touched off efforts to procure better ones. Although the market was scoured, the only other offer received was one of $250,000, made by Loew's, Inc., which operated the theatre under a lease.

The proposed sale was recommended by the referee and every bondholder, lawyer, and bondholder's representative who had appeared at the hearings. Since I had been assigned to this special term only a month earlier, I consulted with the clerk of the part.

"This is my first experience with the sale of the property securing a mortgage," I said. "Is there any regular practice that has been followed in this part?"

"Oh, yes, Judge," he answered. "The practice is to call for competitive bidding—usually by sealed bids, after extensive advertising. In that way you test the market for the best available price. Nobody can come in a month later and complain that he would have bid higher if he had known the building was up for sale."

This impressed me as sensible, and I called in the referee and the attorneys in the reorganization proceedings for a conference. When I told them that I proposed to put the theatre up for sale on competitive bidding, I was met with a storm of protest.

"Rose knows the only other offer is for a quarter of a million," one of the lawyers said. "We've worked him up to where he now offers four hundred thousand. He may withdraw the offer rather than engage in competitive bidding."

"We've listed this theatre with every real estate broker of any standing," said another lawyer. "Among us we've contacted everyone in the theatrical field who's a potential buyer. Not a nibble."

"You see, Judge," explained another, "show business is bad. Besides, this theatre is badly located now; it's neither meat, fish, nor fowl. Although it would cost over a million to build, its economic value is nowhere near that amount."

Nevertheless, I told them I would not depart from the court's established practice. They returned a few days later. The referee had held another hearing and informed Mr. Rose of my decision. He had thereupon increased his offer to $425,000, conditioned, however, upon an acceptance without competitive bidding.

This posed a very perplexing problem. My general objective was to sell the hundreds of millions of dollars' worth of real estate in my jurisdiction under the most favorable circumstances and at the highest prices obtainable. A theatre is known as a specialty building in real estate circles, and has a very limited sales appeal. It would be shunned by the vast army of real estate buyers, because its operation and maintenance demand a specialized knowledge of the intricate theatre business. It does not have a stabilized market value, like an apartment house or office building, which can usually be sold on the general market for perhaps a little less than its market value, but within the same price range. A theatre is definitely not a conventional real estate offering.

I appointed an appraiser, who reported that the market value of the theatre was $450,000. But this was merely an opinion, expert though it might be; and it was certainly possible that a much higher price might be obtained. It was also very possible that if Mr. Rose withdrew his offer, as he had every right to do, no comparable one—or none at all—would ever be made, and the bondholders might suffer a substantial loss. In this case I would certainly be subjected to criticism. Bondholders, who look to results and not motives, can be very voluble.

Faced with this dilemma, I chose the respectable legal compromise. I followed surface precedent, and ordered a court sale on sealed bids. I directed that the proposed sale be advertised in metropolitan newspapers and that prospectuses be mailed to a long list of real estate brokers and to a number of theatre owners who might be interested in extending their holdings. I had no way of knowing whether Mr. Rose would submit a bid, what price the theatre would bring, or if in fact any bid would be made.

Finally came the day that bids were to be opened. I had set twelve o'clock noon as the hour, and the clerk's office as the place where bids were to be submitted. A number of lawyers and bondholders interested in the outcome were in my chambers. At ten minutes past twelve the clerk entered, bearing two sealed envelopes.

An official stenographer was seated alongside my desk. For the record I had the clerk state that he had left his office at five minutes past twelve to proceed to my chambers. At that time just two sealed envelopes, the ones he held in his hands, had been presented. I bade the stenographer mark the two envelopes in evidence, as Court Exhibits A and B, respectively. I then proceeded to open them.

Exhibit A was a letter from Loew's, Inc., offering $525,000, all cash. I breathed a deep sigh of relief. My judgment, whatever animated it, had been vindicated.

With a light heart I opened Exhibit B. This was a letter from Billy Rose, offering $635,000! Now indeed my cup overflowed.

At subsequent hearings in that reorganization proceeding my sagacity was extolled by grateful bondholders. Neither they nor I suspected at the time that were I to be confronted with such a situation today I might handle it differently.

I would weigh pragmatically the chances of procuring a higher price by competitive bidding against the chance of Mr. Rose's withdrawing his offer altogether. I might well come to the conclusion that the wiser business course would dictate caution and the negotiation of a sale with Mr. Rose.

I would recognize and respect the distinguishing features which set this situation apart from those which had established and nurtured the precedent of competitive bidding. My concern would not be with the unorthodoxy of my decision nor with the possibility of criticism. My major inquiry would be directed to whether this decision would impair or destroy a meritorious precedent, and whether a valid distinction could be drawn which, instead of debasing the precedent, might strengthen it.

The point is that I would no longer regard the practice of years as binding precedent—at least, not when different and unusual circumstances indicated the precedent was not applicable. And it is possible that I would have renegotiated a sale for considerably less than was realized by my adherence to precedent.

In the years following the Ziegfeld Theatre incident I have acquired more resourcefulness as well as more assurance. I contrast my worried handling of the theatre situation with the sale of a hotel in the process of reorganization, which I conducted a few months ago.

The sale was held in my courtroom. The bidding was open and oral, as I have found that form better adapted to elicit spirited bidding than the sealed bid method. I had directed that the sale be advertised on the real estate pages of several specified newspapers, on certain specified dates. On one day each week these newspapers featured a real estate news section, containing specialized news items, forecasts, and gossip. The entire real estate fraternity avidly read these pages; and it was upon those dates that I directed publication of the advertisements of the sale. I had also ordered that a prospectus be mailed to every member of the New York City Real Estate Board, and to selected hotel operators.

The property to be offered was an apartment hotel on Central Park West. At 2 P.M., the hour advertised for the sale, the courtroom was crowded. This augured well for active bidding. After several prior hearings, during which I had heard expert testimony as to value, I had fixed an upset or minimum price of $875,000, all cash. I was hopeful the property would bring a little over $900,000.

I announced the terms of the bidding. To qualify as a bidder one had to deposit with the clerk of the court a certified check in the amount of $10,000. The successful bidder was required to deposit within forty-eight hours an additional sum equal to the difference between $10,000 and ten per cent of the amount of his successful bid. Upon the time of closing title, within thirty days after the sale, he had to pay the balance in cash. I also announced that each bidder subjected himself to the jurisdiction of the court. This meant that if the successful bidder failed to go through with the purchase, and had no valid reason for rejecting title, he might be held in contempt of court. Eight potential bidders deposited their qualifying checks. The bidding started at the upset figure of $875,000. It quickly rose, through increases ranging from one to five thousand dollars, to $915,000. At that amount all but three bidders dropped out, and in somewhat slower tempo the figure rose to $930,000, when another bidder signified he had reached his limit. The remaining two raised the amount to $935,000.

At this point one of the two bidders, a well-known real estate operator named Green, crossed swiftly over to the other, a Mr. Brown. He whispered something to his competitor, who had made the last bid. Brown in turn whispered to the two men with him, who were evidently members of his syndicate. Then he looked up at Green and shrugged his shoulders. Green turned toward the bench and asked, "Would Your Honor give us a short recess?"

I had become an old hand at auctioning real estate. I knew most of the participants, and had learned some of their stratagems. It was apparent to me that Green had suggested to Brown that it would be poor business to keep bidding the price up; that since they now had the field to themselves they should take over the hotel as equal partners at the last bid price of $935,000. Brown had probably indicated some interest, and a recess was desired so that they might discuss the partnership possibilities in the corridor.

"There will be no recess at this time," I ruled. "The last bid was nine hundred and thirty-five thousand dollars. Are there any further bids?"

Green conferred with his group; he too represented a syndicate. There was a great deal of gesticulating and sibilant whispering. I rapped the gavel.

"Unless I hear another bid the property will be sold to the last bidder at nine hundred and thirty-five thousand dollars," I announced.

Green had one last frenzied exchange with his associates.

"Can't we have a ten-minute recess?" he pleaded.

"No," I said firmly.

He exchanged glances with his associates. They nodded their heads. He turned to the bench.

"Nine hundred and thirty-six thousand," he said.

"Nine hundred and forty thousand," said his rival.

The auction was alive again. They bid each other up to $970,000, the last sum offered by Brown. Green conferred again with his group. In response to his urgings I noticed dubious shaking of heads. Finally, he turned to me.

"I'm not authorized to go any higher at this time, Judge," he said. "Would you give me an opportunity to telephone?"

I believed him, in part. I believed that he had exhausted his authority and would have to enlist additional backing by telephone to continue any further. I was also certain he would renew partnership negotiations with Brown during the recess. At this stage nothing could be lost by granting the recess, because I was convinced he could not continue the bidding. And if the partnership failed to materialize, and he secured additional backing, the price might be increased.

"We'll take a fifteen-minute recess," I declared. Almost everyone in the courtroom rushed to the doors leading to the corridor. Twenty minutes later the two bidders re-entered the room, but not in each other's company. Brown looked grim and determined; Green was red-faced and flustered.

When everyone was seated I said, "The last bid was in the amount of nine hundred and seventy thousand dollars. Are there any further bids?"

"Nine hundred and seventy-one thousand," said Green.

"Nine seventy-five," sang out Brown.

The amount rose to $990,000, offered by Brown. Green requested another recess. I granted his request. He went out, returned in about ten minutes, and threw up his hands.

"I can't top the last bid, Judge," he said.

I sold the hotel to Brown for $990,000, an amount much higher than the price we had anticipated the property would bring. The proceeds of the sale warranted a distribution to bondholders greatly in excess of the price their bonds had sold for on the market the day before. I directed the attorney for the bank which acted as trustee for the bondholders to print and mail immediately a letter to the several hundred bondholders, informing them of the sale, and what it would mean to them in dollars and cents. This was done to nullify the activities of certain sure-thing harpies, who after a successful sale would somehow secure a list of bondholders, and try to buy their bonds at prices well below the realizable values.

Concluding a satisfactory reorganization is gratifying. Infinite patience and months of hearings are usually required before the conflicting interests of opposing groups of bondholders can be reconciled and a plan of sale approved. Sometimes challenging questions of law are raised. And yet, comparatively, a lawsuit can seldom be packaged so neatly.

The culmination of all these efforts may result in the judge acting as a real estate auctioneer, a role for which I was never trained in law school. But I am sure that my experience in the more conventional functions of a trial judge has made a better auctioneer of me, and that my experience as an auctioneer has made me a better trial judge.

It was not until the summer—a half year after I went on the bench—that I was first assigned to a motion part—called a special term for motions. A motion is generally an application for judicial relief which is made by one of the parties while a lawsuit is moving toward trial. It is usually supported and opposed by affidavits which recite the facts asserted by each side, and by briefs which argue their notions of the prevailing law. Seldom is oral testimony taken in connection with a motion.

Many motions are preliminary or intermediate legal moves designed to clear away the underbrush before trial and explore the real issues clearly and fairly. Thus, to prepare properly for trial, either side may move to examine the adverse party or his witnesses before trial, or may seek a bill of particulars which will amplify and detail his adversary's contentions.

A plaintiff may apply for a temporary injunction, to avert immediate and irreparable damage which would make the ultimate trial academic. He may seek to tie up or attach property of the defendant; in turn, the defendant may move to vacate the attachment. A wife, in a matrimonial suit, may seek temporary alimony and counsel fees, so that she can sustain herself and her children and pay her lawyer during the period she will await trial.

A party may bring on a motion to dismiss his adversary's suit, on the ground that even assuming all the facts he alleges in his complaint, he still has no case under the law. Or, he may move for summary judgment, submitting affidavits and documents which he claims are proof conclusive of his contentions, so that no real issue remains to be tried. And then, there are a number of motions which are disassociated from any trial, and which seek relief which would be final in nature.

But even though comparatively few cases ultimately go to trial, it is the prospect of the trial that stimulates the preliminary activities which absorb much of the court's working time. Since the trial of a lawsuit is the heart of the judicial system, it would follow that the trial feeds and is fed by most of the court processes—and particularly by motions preliminary to trial.

In our court, where seniority is rigidly observed, the junior judges take over the summer motion part assignments. Each actually sits for two weeks, one of which is devoted to deciding contested motions, and the other to signing uncontested orders. At least two more weeks are required to dispose of the work. As a freshman judge, my motion part assignment fell on the last week of July and the first week of August. I now sit two months of each year in the various motion parts, but no longer have any summer assignments.

The trial parts are all closed during the months of July and August. This is not done just to give judges a long vacation. Experience has shown that it would be difficult, if not impossible, to assemble all the necessary participants to a trial in a given courtroom at a given day during those months. Somebody's vacation plans would of necessity be disrupted—lawyer, witness, juror, or judge. Furthermore, trial lawyers, who are under great strain and pressure ten months of the year, welcome and need the summer respite. However, the motion parts operate very busily throughout the summer.

They must remain open fifty-two weeks each year. A forum must always be available to a party who urgently requires immediate relief. A businessman may seek a temporary injunction restraining a competitor from pursuing unfair tactics which, if permitted to persist through the summer, might ruin him. Or a plaintiff may seek to attach property which a defendant is about to remove to a foreign country. Or a mother may sue out a writ for the custody of her child.

During this first week in the motion part my calendars were normal in length, with a normal ratio of difficult and perplexing problems. An average daily calendar will comprise about one hundred and fifty motions. At least half of these will be adjourned to another day. Of the remainder, some are decided almost automatically—upon default or by consent. Others pose no difficult problems of law or fact, but consume time in the reading of the papers. And others present involved questions of law or fact, or vexing problems of policy.

On request of the attorneys, about eight or ten motions will be marked for oral argument; the remainder will be submitted with opposing affidavits and briefs, but without argument. The arguments vary in length, and all together consume perhaps the entire morning.

I literally worked day and night for four steaming, humid weeks to dispose of the contested motions which were submitted or argued before me. But I had few competing demands for my evening hours. My family was out of the city, at our summer home. An empty city apartment in the months of July and August offered little attraction. I therefore worked until midnight every weekday night, and stuffed a briefcase with files every Friday for weekend attention.

During those weeks I had lonely dinners in a near-by restaurant and then returned to the courthouse. When night descends, downtown New York is a desolate area. Restaurants which teem with customers and buzz with excited talk at lunchtime are either closed or now serve only a few stray patrons. Curbs where cars parked bumper to bumper, like files of beetles, are now empty. Streets on which traffic crawled a few hours before are clear, except for an occasional taxicab. Sidewalks are deserted. It is a fine background for intensive work.

I could now do just as much in half the time, and do it just as thoroughly and conscientiously. I know much more law than when I first became a judge, and through experience I have improved my work habits.

As a practicing lawyer I may have handled ten or twenty motions a year. As a judge I pass on close to a thousand motions each year. Therefore, it is to be expected that I am now familiar with all of the leading cases governing the more usual and common motions. Also, I am now conditioned to rendering impartial judgment, where formerly, as a practicing lawyer, I was conditioned to advocacy.

That first year I would read each brief, and then go to the library and read every case cited in the brief. I still read all briefs, but I am now well grounded in many of the legal principles they discuss and the cases they cite, and I need not go to the library to read them.

I now read the affidavits annexed to a motion with a trained eye. I look for certain essential features. For example, as I read the affidavits in a motion for temporary alimony and counsel fee, I am consciously and continuously relating the allegations to the main factors which will govern my decision: what are the applicant's chances for success in the lawsuit itself, what are the needs of wife and children and what are the income and financial status of both parties. Most motions fall likewise into patterns for consideration.

During my first motion part assignment I dictated to the courthouse stenographers all of the memoranda or opinions which accompanied and explained my decisions. Most lawyers never write in longhand, except to sign their names, but they dictate prodigiously and glibly every type of written statement. As a tyro judge, I had carried this habit over into my judicial work. Since all opinions of Supreme Court Justices are printed in the *New York Law Journal,* which is the legal profession's trade paper in the City of New York, I would often impose a third, fourth, and even a fifth draft of an opinion upon a stenographer, until I felt it represented my best effort, by literary as well as legal standards.

In some courts each judge is assigned a stenographer, to do his work exclusively. Our court maintains a stenographic pool, subject to call by judges, law secretaries, and law assistants. This tends toward a more even and uniform distribution of work, and fewer stenographers are required. For example, when sitting in trial term, I may require only a half hour a day of a stenographer's time, to take dictation and type my correspondence. When sitting in my first motion part, I overloaded three stenographers.

I now write out in longhand all opinions and memoranda, and

turn my handwritten product over to a stenographer to be transcribed into a final draft. I have found that the tendency in dictating is to overwrite; and no matter how many revisions, the end result is likely to be too long.

My aim in writing opinions is that lawyers should understand what I have to say. My reasoning should be clear. I try to write with an economy of words, because to overwrite leads to confusion and ambiguities. The very manual effort of writing in longhand discourages prolixity and tautology.

When to write a comprehensive opinion and when not to is a preliminary question which confronts a judge on most disputed motions. The practice among seasoned judges is not to write for general professional consumption unless an issue is one of first impression—that is, a question presented for judicial determination for the first time; or one presenting novel aspects, or possessing elements of great public interest. Otherwise, an experienced judge usually writes only enough to disclose his reasoning to the lawyers in the matter, and to the appellate courts if an appeal is taken. If the reasoning is implicit in the decision, a judge may write only "Motion granted" or "Motion denied," or possibly add the citation of a leading case upon which he relied. Most new judges, however—and I was no exception—believe they must treat every facet of a problem at great length, even though the same propositions have been enunciated more lucidly and more authoritatively many times in the past.

The two publishers of the state's law reports ask for copies of any opinions which they believe will be of interest to the legal profession. They employ eager young lawyers who pore over the output of all of the courts of original jurisdiction, and cull out the opinions they regard as significant. Sometimes a judge is embarrassed when a request is made for publication in the permanent bound volumes of an opinion which he tossed off very casually for the benefit of counsel only. He fears it does not reflect the type of well-developed, polished exposition which he would like to have recorded imperishably in the law reports.

But these discomfitures are mild in comparison with an experience suffered by a colleague a few years ago. He had stewed for weeks over a very perplexing motion. After considerable research and thought, still unable to arrive at a satisfactory conclusion, he had adopted a technique followed by some judges. He had written two comprehensive and closely reasoned opinions. One concluded by granting the motion, the other denied the motion. Then he set them aside for two weeks. When he picked them up and read them after that period, all his doubts became resolved in favor of the opinion granting the motion. So he filed that opinion and gave no further thought to the case.

A few weeks later he received a letter from one of the law publishers asking for a copy of the opinion. He turned it over to his secretary. About a month later that young man entered his chambers, very red of face.

"Judge," he said, "you remember that Roe versus Doe motion you decided a couple of months ago?"

"Of course," said the judge.

"It's in the current advance sheets," said his secretary. Advance sheets are thin, paper-bound volumes, distributed each week by the law publishers, containing a limited number of recent opinions and decisions. The type is held, and when enough material is thus accumulated, a full, hard-covered, permanent volume is printed and published.

"Good! It's an interesting matter," replied the judge. He had devoted a good deal of time and study to that opinion and rather fancied it. He thought his secretary was about to relate some flattering comment he had heard.

"The attorney for the plaintiff just called me," the secretary said. "I'm afraid I've pulled a terrible boner. I sent the wrong opinion to the law reporter. Instead of the opinion you filed granting the motion, they've published the one denying the motion."

A great deal of embarrassed explaining followed, to lawyers and to publisher. With great mechanical difficulties, the proper opinion was substituted in the permanent volume.

The full irony of the situation developed after the decision had been appealed. The appellate court reversed the judge's ruling, and wrote an opinion which paralleled in reasoning the one that he had discarded.

Most motions fall into categories which determine the order in which they will be considered by a judge. In my first summer on the bench I had not formulated any program for priorities in disposition. I picked up the folders containing the motion papers in the order in which they had appeared on the daily calendars. As a result there were a number of interruptions like this one:

My law secretary poked his head inside my chamber door on the third afternoon of this motion assignment and said, "There's a lawyer on the phone who would like to know if we can give him any idea of when Black against White will be decided."

"I can't recall it," I said. "What's so pressing about Black against White?"

"I'll find out," my secretary said. He returned a moment later.

"It's a motion for the appointment of a receiver in connection with an action to dissolve a partnership. This attorney claims the partner in possession is looting the business."

"Very well," I said. "Bring me the file and tell the lawyer I'll try to get it out this afternoon."

Such proddings are rare now, as I have evolved a timetable for the disposition of motions based upon their need for expedition.

For example, I generally give first consideration to injunction applications. They often seek relief which, if delayed, won't ever remedy the situation. In this category are motions to enjoin landlords from evicting tenants, to restrain unfair competition, to enjoin unfair tactics in labor disputes, to restrain the sheriff from executing a levy. On the other hand, motions addressed to the pleadings—i.e., to dismiss a complaint, to strike out portions of a pleading, to direct judgment—can usually be put aside with safety for later consideration. They represent mostly preliminary sparring in cases which are many months away from trial.

It sometimes happens that a motion which is not ordinarily in the urgent category, like an application for an examination of the opposing party before trial, demands immediate attention. The party to be examined may be about to leave the country, or the case may be on the eve of trial. There are several such motions on the calendar each day which I direct the clerk to stamp "Expedite." When a set of papers bearing this magical stamp reaches chambers, my attendant places it on top of the heap.

When I have returned to chambers after hearing arguments in the courtroom, I sort out the pile of motions which has been sent up by the clerk of the part, and read them in the order of their urgency. Difficult and involved motions that require extensive research in the library are laid aside until later, for deliberate and relaxed consideration—unless there are circumstances commanding immediate attention.

When confronted by a knotty legal problem a judge may call upon his law secretary or one of several law assistants in the courthouse to assist him in its study and consideration. I avail myself freely of the services of these law assistants, who are learned, intelligent, and experienced in the trends of judicial thinking. They were especially helpful during my first year on the bench.

Few laymen appreciate the important, often decisive, function of the motion in the average trial court. Many are routine but nevertheless important, because they furnish the applicant with information which limits the issues at the trial or which tends to avoid surprise. Other motions result in a dismissal of the complaint, or the striking of the answer, or the direction of judgment, thereby avoiding the necessity of a trial altogether.

The scope of these motions marks a significant modern trend.

* V *

The Truth Is Not Always in a Trial

IN ALL COURTHOUSES where trials are conducted, the trial is the thing. Here is felt the first head-on impact of the parties. The academic law is not their concern. They want to win a particular case which may affect their pocketbooks, their security, perhaps the future course of their lives.

Through these portals do not issue sterilized dictums. The air fairly throbs with undercurrents of human virtues and human frailties—nobility and meanness, stupidity and shrewdness, gentleness and brutishness. The partisans in each case want their side to prevail. The judges and jurors want their notions of justice under the law to prevail—although their ideas on what constitutes justice in the particular case sometimes differ.

For most cases and most people, the trial court is not only the first forum; it is the final forum. About three per cent of the judgments and orders handed down in my court are carried up on appeal. Only three per cent—in a county where the most important litigation in the country is handled. The percentage is less in other areas, and insignificant in courts of lower jurisdiction. The expense of prosecuting an appeal is partially responsible for the finality of trial court dispositions; but the principal reason, I believe, is that most lawsuits turn upon questions of fact, and the bar recognizes that the trial court's determination of such questions will usually be accepted on appeal.

The dominant concern of a trial court is with facts. Every weekday morning thousands of jurors, witnesses, lawyers, and others toil up the stone steps of the New York County Courthouse. They are bringing their offerings of facts to the Temple of Justice.

Throughout the building witnesses' heads will be bent in last-minute conferences with lawyers. Judges in trial parts will be asking counsel what facts have been presented to warrant submitting a case to the jury. Attorneys will ask jurors to draw inferences of fact from evidence.

In motion parts judges will ask lawyers what facts have been alleged to sustain the complaint, or to warrant so extensive an examination before trial.

Law can be argued, law can be administered, only in relation to facts.

Not that the rule-making role of the law is to be minimized. The law expresses the rights of the parties. However, it cannot rest on a hollow declaration of rights. It has evolved rules to regulate the presentation of evidence tending to prove or disprove alleged violations of these rights. The legal rules are the embankment which restrains the torrent of onrushing facts from overflowing the banks, and channels them into a steady and orderly flow.

Very often, laymen, upon surface consideration, question the utility of these rules.

A friend of mine, who is an intelligent business executive, served on a jury recently, and has been bedeviling me ever since. His chief complaint is that he would never make a business decision on the meager information elicited upon a trial.

"To start off," he said, "you know nothing about the people with whom you're dealing. A fellow testifies for a half hour, maybe two hours, a day. When he leaves the stand a juror still knows nothing about his character or his trustworthiness. Before you take a man's word in business, you really learn something about him."

"A witness can always be questioned as to his credibility," I said.

"What does that mean?" he asked.

"Oh, a witness may be impeached on cross-examination by showing his generally bad reputation for truth and veracity, immoral or criminal acts, inconsistent prior statements, bias, hostility, and so forth."

"Bah!" my friend replied. "That's only helpful in exposing a downright crook or a moron who doesn't know how to parry questions."

"Well, what would you look for in the business world?" I asked.

"Some information you could sink your teeth in. His family setup, whether he owns his own home, is it mortgaged, any judgments against him, his church and communal activities, what charities does he give to, and how much, his income, his credit rating, does he drink, how heavily, does he run around. I'd speak to the people in his trade and to his neighbors. I'd really get a line on him."

"Most of that would be rank hearsay," I said. "And the rest would open up endless collateral channels of testimony."

"What of it? In business and social activities hearsay makes the world go round. When you and I agree that our host here, Joe, is an upright, dependable citizen, that opinion is largely based on hearsay. On what we've heard second or third hand as to how he conducts his business, treats his family and his help. When I hire a salesman, my judgment is formed largely on hearsay."

"A trial, like the weariest river," I answered, "must wind somewhere safe to sea. We must limit issues if a case is ever to be finished. When you're hiring a salesman, you ask him to return in a week if you want to make additional inquiries. But we can't put a trial over for a week to check questionable evidence. As to hearsay, experience has proved it dangerous to accept statements of people who are not produced for the jury to see and appraise, and who are not subjected to the test of cross-examination."

My friend continued, impatiently brushing away my explanation. "We had some accident case. I tried to ask the defendant a line of questions, to find out what kind of a driver he was. How many accidents he'd had, how many traffic tickets, whether he took a drink now and then, and so forth. The judge shut me up so fast I was left with my mouth open."

"Judges don't encourage questions by jurors, as a rule," I said.

"Why? The lawyers didn't object."

"That's one of the reasons. The lawyers didn't dare object, lest they antagonize you or lead you to believe they were concealing something. And our experience has taught us that once a juror asks questions, that encourages others to think up questions. Most of them are objectionable. The lawyers fear to object, the judge tries frantically to sift the questions, and the trial soon becomes a shambles.

"What we generally do is direct the juror to address his question to the court. If it has merit, the judge redrafts the question and asks it of the witness. If not, he shuts it off, as the judge did in your instance. He was probably shielding one of the lawyers from the necessity of objecting to your improper question."

"What was wrong with my question?" he asked.

"Plenty," I answered. "You wanted to know about previous tickets. What proof would that be of what occurred in your case?"

"Supposing it showed the defendant had a record as a reckless driver?"

"The law would not accept that as proof that he had driven recklessly at the time of the accident in your case."

"It would impress me as pretty good proof."

"That's why we exclude it. Let's take an extreme example. Your defendant was given a ticket for speeding five minutes before the occurrence of the accident in your case, and he later pleaded guilty to it. It had no other relation in time or space to the happening of your accident. Now, different jurors and different judges would view that circumstance in different ways. Some might reason he was a reckless driver generally and must have been at fault in the accident that happened five minutes later. Others might feel that so soon after receiving a traffic ticket he would be proceeding most cautiously and carefully. The law reasons that the fairest and safest course is to exclude such speculative and uncertain considerations altogether."

"You ask us to use our experience freely in drawing inferences, and then you deprive us of the facts to which we could apply our experience," my friend protested. "It's like putting a man in a strait jacket, and then telling him he may use his limbs freely."

"Nonsense!" I said. "Nobody pretends that a trial is a precise formula for finding the truth. In laying down the rules that govern a trial, it's preferable to exclude highly speculative and dangerous evidence, although our standards as to what is too dangerous to receive are constantly changing.

"But there is ample room at a trial for the extensive play of an intelligent juror's faculties and experience. Sometimes he must work hard to reconstruct what really happened. He must look for clues, grasp the glints and shadings offered by astute counsel. If he sits back waiting to be hit by a sledgehammer of proof, he'll miss a good deal. If he's on the edge of his seat, following the ball in play, he'll acquire a surprising amount of information."

"I didn't," grumbled my friend.

"I'll wager you brought your experience into play more than you realize," I said. "Tell me something about the defendant in this accident case you're grumbling about."

"There were two defendants. A bus company and the bus driver."

"Couldn't have ordered it better for my purposes," I said, and smiled. "What was the bus driver charged with doing?"

"Closing the door and starting the bus in motion before a passenger had alighted. Her foot was caught, she was thrown off the steps and fractured her ankle."

"You found in favor of the plaintiff?"

"Yes. She made a good impression and had a witness who bore her out."

"Did the defendants have any witnesses?"

"Yes, some passenger who said the plaintiff slipped on the icy pavement after she had walked away from the bus. And, of course, the bus driver. But we paid little attention to him."

"Why?" I asked.

"First, he was an interested witness. But also, we all knew how these bus drivers act."

"How do they act?"

"They're always in a hurry. They have to receive fares, make change, open and close doors, and make the trips inside a time schedule. I'll admit theirs is a tough job. But while I've never seen an accident like this happen, I've seen bus drivers slam doors in people's faces and narrowly miss hitting passengers getting off."

"And those observations had some influence on your appraisal of the bus driver's testimony and on your ultimate verdict?"

"Yes," my friend said. "I see what you're getting at."

"Of course. Whether you were right in your conclusions is not our concern just now. The fact remains that you drew on your experience and that experience influenced your verdict.

"I'll ask you one more question. You're a city cliff dweller. Suppose you lived in a rural community. Bus drivers are very friendly and co-operative in such areas. They relay messages, wait for expected passengers, even deliver keys and packages. If your impression of bus drivers had been gained from experience on rural buses, might your vote have gone the other way on this trial?"

He pondered. "I honestly don't know. It might have."

Had this conversation taken place in my library, I could have quoted the following dictum to my friend, from an opinion of Mr. Justice Benjamin N. Cardozo:

"It is for ordinary minds, and not for psychoanalysts, that our rules of evidence are framed. They have their source very often in considerations of administrative convenience, of practical expediency, and not in rules of logic."

The watchword of the law in admitting evidence is safety. Proof is introduced in a taut, unnatural atmosphere, in a contest ringed round with rules. Because of the convergence of time and space, there is scant opportunity to investigate and disprove unexpected evidence.

Conscious perjury is always difficult enough to detect or expose. But there are what Dean Wigmore, the keenest analyst of the rules and law of evidence in this generation, has described as the "possible errors underlying a plausible, positive testimonial assertion—errors latent in the processes either of Perception, Recollection or Narration." Honest men will testify erroneously because of defective functioning of one or more of these processes.

Hugo Münsterberg, the noted psychologist of a generation ago, cites two so-called tableau experiments to illustrate how treacherous observation and memory may be, and how, with the best of intentions, honest witnesses may err in relating an incident.

In the classroom of Professor von Liszt, a famous Berlin criminologist, a student suddenly shouted, "I wanted to throw light on the matter from the standpoint of Christian morality!" Another student yelled, "I cannot stand that!"

Further angry words were exchanged between them. They culminated in the first student's drawing a revolver and the second one's charging upon him. The professor stepped between them and, as he grasped the first student's arm, the revolver went off. Of course, the classroom was seething with excitement.

The entire incident had been planned, rehearsed, and staged as an experiment in observation and recollection. Professor von Liszt restored order and asked some of the students to write an exact report of what had occurred. Some students were asked to write their reports during the ensuing week, and others related their observations orally and subject to cross-examination.

The omissions, alterations, and erroneous additions were counted as mistakes. The ratio of mistakes ranged from twenty-six per cent to eighty per cent!

The closing and climactic half of the scene was of course more tense and exciting; the reports averaged fifteen per cent more mistakes for that half than for the opening part.

Münsterberg relates another experiment in which the audience was not only unaware that the scene was sham during its enactment, but where reports were procured while the onlookers still believed in the reality of the episode. The incident was staged during a meeting of a scientific body composed of jurists, psychologists, and physicians—all, as Münsterberg points out, men well trained in careful observation.

A carnival was in progress in the neighborhood of the meeting hall. In the midst of this meeting of trained observers, the doors burst open, a clown in costume rushed in, followed by a Negro with revolver in hand. What followed is thus described by Professor Münsterberg in his book *On the Witness Stand:*

"... In the middle of the hall first the one, then the other, shouts wild phrases; then the one falls to the ground, the other jumps on him; then a shot, and suddenly both are out of the room. The whole affair took less than twenty seconds. All were completely taken by surprise, and no one, with the exception of the President, had the slightest idea that every word and action had been rehearsed beforehand, or that photographs had been taken of the scene. It seemed most natural that the President should beg the members to write down individually an exact report, inasmuch as he felt sure that the matter would come before the courts. Of the forty reports handed in, there was only one whose omissions were calculated as amounting to less than twenty per cent of the characteristic acts; fourteen had twenty to forty per cent of the facts omitted; twelve omitted forty to fifty per cent. But besides the omissions there were only six among the forty which did not contain positively wrong statements; in twenty-four papers up to ten per cent of the statements were free inventions, and in ten answers—that is, in one-fourth of the papers—more than ten per cent of the statements were absolutely false, in spite of the fact that they all came from scientifically trained observers. . . . The scientific commission which reported the details came to the general statement that the majority of the observers omitted or falsified about half of the processes which occurred completely in their field of vision. As was to be expected, the judgment as to the time duration of the act varied between a few seconds and several minutes."

Wigmore tells us that the oath "used to be regarded as a summoning of Divine vengeance upon false swearing, whereby when the spectators see the witness standing unharmed they know that the Divine judgment has pronounced him to be a truth-teller. But it is now conceived as a method of reminding the witness strongly of the Divine punishment somewhere in store for false swearing, and thus of putting him in a frame of mind calculated to speak only the truth as he saw it."

We have noted that the relating of an incident or a transaction truthfully under oath is not entirely a matter of the witness's own volition. Every false statement under oath is not conscious perjury. Perhaps the implications in the words "so help you God," with which most witnesses' oaths conclude, should be extended so that they will not only be a reminder of Divine punishment but also beseech Divine guidance for truthful narration by honest but human witnesses.

One of the best statements on the difficulties of truth telling which I have ever seen is made by the hero in a mystery story written by Charlotte Armstrong. The character said:

"We know that to tell the truth is not merely a good intention. It's a damned difficult thing to do. It's a skill, to be practiced. It's a technique. It's an effort. It takes brains. It takes watching. It takes humility and self-examination. It's a science and an art. . . ."

Then, too, recollection of an occurrence may be erroneous, even though the original observation was correct. Recollection is dependent on memory, and memory is notoriously faulty and elusive. A witness's recollection may be molded by his interest in one of the parties, by a similar personal experience, by prejudice, by imagination, lack of imagination, or a score of other factors. Münsterberg has said that we "never know whether we remember, perceive or imagine."

Investigators, who are trained to wring testimony from the reluctant lips of hostile witnesses, are especially aware of how treacherous such testimony can be. I do not refer necessarily to the lies or sullen denials of witnesses or suspects under examination. The most serious consequence of such obstructionism will be that a case will not be cracked nor an indictment procured.

But a conscientious investigator or prosecutor really begins to worry when a witness breaks, and the torrent of confession is released; when the testimony overflows the banks of self-incrimination and begins to incriminate others. An experienced prosecutor is aware of the many incentives and impulses which will move a witness to implicate others: hope of lenient treatment, desire to please vested authority, vengeance or pique motives, weakness of character, exhibitionism, and many others.

The law recognizes the vulnerability of testimony of an accomplice and requires that it be corroborated by independent evidence tending to connect the accused with the commission of the crime. Slight corroborative evidence will generally satisfy the requirements of the law. But it will not satisfy a cautious and scrupulous investigator. Before accepting the story of an accomplice or complaining witness he will examine and cross-examine him in a search for flaws in his charges; and he will conduct an external checking investigation of the story.

Many years ago I conducted an accident fraud investigation, under the auspices of the bar associations of the City of New York. In the course of the inquiry my staff uncovered an amoral rogue named Sam. He had never done an honest day's work in his misspent life.

Sam had gathered together a dozen compatible characters and formed an accident-manufacturing ring. It operated on the principles of a theatrical stock company. A different accident would be staged every week. The members of the ring interchanged roles and were rehearsed carefully in their parts.

Sam employed many lawyers and doctors in preparing and presenting his claims. Some were highly suspect, because of the number of faked cases they handled, and because they had represented or treated the same member of the ring under different names. However, it was not unlikely that other doctors and lawyers had been innocent and imposed upon by Sam and Company.

After Sam had been apprehended he finally broke down and implicated his leading associates. I then turned him over to several assistants, to question him in relays from the voluminous files that had been seized. The next day one of these young men walked into my office, looking very troubled.

"Say, chief," he said, "I don't know what to do about Sam. If he keeps on he'll implicate half the lawyers and doctors in town. In every case he says the doctor and lawyer knew it was a phony. And in some the facts just don't seem to bear him out."

We immediately looked into the situation and found out what had happened. The day before, when Sam was being questioned by another assistant, he had maintained stoutly that none of the doctors or lawyers knew that the claims were spurious. The evidence in some of the files indicated otherwise. Sam confided to me later he had hoped to hold out their names for future blackmail purposes. He had intended to visit these men after he was released on bail and threaten to turn them in unless he was paid substantial sums. Finally, a detective sitting in on the questioning had taken Sam into a front room with windows facing Tombs Prison.

"Sam," he said, "how do you like the Tombs?" pointing to that grim edifice.

Sam shuddered. "It's terrible."

"Well, Sam," said the detective, "if you don't come clean, you'll spend a long time there."

"What d'you want me to say?" Sam whined.

"We want you to put the finger on those crooked lawyers and doctors. And if you hold out on us, don't look to us for any help with the judge."

The police officer's threat was susceptible of more than one interpretation. He was really trying to frighten Sam into telling the truth. Thoroughly cowed, Sam mistook it for a mandate to implicate everybody. Long and patient explaining was required before his warped mind, always looking for "angles," grasped that we wanted only the truth.

Some years later, by appointment of Governor Lehman, I conducted the New York State Printing Inquiry. It was soon disclosed that the state was being mulcted of close to a million dollars yearly in excessive printing costs. The principal figure in these frauds was the president of a large New York City printing firm who was questioned so often that all the members of the staff called him Joe.

There were a number of jokers or "sleepers" in the specifications which the State Printing Bureau issued for competitive bidding.

Joe had figured out these loopholes in the specifications; his competitors had not. As a result, the bidding was not really competitive. Most printers were afraid of bidding for a pig in a poke.

Part of our job was to revise the specifications so that they would be intelligible and fair to all bidders. Joe confessed to bribery and a conspiracy with other printers to defraud the state. But he was very chary of telling us the jokers in the specifications. One assistant threw up his hands in disgust, after making no progress. So I assigned Joe to another assistant.

This young lawyer began to get results. I strolled into his room while he was questioning Joe, to find out how he did it. The questioning went something like this:

ASSISTANT: Now, Joe, we come to Group B, Item 6. Workmen's Compensation claim forms. You've won that job for seven years straight. What's the angle?

JOE: No angle. I was always the low bidder. And I always made a very reasonable bid. Ask any printer if my price for the job wasn't always a fair one.
(My assistant had previously checked with our printing expert, who affirmed that the bids were reasonable, even a little on the low side. That was why we wanted to find out whether there was a joker in the specifications.)

ASSISTANT: I know it's low, Joe. That's why I can't figure your bids. You've always told me you're not in business for the glory.

JOE: Oh, once in a while I gave the state an even break.

ASSISTANT: Look, Joe, you're the smartest guy I've ever met. I've told you that before. Smart guys don't give suckers an even break.

JOE: Aw, I managed to get along.

ASSISTANT: No, you're absolutely the smartest fellow I ever met. That's why I'm convinced there's a gimmick in the specifications. If it were any other dumb cluck of a printer, I'd pass it by. But the smartest baby of them all wasn't in there bidding for his health.

JOE: Aw, you're rating me too high.

ASSISTANT: No, I'm not. How about it, Joe? Give me the low-down on this one and we'll call it a day.

JOE: Oh, all right. This is the gimmick. There was a lot of confusion when the state was handling the social security program and no bids were asked for the application forms. Well, when the state fails to award a yearly contract for a certain type of printing, that work goes to the printer with the contract for the kind of job that comes closest to it. I knew the compensation form was closest to the social security one, so I made sure I'd get both jobs by bidding low in comp. The social security forms are much cheaper to turn out—and there are many more of them. I've been charging the comp price for the social security work, and there's a lot of gravy in the cost difference.

I cite these instances only to illustrate of what volatile matter evidence is made. It may be, as in these illustrations, the result of fear or flattery, or of conscious fraud or subornation of perjury. Or, it may be an honest mistake made by a conscientious witness.

Although not always successful in its quest, the modern trial is designed as a regulated, disciplined search for the truth. But just as men have not always sought to ascertain truth in the same way we do, the trial process has not always been the same as it is now. In fact, the trial as a search for truth is a good barometer of the degree of rationalism, possibly civilization, attained by a given society.

When men are brutes, law employs the primitive techniques of the tribal hue and cry, lynch law, or the witch hunt. When men are deterministic and repose their faith in miracles, Divine intervention, and supernatural powers, they look to trials by ordeal, compurgation, or battle to determine the truth. When men mature into a belief in the powers of reason, free will, and scientific method and inquiry, they depend upon rational modes of proof and trial to ascertain the facts. And when institutions become decadent and removed from the reality of ordinary men, then the trial process becomes an incomprehensible, dreamlike experience, such as that described in Kafka's *Trial*.

Eight or nine centuries ago, in Europe, trial by ordeal was an accepted method for determining the guilt or innocence of an accused. The theory underlying the ordeal was that the Almighty, when invoked in proper form, would reveal the truth concerning the accusation. No matter what the challenge, it would be met by the innocent, with Divine aid. Professor Wigmore states that at some stage or other of its history every people in the world has employed the ordeal as a mode of trial, as a test of truth. Natives of retarded development in Africa still believe in its efficacy.

The ordeals of boiling water, of fire, and of hot iron were employed most frequently. When tried by the ordeal of boiling water, the accused was required to plunge his hand into the seething vessel, and sometimes to remove a stone from the bottom of the caldron. After the accused lifted his hand out of the caldron, it was wrapped in cloths, which were sealed by the judge or priest officiating at the ordeal. Three days later the wrappings would be removed, and the hand examined. If the wound was found to be clean, as willed by the Almighty, the accused was declared innocent. If it were unclean, he would be found guilty.

In the ordeal of the hot iron, the accused was placed in front of a fire in which an iron bar was heated until red hot. Then he removed the iron from the fire with his bare hands and carried it a prescribed distance. When he laid down the iron his hands were wrapped with cloths and sealed. As in the ordeal of boiling water, the cloths were removed three days later; and his guilt or innocence was adjudicated according to the condition of his hands.

In the ordeal of fire the accused was subjected directly to the flames. Sometimes he simply thrust his hand into the flame. In more elaborate forms he walked through flames or between flames or upon plowshares with bare feet. When administered by the church authorities, the ordeals were preceded and accompanied by fasting, elaborate rites, and prayers for Divine intervention.

Trial by compurgation, prevalent in one form or another in the early history of many peoples, also derived from the same belief that the gods would punish the evildoer and preserve the righteous. Compurgators were sworn, who were neighbors of the person accused. They would swear that they believed what the defendant said under oath. No evidence of any facts was taken. If a defendant could procure a given number of compurgators, he would be cleared of the charge. The belief was that if a compurgator swore falsely, he would be punished from on high.

So strong was the primitive belief in the immediate vengeance of the gods that another method was to require the accuser and the accused to take a mighty and awe-inspiring oath. Everyone was confident that frightful punishment would be visited upon the perjurer. And trial by battle was also based upon the conviction that the Lord strengthened the physical arm of the righteous.

No doubt there were occasional manifestations which served to confirm the people's belief in these forms of truth finding. Last year an incident happened in my courtroom which, had it occurred a few hundred years ago, would have been heralded far and wide as an example of Divine intervention.

A doctor had testified on behalf of a plaintiff in an accident case. He was an orthopedic surgeon of some renown. His specialization brought him into court occasionally, and therefore both the lawyers trying the case and I knew him fairly well. He was an honorable, amiable gentleman, whom we liked and respected.

This doctor was cross-examined very rigorously by the attorney for the defendant. While being questioned about his diagnosis of the plaintiff's injuries, he suddenly slumped in the witness chair and commenced to gasp for breath. He was assisted to a bench in the rear of the courtroom, where he lay down, but writhed in evident agony, and retched. An ambulance was called, but on the way to Downtown Hospital he died, of a heart attack.

We learned that this doctor had suffered from a heart condition for a few years, and had been warned against subjecting himself to the severe strains of testifying in contested lawsuits. We were all shocked, and the lawyer who had cross-examined him felt miserable. And we knew, in view of his previous cardiac condition, that it was not unnatural that his death should occur as it did. But would our ancestors think so when a compurgator died of a heart attack under the stress of swearing to an awesome and mighty oath, or would they ascribe it to supernatural causes?

The trial procedure of today heavily emphasizes a rational inquiry for the truth. However, it must not be concluded that the trial process originated for the major purpose of rendering justice, or that even today its exclusive function and end product is the dispensation of justice. Originally, and in some primitive societies today, conflict was resolved by personal or clan warfare and, in some instances, by vendetta or blood feud. These techniques combined the notion of self-help and the motivation of revenge. They came to be replaced by a process combining compensation for injury and a set, regulated, and orderly procedure.

Thus, where private injury was suffered, the emphasis shifted from punishment of the wrongdoer to compensation of the one who sustained a loss. And with the development of a state machinery, of course it became unthinkable that conflicts between parties should be resolved by force. The existence of a state presupposes that the government possesses the right to exert physical force in execution of its mandates. Consequently, the development and emergence of a trial court is a necessary extension of the emergence of a formal state structure.

Moreover, the substitution of a trial process for self-help in order to accomplish a peaceful resolution of conflict may to some extent have been dictated by the simple desire of a community for self-preservation. Wise men were apprehensive that the unbridled revenge impulse would lead clans or communities to self-destruction. Even the great ethical teacher Mohammed is said to have given this as a major reason for banning blood feuds. And to this very day a vital function of a trial court is to resolve conflict peacefully.

The trial process, however, cannot assure a revelation of truth or a just result. We have observed that witnesses may testify honestly but not truthfully. It is difficult enough for the fact finders, whether judge or jury, to detect falsity when the witness himself is unaware of it. It is difficult enough, we have noted, for investigators with facilities and freedom of action not available at any trial to wring the truth from witnesses.

How much more difficult is it to expose the heavy perjury content in court testimony which is the result of conscious lying and careful planning. I need not treat with perjury at any length, since this is an obstacle to fact finding which comes readily to mind. Just one example of a witness who was fortuitously unmasked is enough to illustrate how the detection of perjurious testimony within the rigid limitations of a court trial is fraught with uncertainty and often dependent upon luck.

The plaintiff in this case was a good-looking, well-spoken young man in his late twenties. He testified that he was an engineer, a graduate of Notre Dame with a Bachelor of Arts degree, and of Massachusetts Institute of Technology with an engineering degree. The defendant was a manufacturer of a certain type of industrial machinery. The plaintiff claimed he had made an arrangement with the defendant under which he was to receive thirty-five per cent of the net profits, in exchange for devoting his full time to the technical improvement of the defendant's products. In his opening statement the defendant's lawyer stated he would prove the plaintiff had been hired as a salesman, had failed to make any sales, and had been discharged. The only agreement made with him, according to the defendant, was to pay him a small salary and commissions when earned; and whatever was due him had been paid.

Upon direct examination the plaintiff narrated a plausible story of how he was in a small but prospering business of his own. The defendant had persuaded him to give up his business and become his associate, under promise of an eventual partnership. He had made this great sacrifice, worked day and night in designing improvements in the defendant's products, and then, without explanation, he had been discharged. By that time, he stated, he had remodeled the defendant's entire line of machinery. He testified simply, without evident embellishment or rancor, and apparently created an excellent impression of a technician whose brains had been picked. He appeared clean-cut, ingenuous, and inexperienced.

Upon cross-examination the defendant's counsel seemed to

ramble a good deal. He asked the years during which the plaintiff had attended Notre Dame and the Massachusetts Institute of Technology. The case was adjourned to the following morning before he had concluded his cross-examination. The next morning the examination was resumed.

LAWYER: Where did you live while you attended Notre Dame?
WITNESS: South Bend, Indiana, of course.
LAWYER: Where in South Bend?
WITNESS: In one of the dormitories.
LAWYER: Which one?
WITNESS: The name escapes me.
LAWYER: Where was it located?
WITNESS: Oh, on the campus.
LAWYER: Where did you live while you attended M.I.T.?
WITNESS: Also in a dormitory.
LAWYER: Has that name escaped you too?
WITNESS: I must confess it has.
LAWYER: Who was the president of Notre Dame when you attended there?
WITNESS: I don't remember.
LAWYER: Remember the president of M.I.T.?
WITNESS: No.
LAWYER: Did you receive a diploma from either university?
WITNESS: Yes.
LAWYER: Where are they?
WITNESS: At home.
LAWYER: Could you bring them to court?
WITNESS: (turning to bench) What have they to do with this case, Judge?
COURT: The witness will produce the diplomas.
WITNESS: Then may I go home now and get them, Your Honor?
COURT: No. This case will consume at least another day. You will bring them to court tomorrow morning.
WITNESS: May I be excused to make a telephone call?
COURT: Surely. We'll take a short recess.

The witness hurried from the courtroom—and did not return. After waiting half an hour the defendant's attorney ventured the opinion that he would never return. He showed me two telegrams from the registrar's office of each university. Each contained the message that no student by the name of the plaintiff had been registered during the years he claimed he had matriculated.

I adjourned court to the afternoon and dispatched the plaintiff's lawyer to find his client. He returned that afternoon and informed me that he had visited the plaintiff's home, where he lived with his parents. The mother told him her son had come home that morning, said he had to make an out-of-town business trip, packed a bag and rushed out.

The plaintiff's lawyer agreed to a dismissal of the case. I congratulated the defendant's lawyer upon the instinct which had prompted him to probe the vital defect in the plaintiff's testimony.

"Don't congratulate me, Judge," he said. "My client deserves all the credit. When we left court yesterday afternoon he said to me, 'Ben, if that fellow's an engineer, I'm a lawyer. He knew simply nothing about the technical end of our business.' So I took a chance and sent telegrams to both colleges."

It would appear, therefore, that the description of a trial as a *search* for the truth is a somewhat loose definition. The ascertainment of the truth has always been the ideal objective of a trial—whether trial by ordeal, inquisition, compurgation, or in a modern courtroom. Often, as will be illustrated in the next chapter, a jury or a judge cannot determine where the truth lies; yet they can nevertheless return a verdict. There has at least been a resolution of a conflict without resort to force.

* VI *

Most Trials Are Private Fights

TRIAL BY COURT or jury is not accepted universally as the most efficient fact-finding medium. The trial process is usually weighted on the side of the defending party.

This may be because inarticulately, perhaps unconsciously, the law has striven to place a heavy burden upon the complaining party who would enlist its processes to obtain relief at the expense of the defending party. Or, it may be that the modern trial continues to perpetuate those safeguards which were developed to protect individual defendants from tyrants and other oppressors who sought to use the courts in aid of their harsh objectives.

A defendant in a criminal case, for example, is clothed with the potent presumption of innocence. The rules for the exclusion of evidence employed in civil as well as criminal cases, though not manifestly designed to benefit the defendant, generally work a greater hardship on the complaining party. He usually has to bear what is known as the burden of proof. Consequently, the initial impact, at least, of our evidentiary rules is usually felt by the plaintiff.

In his provocative book, *Courts on Trial,* Jerome Frank calls a lawsuit "a kind of fight or combat." Few trial judges will disagree.

If Smith sues Jones on a contract and Jones denies making the contract, it is up to Smith to persuade the jury that Jones entered into the contract with him. In the main, it's his fight with Jones; the law does not take sides. If he fails to sustain his burden, the verdict should be in favor of the defendant Jones. In charging a jury a judge always states that if the evidence on the plaintiff's case is evenly balanced, the defendant is entitled to the verdict.

In a civil case the party bearing the burden of proof must prove his version of the issue by a fair preponderance of the evidence. In a criminal case the People must prove the defendant guilty beyond a reasonable doubt. The burden of proof has been described as the "allocation of the risk of nonpersuasion."

Many a guilty defendant has been acquitted because the burden of proof rested upon the prosecution. There is no quarrel with this rule. In the words of Blackstone, "The law holds, that it is better that ten guilty persons escape, than that one innocent suffers."

A number of years ago, when I was an assistant district attorney, I prosecuted a defendant accused of robbery in connection with a holdup. He was identified after a fashion by two quaking witnesses to the occurrence. The jury did not know that for weeks these witnesses had received mysterious telephone calls, threatening dire consequences if they identified the defendant in court.

I was opposed by a canny veteran of the criminal courts. His client had a long record of convictions for felonies and misdemeanors. He would have pleaded him guilty to a lesser felony charge, were it not for the fact that the defendant would then have been imprisoned for life, as a fourth offender. I was confident that he would not take the stand, that he would be fearful lest I question him about his convictions. Such questions are allowed only as affecting the credibility of a witness—weakening the weight of his testimony by showing the prior criminal acts. If a defendant does not take the stand, there is no way of bringing his past record to the attention of the jury.

When I said, "The People rest," the defendant's attorney put on quite a display of histrionics. He rose slowly from behind the counsel table, looking as though he could not trust his ears. He queried, "You rest?" as though only by the greatest restraint could he contain himself from adding "on such paltry evidence."

I was inexperienced then, or I would have grinned and joshed him to break the spell of his acting. As it was, I said weakly, "Of course."

He thundered, "Your Honor, I'll make no motions," as though he couldn't be bothered with technicalities in so absurd a case. He was really fearful that the experienced judge would puncture his dramatics with a caustic denial of the motion to dismiss the case because of insufficient evidence.

He gestured to his client, and to my surprise said, "Take the stand." As his client started to walk toward the witness chair, the lawyer paused irresolutely, and then said, "On second thought, Your Honor, the defendant will also rest." Of course, he had never intended to put the defendant on the stand.

In his summation he stressed the People's burden of proving the defendant guilty beyond a reasonable doubt and that no inference could be drawn from his client's failure to take the stand. He told the jury not to take his word for these rules of law but to listen for them in the judge's charge. Since his client's convictions were not part of the record, I could not properly comment upon them in my summation. Nor could I convey to the jury the slightest hint as to why his client had not dared take the witness stand. The jury returned a verdict of "not guilty."

When the verdict was returned the judge was free to tell the jury how it had been beguiled by the defendant's lawyer. This he proceeded to do with great relish. He read slowly, from the criminal identification sheets, the record of arrests and convictions of the defendant. He then excused a crestfallen group of jurors. None of them ventured to suggest to the judge that he was reproaching them for not ignoring his charge. Under the law as it had been presented to them by the defendant's lawyer, and later reaffirmed by the judge himself, they could draw no unfavorable inference from the defendant's failure to take the stand, and they were therefore justified in acquitting upon the otherwise weak case of the prosecution.

About two weeks later I prosecuted a bucket shop owner, charged with larcenously converting an old woman's securities. This man had never been convicted of a crime. However, he had been interrogated for days by the State Attorney General, under a law permitting such preliminary inquiries. His attorney was afraid that he had made some damaging admissions. He had a close decision to make, but finally decided to keep his client off the stand.

Several members of this jury had sat in the first case. A verdict of guilty was returned in less than half an hour. The next day one of the jurors said to me, "That lawyer didn't fool us. We knew his client had a long criminal record."

On the surface it would appear that the prosecution had failed to sustain its burden of proof in the first case, but had succeeded in the second. Sometimes unpredictable factors will conspire to frustate the uniform application of a rule of law designed to effect justice in the generality of cases.

There are many reasons for court rules and procedures tending to exclude evidence which would be regarded as relevant in our everyday affairs. They are bred from necessity and realities. One dictates that a trial cannot be permitted to prolong itself indefinitely. All factors of a trial converge upon a fixed place—the courtroom—and a fixed time—the date of trial. Mainly through narration, transactions years past, which may have covered a span of years, must be presented in the courtroom in a matter of hours or days. The rules are designed to permit such a presentation of what hard experience has proved to be the essentials of the average case.

Play construction is not unlike case construction. Limitations of time and space require the exclusion of instructive and entertaining material. The playgoer may complain that a theme was inadequately developed, or a promising character was subordinated. The management cannot raise the curtain and have the players develop that theme or character for him.

Neither may the jurors be heard to complain that they cannot decide the case intelligently on the skimpy evidence presented to them; that they would like to have a neglected line of testimony developed, or an eyewitness whose name was mentioned but who did not testify produced in court, or have the allegedly defective material tested in a laboratory. Once both parties rest, the curtain has dropped on the introduction of evidence. No further evidentiary excursions or inquiries are permitted. A jury can then ask a judge for further instructions on the law of the case; but it may not ask for the introduction of additional evidence.

In a jury trial, at least, there is no other alternative. Additional evidence requires time to prepare, additional witnesses require time to procure. Jurors serve for definite periods—a week, two weeks, a month. When called, many gird themselves at considerable personal sacrifice to perform a civic duty. They often experience great difficulty in accommodating their business and household affairs to jury service.

It would be unthinkable to require them to return repeatedly to the courthouse after their terms had expired, to hear additional testimony. It would also be unhealthy to reassemble them after long intervals, expect them to retain the skein of evidence in mind, and finally render a verdict as a cohesive unit. Of course, in his discretion, a judge may allow wider latitude in a nonjury case.

A case was once tried before me in which the plaintiff sued a manufacturer of precision instruments for $200,000. He stated that he was a business engineer—whatever that means—and that he had been hired by the defendant, during World War II, to serve as adviser in the management of its war contract department. He testified to an oral agreement with the president of the defendant corporation, under which he was to receive five per cent of the amounts received by the defendant on its war contracts.

It was conceded that the plaintiff had been paid $25,000 by the defendant; also, that the defendant had received about $4,500,000 on its war contracts. The plaintiff claimed five per cent of that figure, or $225,000. After giving the defendant credit for the $25,000 he had been paid, he sued for $200,000.

The plaintiff did not testify to any experience which would qualify him for so remunerative a job with the defendant. In a short and very gingerly cross-examination by the defendant's lawyer he was not questioned as to such qualifications.

The defendant's president testified that the plaintiff had been hired for a flat sum of $25,000, to advise in setting up a government contracts department. He too was cross-examined very warily by the plaintiff's lawyer.

Only these two men testified. Apparently both sides were content to let the jury decide a $200,000 lawsuit upon just two conflicting versions of a few conversations. I suspected the legality of the agreement, a distrust heightened by the manner in which two competent lawyers shied away from obvious and inviting channels of examination.

Ordinarily, a judge will respect a lawyer's management of his client's case; and he will refrain from peppering a witness with questions, lest he mar the lawyer's trial strategy. In this case, because of my suspicions, I had no such scruples. The jury was entitled to some enlightenment as to whether this was an agreement contemplating payment of $25,000 or $225,000.

I recalled both witnesses to the stand and questioned them. My skepticism deepened, but little additional light was shed on the major issue in the case.

"What experience have you had in the manufacture of precision instruments?" I asked the plaintiff.

"Well, none in that line," he said.

"Have you had any experience in the manufacture of any similar product?"

"No—not exactly. I was hired because I knew the ropes on the government regulations."

"On the government regulations for performing or procuring contracts?" I asked.

"Oh, no, Judge, for performing them. I had nothing to do with getting the business."

From there on the plaintiff took frequent refuge in a poor memory. The defendant's president was just as evasive.

"When you were discussing the possible employment of the plaintiff, did you question him about his experience?" I asked.

"Probably."

"What did he tell you?"

"I really don't remember, Judge. It was a few years ago. Besides, I do remember he was well recommended by someone in the industry."

"Who?" I asked.

"Gosh, now that name escapes me, Judge."

I finally gave up and the case went to the jury. It promptly returned a verdict in favor of the defendant. The jury was not required to ascertain the truth in the case. In that event it might never return a verdict. Some of the jurors told me later that they had surmised that the plaintiff was a Washington "five percenter"—a man who exerted influence to procure government contracts for five per cent of their face amount. But they decided, quite correctly, that it was not their concern upon this trial whether the parties entered into an illegal contract for $25,000 or an illegal contract for $225,000. It was enough that it could and did find that the plaintiff had failed to sustain his burden of proof—to satisfy them by a fair preponderance of the evidence that he had made an agreement such as he claimed.

If you were a juror in that case, would you ever think of addressing yourself to the court as follows:

"Judge, we're not able to decide what these parties really agreed upon. At this point we can't accept either side's version. We'd like you to put this case over for a few weeks and order some further investigation and proof. We'd like to hear the defendant's factory manager testify about what help, if any, he got from the plaintiff. We'd like to see the actual government contracts, and decide how difficult they were to perform. We'd like to hear the Washington officials who awarded the contracts," etc., etc.

Or, "Judge, the evidence is pretty evenly balanced and we can't decide which side is telling the truth. How about calling it a draw and giving the boys a return match in two weeks?"

In practice, individual jurors never call it a draw. They always plump for the plaintiff or defendant. Collectively, however, the jury occasionally calls it a draw by disagreeing among themselves. Some persist in voting for the plaintiff, some for the defendant; then they must be discharged and a new trial ordered before another jury. Considering the difficulty in getting any group with diversified backgrounds and prejudices to agree on any controversial issue, the insignificant incidence of "hung juries" is amazing.

Another important characteristic of the Anglo-American trial is the rule that the parties to the lawsuit must produce the proof. That is their burden in a competitive, adversary concept of litigation. This is the self-help theory in trials. If a party's lawyer is less skillful than his opponent, he will present his client's evidence in a less favorable and inferior fashion. His client will often be at a disadvantage, in much the same manner as he would be at a disadvantage if his factory manager produced a product inferior to his competitor's, or if his salesman or advertising manager presented his product less attractively.

In these contests the state has been relegated largely to the function of furnishing the stadium and the referees; of booking, staging, and deciding these civilized fights; and of participating, if at all, in nonpartisan fashion. This role might be accepted superficially, although not justifiably, in civil litigation, on the ground that the state has no direct stake in the result; that in matters involving property rather than society, a judge should not take the case out of the hands of the parties, who, out of self-interest, can be trusted to present and protect their rights. This presumes that society has no stake in doing justice among two or more of its people, even though their pocketbooks, and not the state's, are affected by the result.

What about the workman injured in an accident, whose family is on relief during his disability? What about the matrimonial action, in which the custody of children, wards of the state, hangs in the balance? Many other types of private litigation affect directly the more commonly recognized responsibilities of society.

And the private fight concept has invaded and captured areas of the trial of criminal cases. No prosecutor will prosecute consciously a defendant whom he considers innocent. But few prosecutors will seek out evidence favoring the accused with anything like the zeal with which they ferret out incriminating evidence. And once the case goes to trial, the pattern of the private combat is followed. True, there are certain burdens cast upon the prosecution and there are presumptions of innocence which are designed to favor a defendant. But the defendant is at a disadvantage if the prosecuting attorney is more zealous and skillful than his lawyer—particularly if the former is ambitious. The prosecutor has facilities for investigation and preparation which cannot be matched by a private party. An ambitious prosecutor will unconsciously rationalize his own aggressive trampling upon human rights. On the other hand, the defendant is aided greatly if the prosecutor is indifferent or inexperienced.

The Supreme Court of the United States, in *Berger* v. *United States,* has thus defined the duty of a prosecutor to protect the innocent as well as prosecute the guilty:

> "The United States attorney is the representative not of an ordinary party to a controversy, but of a sovereignty whose obligation to govern impartially is as compelling as its obligation to govern at all; and whose interest, therefore, in a criminal prosecution is not that it shall win a case, but that justice shall be done. As such, he is in a peculiar and very definite sense the servant of the law, the twofold aim of which is that guilt shall not escape or innocence suffer. He may prosecute with earnestness and vigor—indeed he should do so. But, while he may strike hard blows, he is not at liberty to strike foul ones. It is as much his duty to refrain from improper methods calculated to produce a wrongful conviction as it is to use every legitimate means to bring about a just one."

This opinion defines an ideal which is not always followed in practice.

Sometimes a judge feels that his duty requires him to take a hand in this private fight. Problems arise when the judge ventures across the line marking the traditional division of labor between lawyer and judge. Most common is the question to what extent, if at all, a judge should question witnesses. At one extreme is the judge who "takes the case away from the lawyers on both sides." At the other extreme is the judge who is strictly an umpire; he calls and rules on the plays, but never takes a part in the game.

Advocates of the laissez-faire school of thought not only question the propriety of a judge's intervening actively in the trial, but also dispute his power to do so. They point with alarm to French jurists, who sometimes cross-examine witnesses as vehemently and acidly as do opposing lawyers in England and America.

It is generally accepted that a judge has the power to call forth evidence and that it is proper to exercise that power reasonably. The courts have refused to sanction "the reduction of the trial judge to the helpless referee of an unscrupulous combat between skill and ignorance."

Or, as Edmund Burke said: "A judge is not placed in that high situation merely as a passive instrument of parties. He has a duty of his own, independent of them, and that duty is to investigate the truth."

But plainly, no legal compulsion rests affirmatively upon a judge to take part in the production or presentation of evidence.

Most often a judge's questions will be prosaic and harmless enough. They will be asked to supply technical omissions, such as identification of the signatures to a contract, proof of mailing of invoices or notices or similar evidence to remedy the oversights of overburdened lawyers.

But if an inexperienced lawyer is unable to frame a proper hypothetical question, or is unable to qualify his expert witness to establish the market price of the defective goods, should a judge suffer him and his client's case to perish in his own ineptitude? Surely a judge should step in and release the evidence dammed up only by the lawyer's inadequacies.

The perplexing problems arise when a judge possesses some specialized knowledge which causes him to doubt a witness's testimony. He will wait, hoping that on cross-examination opposing counsel will at least challenge that phase of the testimony. If he fails to do so, there is posed a judge's dilemma. The average judge will resolve it by questioning the witness only to avert grave injustice.

On one occasion a doctor, under skillful guidance by the plaintiff's attorney, testified in impressive professional phraseology to a number of injuries which could have been termed scratches and bruises.

Then the plaintiff's attorney asked, "Did you find anything else upon your examination, Doctor?"

"Yes," said the doctor, consulting his notes. "I found the plaintiff to be suffering from a congenital scoliosis."

"What is that, Doctor?"

"That is a derangement of the spine."

"Is this a pronounced derangement?"

"Oh, yes. A very bad one."

"Is it visible on X-ray?"

"Certainly."

"So there is no speculation about your diagnosis?"

"Oh, no, none whatsoever." The doctor then described at some length the limiting and crippling effect of the scoliosis, its permanency, and so on.

This evidence was not connected with the accident, and was clearly inadmissible. Still, the defendant's lawyer did not object. I did not interfere, thinking that maybe he reasoned that the higher the doctor built up the scoliosis symptoms, the greater would be his eventual tumble in the jury's eyes. But to my surprise, he did not touch upon the scoliosis testimony on cross-examination. As the doctor was about to leave the stand, I intervened.

"One moment, please," I said. "Doctor, you testified that this scoliosis condition, or derangement of the spine, was congenital?"

"Yes, Judge."

"What do you mean by a congenital condition?"

"Well, Judge, I didn't mean to imply that the scoliosis was necessarily the sequela of trauma," he replied.

This of course was an absurd evasion of my question.

"Doctor," I went on, "by congenital didn't you simply mean that the plaintiff was born with this condition—that he was born with a derangement of the spine?"

"Yes, Judge," he said, uncomfortably.

"And, Doctor, isn't it the fact that this congenital scoliosis could not conceivably have resulted from the accident?"

"Of course not, Judge. I never said so."

"That will be all, Doctor."

Probably the jury had grasped the full import of the doctor's testimony without my intervention, but I could not take the chance. After all, the defendant's attorney had somehow overlooked it.

Sometimes special circumstances, in addition to special knowledge, impel a judge to intervene. Our court is presently flooded with claims, in accident cases, of head injuries resulting in lasting neurological consequences. We are morally certain, from pretrial experiences and off-the-record talks with lawyers, that many of these claims are exaggerated—at least in so far as the head injuries are concerned. They are almost impossible to expose. A plaintiff will testify about certain complaints, such as dizzy spells, headaches, loss of memory. These are subjective complaints—an examining physician cannot detect them by sight or by X-ray or by feel.

Now, judges are aware that there are genuine head injuries. They do not desire to prejudice an honest claimant because of the suspicion attaching generally to this type of injury. Yet they desire that the jury be as fully informed as possible on the medical aspects of the case, so that it can determine sensibly for itself whether the claim is fraudulent or authentic. So judges will take over the examination on claimed head injuries more freely than in other types of testimony.

The following is an example of a line of testimony which many judges in our court would decide invited limited questioning on their part. It is taken from an actual case tried before me, and can be duplicated many times during any court year.

The plaintiff was a young lady who had been thrown forward while riding in a car that had been involved in a slight collision. There was no history of unconsciousness given to the police officer who came to the scene of the accident. All the plaintiff had said was that she had hurt her elbow. She was taken to Fordham Hospital following the accident, where she was treated for the bruised elbow. No complaint was made there of any head injury.

She was given first-aid treatment and sent home. Fordham Hospital is a first-rate institution. Had there been the slightest suspicion of a serious head injury, the plaintiff would have been detained for a complete check. This is basic hospital practice, throughout the country.

Her family doctor sent her back to Fordham Hospital the next day, for an X-ray of the elbow. Again, there was no suspicion of a head or neurological injury. On direct examination at the trial, however, the only serious injuries which the family physician attributed to the accident were neurological in nature; and they included cerebral hemorrhage with the very serious consequence of a changed personality.

The plaintiff, friends, relatives, and her husband—the last-mentioned acquired after the accident—had testified that before the accident she had been gay and bright. She had been the life of every party. She used to love movies, parties, people. Now she shunned all, and was a veritable recluse.

The family physician, reading from his record of treatments, testified that he had treated her in all for about a month. The emphasis in treatment seemed to be on the elbow injury. True, he did state that she had complained of headaches. When asked on cross-examination what he had prescribed for this condition, he said phenobarbital. But he testified firmly that shortly after the date of the accident he had diagnosed the plaintiff's injuries as a cerebral concussion, with changed personality as an aftermath.

In addition to the other reasons which led me to believe that this diagnosis should be examined carefully, I could not reconcile the plaintiff's change of personality with her marriage. Her husband was twenty-one years old and appeared to be no more steadfast or devoted than the average boy of that age. They had married six months before the trial, about two years after the accident had occurred. I doubted that their courtship would have survived, or burgeoned into marriage, had she been half as melancholic during the two-year wooing period as her husband and other witnesses portrayed her.

I weighed the advisability of questioning the family doctor. I regarded my specialized experience as complementary to the general experience of the jurors. Did the need for clarification or amplification outweigh the dangers to the parties from judicial interference?

I decided to put the question.

"Doctor," I said, "you have testified that within a few weeks after the accident you had diagnosed the plaintiff's case as a cerebral hemorrhage with serious sequelae, such as changed personality, and so forth. Is that so?"

"Yes," said the doctor.

"Have you any uniform practice, Doctor, with regard to referring patients suffering from such injuries to a qualified neurologist?" I asked.

He hesitated. "I usually do that," he said. "But in this case I decided not to do so."

With that I let him go. I had barely touched upon what might be a source for consideration by the jury, or for either lawyer to pursue further if he so desired. Both lawyers were evidently fearful of asking him his reasons for not sending the plaintiff to a neurologist. I thought I had gone as far as necessary in opening this avenue of deliberation for the jury. To go further might betoken partisanship. I had no interest in which party won the lawsuit.

A neurologist was also called by the plaintiff. He had been retained by her lawyer a week before the commencement of the trial, to examine the plaintiff and testify at the trial. He testified to an imposing list of permanent, postconcussion neurological injuries. He was about to leave the stand, without having been asked certain questions I had in mind. I decided to ask him those questions.

"Doctor," I said, "is there any recognized treatment for the condition from which you found the plaintiff to be suffering?"

"Oh, yes," he said.

"Did you prescribe that treatment?" I asked.

"No," he said. Then he volunteered hastily, "I wasn't asked."

I held my peace thereafter. It is not often that a judge will take over a critical part of a witness's examination. Judges are wary about questioning witnesses on fundamental issues.

Sometimes such a start sucks a judge into a position in which he becomes virtually associate counsel for one side. If an experienced, able lawyer overmatches his incompetent opponent, the judge may find himself taking over witness after witness on examination. This he does not to influence the jury's verdict but to elicit pertinent testimony which the less skillful lawyer has overlooked or seems unable to bring out clearly.

And sometimes, with and without justification, the lawyer does not feel that the judge's helpful hand is particularly helpful, or he resents the interference.

A small-scale manufacturer was suing on a theory of breach of warranty, claiming that defective merchandise had been shipped him by the defendant. When the plaintiff's lawyer rested his case, and before the defendant's attorney could move to dismiss, I called both lawyers to the bench.

"I don't think you've proved any damages, as yet," I said to the plaintiff's lawyer. I went on to explain that it appeared to be a technical omission, and I was sure that if he reopened his case and recalled his client to the stand he could remedy the defect in his proof.

"Judge," he replied, "I'm sure I've made out a case." He cited two cases in support of his contention.

"I've read those cases," I said. "They're in your brief. I don't think they apply in this case."

"I'm certain they do, and I'm willing to back my judgment," he persisted.

"But you can't possibly prejudice your case by recalling your client, and then there'd be no question about the case going to the jury," I said. "Even if you're right, and I have grave doubts on that score, you have no right to gamble needlessly with your client's case."

The plaintiff's lawyer was young and inexperienced, and possessed a doggedness which might have been admirable under other circumstances.

"It's my responsibility and not yours, Judge," he answered. "If I'm wrong it's my funeral."

This bordered on insolence. It was on the tip of my tongue to snap, "Very well, so it is your funeral. Case dismissed!"

But I checked this impulse by looking at his client. Such a decision would be his funeral. He appeared to be a gnarled, hard-working small businessman. He had impressed me favorably as a witness.

I sent the lawyers back to the counsel table and recalled the plaintiff to the stand. While his attorney fumed I asked him the few questions required to remove all doubt as to the legality of his claim. The case continued and the plaintiff procured a verdict from the jury.

Whenever roiled by an attorney—and it is very seldom—I always associate the client with the case before taking any action. This is a device I have found useful as a check on hasty or unconsidered reaction. It is exactly the opposite of what I did as a prosecutor. Then I sought to block out the personality and personal history of the defendants, except to the extent necessary to try my case. It is less rending to prosecute a cipher than a human being with the normal complement of family, friends, and temptations.

At times experienced and well-controlled lawyers are fearful of a judge's intervention in a lawsuit.

Serjeant Ballantine, a great English barrister of the nineteenth century, told of the time when an experienced judge interrupted him while he was cross-examining a witness, saying, "Really, this is a long way from the point."

"I am aware of that," said Ballantine. "If I were to begin any nearer, the witness would discover my object."

Another story is told of a judge who took the case out of the hands of the lawyers, and examined and cross-examined witnesses at great length and with great vigor. Finally, one of the lawyers could not contain himself any longer, and blurted out: "Judge, I don't mind your trying the case for me, but for God's sake, don't lose it!"

* VII *

Trials and Tribulations

IF THERE WERE efficiency engineers for courthouse operations, one might express this opinion:

"You've got a pretty good plant and some fine products. Your substantive laws, which define rights and duties, are excellent. In the main they reflect sensibly the wisdom and experience of mankind. But your production of facts isn't half as efficient as your production of laws. This trial you're all so proud of often debases rather than strengthens your laws. In its present form the trial sometimes operates as a bottleneck and throttles your production of facts."

As in so many fields, it is easier to voice the criticism than suggest the remedy. But gradually, surely, the courts have been responding to this challenge. Witness such revealing procedures as bills of particulars, alibi disclosures, physical examinations of plaintiffs in personal injury cases, and many others which are accepted and taken for granted today.

Legal fact finding has always striven to become more comprehensive, more reliable and true. But it has been slow and tortuous progress. Recently, an important development has been the shifting of the center of gravity of the trial to the pretrial preparation. Slowly the frontiers of a trial are being advanced to the time when the complaint and answer have been served. The trial has really been in progress during all of the months or years of pretrial preparation.

The courts are becoming increasingly liberal in requiring the parties to a lawsuit to inform each other substantially of their evidence in advance of trial. The object is to make the trial less of a game of wits, and more of an informed search for truth.

Some courts, notably federal courts, grant a party in civil cases a sweeping examination before trial of his adversary on all matters in issue. They no longer flinch from giving a party a license for a "fishing expedition" into the details of his opponent's case. More and more cases are won, lost, or settled on pretrial disclosures.

There is a tendency in litigation to level off the advantages of the technical superiority or individual brilliancy of lawyers. The fact's the thing—not the lawyer. And the function of the trial is to elicit the facts—unobstructed and unenhanced by professional ineptitude or excellence.

The area of dispute in civil cases becomes narrowed—so narrow that there is less and less room or need for the brilliant maneuvers or opportunism of expert trial counsel. The area of the unknown also contracts. The trial loses some of the aspects of a game. I believe the romantic era of the trial lawyer is drawing to a close—and that it will never revive in the full flower of nineteenth-century rhetoric.

The trial itself will become more of a medium for the laboratory assembling of tested factors. There will be a minimum of surprises, gaps in evidence, gnawing doubts. The hazards inherent in finishing a trial at a given place, within a given, uninterrupted period, will be reduced by the pretrial inquiries. The trial's boundaries of time and place will be broadened.

It might be argued that when a litigant exposes his entire case, down to the last detail, he bares his chest to an unscrupulous adversary; that such an opponent, knowing the other side's evidence, will be free to fabricate evidence and suborn perjury to overcome it. This, of course, could be a decided and unfair advantage, since an honest adversary will not stoop to such tactics.

But fraud and perjury have an advantage now, under the hampering conditions of the traditional trial. Scrupulous litigants must cross-examine blindly and scurry about frantically for last-minute evidence with which to combat the knavery. If, however, the fabricated evidence is revealed by pretrial disclosure, it will be known to the opposing party well in advance of trial. The honest party can test the dubious evidence minutely, comprehensively, and in his own good time; he will have months, instead of hours, for collateral investigation. It seems to me the advantage in early discovery of the other side's evidence rests with the honorable litigant.

The strictures of time and the lack of facilities for investigating suspect evidence during a trial tend to frustrate the discovery of perjury. When uncovered, it is usually the result of luck or inspiration. The bogus engineer mentioned two chapters back, who claimed degrees from Notre Dame and M.I.T., was exposed through the defendant's inspired hunch; and luckily, the information for confounding the plaintiff was procured overnight. If the demolishing evidence had not been readily available, the plaintiff's claims would have gone unchallenged. But, had he made those claims during a pretrial proceeding, months or years before trial, there would have been ample time to check his qualifications, and the chances of exposure as a routine litigation consequence would have been much improved.

I recall another case in which bold perjury was uncovered only because of a coincidence—or call it luck. In this case a witness was discredited upon cross-examination in the trial of a matrimonial suit.

A private detective, hired by the plaintiff's wife, testified that he had trailed the defendant husband on a certain night. He told of following him from his office to a residential hotel, from which he emerged in the company of a young woman. He testified that they went to a night club, where they remained for a few hours, and that they left in a taxicab, the detective following in his car.

According to the detective, the taxicab parked about a block from the hotel where the young woman presumably lived. He said the couple had remained in this taxicab about half an hour. He watched from his car but observed nothing of what went on inside the taxicab. After the passengers left he stated that he hailed the taxi driver and had a conversation with him. No effort was made to introduce any testimony of this conversation.

The next witness produced by the plaintiff was the taxi driver himself. He said that the defendant had directed him to park by the curb for a while, and to keep his taxi meter running. He bore out the detective's testimony that he had remained there for half an hour; and he gave a lurid recital of the love-making he had observed in the back of his car, with no details omitted. He was relinquished for cross-examination.

LAWYER: You make notes of every call you receive on what is known as a trip card, do you not?

WITNESS: Yes.

LAWYER: Have you the trip card for this particular night?

WITNESS: Nope. I gave it to the checker when I turned the cab in.

LAWYER: Could you get it and bring it to court this afternoon?

WITNESS: Oh, the company only keeps them three months under the law and then throws them away.

LAWYER: Did you ask the company to hold this particular trip card?

WITNESS: Nope. Why should I?

LAWYER: Well, you knew you were going to be called as a witness in this case.

WITNESS: No, I didn't.

LAWYER: You had given a statement to the private detective. You knew there was some chance you'd be called as a witness.

WITNESS: So what! What's that got to do with a trip card?

LAWYER: I suggest it might be some proof that you actually made this trip to the hotel. But we'll pass on to something else. Wasn't it pretty dark where you were parked?

WITNESS: Light enough to see what was going on in back. We weren't far from a street lamp.

LAWYER: How did you observe this couple? Did you turn around to look at them?

WITNESS: Look, counselor, I wouldn't do that. I'm a gentleman. I seen them through my rear-vision mirror.

The defendant's attorney questioned him at length, but fruitlessly, in an effort to shake his story. The driver was still under cross-examination when the luncheon recess was declared. After lunch the defendant's lawyer resumed the examination; a fresh eagerness was evident in his entire bearing.

LAWYER: This morning you testified you saw the defendant and this young woman through your rear-view mirror.

WITNESS: That's right.

LAWYER: You're sure you didn't turn around and look at them?

WITNESS: I'm positive. I seen them through the rear-vision mirror.

LAWYER: Where was the mirror located?

WITNESS: On top of the windshield—near the middle.

LAWYER: Inside the cab?

WITNESS: Sure.

LAWYER: The taxicab you were driving was owned by the City Taxi Company, was it not?

WITNESS: Yes.

LAWYER: And, of course, you were employed by that company.

WITNESS: Yes.

LAWYER: Mr. Witness, isn't it a fact that on this night, and for a number of weeks before that, none of the taxis operated by the City Taxi Company had rear-vision mirrors?

WITNESS: (uneasily) That was some other time.

LAWYER: Isn't it a fact that on this night the cab was equipped with outside mirrors only, which gave the driver no view of the rear interior of the cab?

WITNESS: They stripped the cars of the inside mirrors for a while, but I think it was some other time—not this night.

LAWYER: You think! Are you sure?

WITNESS: Now, counselor, I'm getting confused. I won't swear to it.

LAWYER: Mr. Saunders, please stand. Mr. Witness, do you know this gentleman?

WITNESS: Yeah. He's with the company, in the office.

LAWYER: If I told you that his records indicate that the rear-view mirrors were off on the night in question, would that refresh your recollection?

OPPOSING LAWYER: I object. Oh—I'll withdraw the objection.

JUDGE: You may answer.

WITNESS: Honest, I don't know no more. Maybe I turned around and looked.

By the time the cross-examination was concluded the witness was in an abject state. On the defendant's case the company records were introduced. They indicated that the inside rear-view mirrors had been removed from all cabs some months before the fateful night, and that they had not been replaced until two months later.

After the jury had returned a verdict in favor of the defendant, I spoke with his lawyer.

"How did you ever light on that information about the rear-view mirrors?" I asked.

"Judge, it's one of those coincidences that happen once in a professional career," he said. "Joe Harkness, who's an old friend, represents the defendant in the case that you are holding to follow mine. Joe is attorney for half the taxi fleets in town. I met him in your courtroom this morning and we made an appointment for lunch. He was sitting here waiting for you to declare a recess, while the taxi driver was testifying.

"On the way to the restaurant Joe said to me, 'I have a hazy recollection that about a year or two ago a few taxi companies, including City Cab, experimented for several months with the removal of the interior mirrors. They had an idea that passengers would favor their elimination, and that drivers were paying more attention to what was going on in the back of the cab than to what was going on in the roadway. After a few months drivers squawked that they needed the interior mirrors for backing up and other purposes and that the passengers weren't even aware of the change, so they restored them.'

"Joe knew some of the City Cab people," continued the lawyer. "He was good enough to call up, from the restaurant, and verify his hunch. You know the rest from what happened in the courtroom."

I recall another case in which the plaintiff sued his brother for twenty thousand dollars. The plaintiff introduced into evidence his canceled check in that amount, payable to his brother and bearing the written notation "Loan to be repaid within three months." The defendant claimed the check represented his brother's investment in a business partnership which did not fare well; that since they were brothers they had not reduced their arrangement to writing.

The defendant claimed that the notation was not on the check when his brother gave it to him. He asked an opportunity to subpoena the records of the plaintiff's bank, which I gave him.

Unfortunately for the plaintiff, his bank made microfilm copies of all checks it honored. The minute copy of the check in evidence was blown up to full check size. Unlike the original check produced by the plaintiff in court, it bore no notation indicating that it represented a loan. The plaintiff had written in those important words after the canceled check had been returned to him.

I impounded the exhibits in this case with the clerk of the court and referred the entire matter to the district attorney. It is seldom that evidence of perjury is clear enough to warrant prosecution. Ordinarily a judge may be morally certain that a claim is spurious or a witness is lying; however, his certainty may be based upon a number of indicia which are significant to the judge but have no status as evidence. Very often in a case, two sets of witnesses tell conflicting stories. Which is lying, which is telling the truth? Without substantial collateral evidence to support one side, no prosecutor would dare seek an indictment for perjury.

Of course, in the check case the microfilm not only was decisive corroboration of the defendant's version of the matter, but also independent evidence of deliberate perjury.

In this case too it was not until the time of trial that the defendant first knew of the all-important notation which had been made upon the check. The pretrial procedure would have revealed it long before trial. Pretrial examinations also discourage the use of trumped-up evidence by litigants who hope to put over perjury in the hurry and excitement of a trial.

In a leading case, the United States Supreme Court has said:

"We agree, of course, that the deposition-discovery rules are to be accorded a broad and liberal treatment. No longer can the time-honored cry of 'fishing expedition' serve to preclude a party from inquiring into the facts underlying his opponent's case. Mutual knowledge of all the relevant facts gathered by both parties is essential to proper litigation. To that end, either party may compel the other to disgorge whatever facts he has in his possession. The deposition-discovery procedure simply advances the stage at which the disclosure can be compelled from the time of trial to the period preceding it, thus reducing the possibility of surprise." (*Hickman* v. *Taylor,* 329 U.S. 495, 507.)

This book treats mostly with the trial of today. This is my obeisance to reality, since I am convinced the trial will retain its present pre-eminence in the juridical structure for a long time. But a glimpse of the trial of yesterday will help us understand the evolution of the trial of today and tomorrow.

I wish to convey some idea of how thoroughly the lawmakers munch and digest all proposed changes. The process seems tedious and slow, but has its advantages.

As Mr. Justice Frankfurter has said: ". . . much long-headed thought and patient experimentation are demanded lest uncritical use may lead to hasty jettisoning of hard-won gains of civilization. The rational process of trial and error implies a wary use of novelty and a critical adoption of change."

I shall discuss sketchily two well-known rules of law among those which govern the trial of a lawsuit. Like so many other rules, they have been born and shaped out of hard experience. I give no assurance that they will not be revised or eliminated completely at some future time, nor do I indicate my unreserved approval of them.

The law holds that it is unsafe and unwise to admit certain types of proof. When the law is uneasy lest the perils of fraud or mistake corrupt the usefulness of evidence, it will often exclude such evidence. Call it excessive caution if you will; call it distrust of the perceptions and common sense of jurors and judges. At any rate, it is a historic development.

At one time the parties to a lawsuit, and any witnesses who had an interest in its outcome, were disqualified from testifying. This disqualification had its origin in a belief that persons having a financial interest in the result of a lawsuit were especially likely to testify falsely. So strong was this conviction that the bars to the witness stand in England were not lifted for interested witnesses until early in the nineteenth century; and parties, their husbands and wives, were not permitted to testify until some time after. Imagine a contemporary lawsuit in which the plaintiff, the defendant, and the most vitally interested witnesses were unable to testify!

No longer, in Anglo-American jurisprudence, is such testimony regarded as so dangerous that it must not be received under any circumstances. The modern rule holds that the witness is competent to testify and that his testimony should be received; but his interest may be considered in weighing the value of his testimony and his credibility.

Now this change was not effected overnight. A legislature, commission, or board of judges did not sit down and decide, "These disqualifications are unsound. A financial stake in a case does not necessarily mean that a witness will perjure himself. The injustice worked by the exclusion will often outweigh the possible dangers. We shall therefore remove the disqualifications."

Instead, lawyers, judges, and others studied, pondered, and debated the proposed changes. No snap judgments were made. The experience under the existing rules was analyzed and appraised. Arguments were made pro and con by the best minds of the times.

A legal writer of the early nineteenth century thus presented the core of an influential body of thought:

"This rule of exclusion, considered in its principle, requires little explanation. It is founded on the known infirmities of human nature, which is too weak to be generally restrained by religious or moral obligations, when tempted, and solicited in a contrary direction by temporal interests. There are, no doubt, many whom no interests could seduce from a sense of duty, and their exclusion by the operation of this rule may in particular cases shut out the truth. But the law must prescribe general rules; and experience proves that more mischief would result from the general reception of interested witnesses than is occasioned by their general exclusion."

Jeremy Bentham, the great English law reformer, answered:

"In the eyes of the English lawyer, one thing, and one thing only, has a value; that thing is money. . . .

"If you will believe the man of law, there is no such thing as the fear of God; no such thing as regard for reputation; no such thing as fear of legal punishment; . . . weighed against the interest produced by the value of a farthing, the utmost mass of interest producible from the action of all those affections put together, vanishes in the scale. . . . This in Westminster Hall is science; this in Westminster Hall is law."

And later, when discussing the impact of the law upon the parties to a lawsuit, he said:

"A party is not suffered to be examined on his own behalf. Observe the consequence; he is delivered without mercy into the hands of a mendacious witness on the other side. Your adversary, to make evidence for a suit he means to bring against you, sends an emissary to you to engage you in a conversation, that, when called upon as a witness, he may impute confessions to you such as you never made. When the evidence comes to be given at the trial, the witness tells what story he pleases: as for you, you must not open your mouth to contradict him, although, were you admitted to state what passed, it might be in your power to satisfy the judge, that the account given of the conversation by the witness could not possibly have been true. . . . Every defendant is a liar. But every human being may, at the pleasure of every other, be converted into a defendant. Therefore, and by that means, every human being may, at the pleasure of every other, be converted into a liar, and, in that character, his capacity of giving admissible testimony annihilated. . . . In principle there is but one mode of searching out the truth: . . . Be the dispute what it may, see everything that is to be seen; hear everybody who is likely to know anything about the matter; hear everybody, but most attentively of all, and first of all, those who are likely to know most about it—the parties."

These disqualifications have now been removed, except that, in almost every state, including New York, a person interested in the outcome of a lawsuit may not testify about a conversation or a personal transaction with a deceased or mentally incompetent person. Some states permit such testimony but require corroboration from a disinterested witness. The kind of interest which will disqualify a witness is usually a monetary one, not an intellectual or emotional interest.

As in the case of its broader ancestor a century ago, this rule is presently under sharp attack. It is urged that we should not attempt to protect the estates of decedents and incompetents at the expense of the living. And many of the arguments of one hundred and fifty years ago are echoed today. Prominent is the contention that the right to cross-examine the survivor to the conversation or transaction is an adequate safeguard for the estate.

The question posed involves a nice balancing of advantages and disadvantages. If the rule is retained, many plaintiffs will be forever barred from proving a transaction essential to their case. If the rule is eliminated, many an estate will be mulcted, because the voice to refute the perjury has been stilled by death or derangement. Such is the crucible in which our rules of law are fashioned.

As a young law clerk I witnessed the trial of a case in which the plaintiff, a lady of dubious repute, sued the estate of her former patron, who had been a wealthy broker. During the last few years of his life he had maintained her in fine style, and had given her a generous monthly allowance. She claimed an arrangement, for services rendered, under which this allowance was to be paid for the remainder of her life. (Such claims are now barred in New York.)

The plaintiff was plainly disqualified from testifying as to any conversation she had had with her late benefactor. Her sister, who, in the eyes of the law, had no interest in the lawsuit, suffered from no such disability. Accordingly, she took the witness stand and testified to a series of conversations she had overheard at her sister's apartment. She stated that the deceased had asked the plaintiff to watch after him and said that in return he would provide for a continuance of the allowance for the remainder of her life. There were some ambiguous writings introduced into evidence, but the outcome of the case hinged on the credence given to the sister's story by the jury.

On cross-examination, it appeared that the lawyer representing the estate doubted that she had ever met the decedent.

"Will you please describe the late Mr. J.?" he asked.

"Certainly. When I first met him, when he made these promises to my sister, he was a fine-looking man in his late forties."

"According to your testimony that was about nine years ago—about seven years before he died?"

"That's right," answered the witness.

"Please describe him further," directed the lawyer.

"Well, he had dark hair, kind of gray around the temples. He was very distinguished-looking. He had a dark, cropped mustache with some gray in it."

"Did he wear glasses?"

"Oh, yes, he always wore dark tortoise-shell ones."

"Now, madam, I don't want to trick you. Did he wear glasses when you first met him seven years before his death?"

"Er—no, I'm not too sure about that. He may have started wearing them later."

"Hm. Are you as uncertain about his mustache?"

"Oh, no," she trilled. "He always had a mustache."

"Would it surprise you to learn, madam, that Mr. J. did not grow a mustache until three years before his death?"

"I object," the opposing lawyer snapped.

"Oh, why waste time?" said the examining attorney. "Ask your client."

The plaintiff forlornly nodded her head.

"I probably mixed up my dates," volunteered the witness.

"I'm sure of that," her questioner agreed grimly. "I suggest, madam, that the first time you ever visited New York was two years before Mr. J.'s death, and that it was then you met him for the first time."

Evidence was later presented which indicated that the witness had been in her home state of California when the alleged conversations had taken place. The jury returned a verdict in favor of the defendant.

I relate this incident realizing that it can be cited by both proponents and opponents of the modern rule. It can be argued that were it not for the rule the plaintiff would have testified to the conversations with the deceased, with the likelihood that she would not have been trapped and discredited. Or, it can be urged that the rule is only a theoretical safeguard, that an unscrupulous litigant can always supply the deficiencies in proof, and that only skillful cross-examination had exposed the plaintiff's sister.

Another example of the law's concern with limiting a trial to verifiable evidence is the familiar hearsay rule. Hearsay evidence is defined as "evidence of the existence of a fact based not on the witness's own personal knowledge or observation but on what someone else said." The witness testifying to a hearsay statement usually says that he heard someone else state a fact relating to the issues of the case; and his testimony is offered as proof of that fact.

For example, the plaintiff in the bus door case in which my juror friend sat could not have testified that she overheard one of the passengers say that the operator had closed the door before the passenger had alighted. Such a statement would have been inadmissible as hearsay. The passenger to whom the remark was attributed could come to court, however, and give direct testimony under oath as to what he or she had observed and, in turn, submit to cross-examination.

The traditional reason for barring hearsay evidence is the desirability of testing all assertions of fact by oath and cross-examination. As already indicated, the understanding, memory, and narration powers of the witness may be faulty. But he at least may be examined as to the strength of his recollection and his disposition to speak the truth; and his demeanor could be observed, upon direct as well as cross-examination. There is no way to test the trustworthiness of the statement attributed to an absent person. He may be an irresponsible character. He may have certain obsessing prejudices. His perceptions and memory may be poor; he may have been boasting, exaggerating, or lying. He may even have based his positive assertion on something told him in turn by one or more other and anonymous persons. The law guards its portals jealously against such untestable testimony.

One may perceive the modern rule in the process of formation as we read the record of Sir Walter Raleigh's case. Raleigh was tried in 1603 for a treasonable conspiracy. The chief witness against him was Lord Cobham, who had confessed his own guilt and in a sworn statement before trial implicated Raleigh. Cobham was not produced on the trial and only his statement was offered. Raleigh's protest against the use of this statement, as depriving him of the right of confrontation and cross-examination of Cobham, was a precursor of the present hearsay rule.

"But it is strange," said Raleigh, "to see how you press me still with my Lord Cobham, and yet will not produce him; it is not for gaining of time or prolonging my life that I urge this; he is in the house hard by, and may soon be brought hither; let him be produced, and if he will yet accuse me or avow this confession of his, it shall convict me and ease you of further proof."

To this most reasonable request, the judges ruled "that in respect it might be a mean to cover many with treasons, and might be prejudicial to the King, therefore, by the law, it was not sufferable. . . . Where no circumstances do concur to make a matter probable, then an accuser may be heard; but so many circumstances agreeing and confirming the accusation in this case, the accuser is not to be produced; for, having first confessed against himself voluntarily, and so charged another person, if we shall hear him again in person, he may, for favour or fear, retract what formerly he hath said, and the jury may, by that means, be inveigled."

It was upon such evidence, or lack of evidence, that Raleigh was sentenced to execution. However, public indignation at the sheer iniquity of the procedure did much to pave the way for the establishment of the hearsay rule. Legal writers have pointed out that the rule reflects a wisdom as old as the Bible, where, in the 18th chapter of Proverbs, we read that "He that pleadeth his case first seemeth just, but his neighbor cometh and searcheth him out."

There are certain exceptions to the hearsay rule. The law is adaptable and realistic, and strives to meet the challenge of changing times and conditions. Under certain circumstances, account book entries made in the regular course of business are admissible in evidence, although they are written hearsay evidence. The rule has been relaxed for two reasons.

First, by reason of necessity. Commercial litigation requires submission of proof through books of account. It would be almost impossible to trace each item back to the employee who handled it, and produce such employee in court. Second, experience has proved the reliability of such accounts, when the entries have been made at or reasonably near the time the transaction occurred. The core of this reasoning is that the entries were made when presumably there was no incentive to falsify, when the dominating desire was for accuracy.

Still, the courts and legislators have surrounded the admission of such entries with many safeguards.

These rules of law are bred from common experience, not from the fevered imagination of judges. You apply the hearsay rule repeatedly in your daily life.

A vase in your living room has fallen and shattered. At the time your teen-age son and daughter were practicing a dance step to music from a recording. Each accuses the other of having brushed off the vase. You cannot decide which of them is at fault.

Finally your daughter blurts out, "Emily Smith was visiting me and she saw what happened. She told me she saw John knock off the vase."

John shouts, "She said nothing of the kind."

It isn't likely you'd accept your daughter's hearsay statement of what Emily Smith saw. You'd reserve decision until you had an opportunity to speak with Emily. You'd want to find out what she observed. If it transpired that she did place the blame on Johnny, you'd bear in mind that she was your daughter's friend. You would probe the depth of her disposition to aid your daughter.

This is what you would probably do in reaching a decision within your own household. You would reserve judgment, even though you had long before formed an opinion as to your daughter's truthfulness and trustworthiness based upon a lifetime of intimate association. Should jurors or a judge to whom your daughter is a complete stranger be permitted to consider such testimony?

In the course of a recent hearing held in the City of New York, dealing with the connection between politics and local crime conditions, an examiner asked this question of a district attorney who was on the witness stand:

"Did you ever hear that this man Moran . . . in the mayoralty campaign of 1948-1949 went on the road and demanded a cash contribution from many of the gamblers hereabouts to promote the O'Dwyer candidacy, from bookies, and got them in large amounts?"

"I have heard stories to that effect," answered the district attorney.

Of course, it is well-nigh impossible to refute such an answer. A rumor is bred from common talk. What witnesses does one call to rebut an inference drawn from common talk?

But aside from other legal defects, this question illustrates the dangers inherent in hearsay answers. There are implications in the alleged rumor that large contributions to a political campaign were coerced from gamblers. How can one disprove such an inference? It would be difficult enough if the gamblers who made the rumored contributions were named by the witness. The accused could at least produce the same opposing proof as though the named gamblers had appeared in person and testified to making contributions; only he would not have the opportunity to confront and cross-examine his accusers. However, the only way he could meet the hearsay innuendoes in the quoted question would be by calling every bookmaker in the City of New York to the witness stand—an obvious impossibility.

Thousands of opinions have been written, weaning and developing these exclusory rules, expanding and contracting them. The hearsay rule has also been assailed and defended bitterly and strongly for generations.

If you sat in a courtroom and heard the application of one of these rules being argued, it would probably sound bewildering and technical to you. Yet, as we have observed, they are the products of our experience and common sense; and they reflect in great measure your own thought processes.

We have all heard the flip dismissal of rules of evidence as designed to impede the search for truth and make of a trial a game of chance, a set of mystifying rules conceived so that they can be decoded only by professionals. In the main, the rules of evidence exclude unreliable matter which you in your own daily affairs would equally view very guardedly as evidence of the facts to be proved.

Efforts to relax these rules are being questioned right now. Injustices appear in the nonjudicial trial procedures of administrative agencies—such as the National Labor Relations Board, congressional committees and the like—which were designed to serve their broad purposes unhampered by the restrictive and protective body of rules developed over the years by the courts.

In fact there is growing agitation for some restraint in the conduct of these nonjudicial hearings, fed by community displeasure with instances of unfairness and indignity to persons involved in their proceedings. The arguments for reformation are not unlike those which nudged the Anglo-American law over to the side of the defendant; strikingly similar is the contention that the extra-judicial processes lend themselves to abuse by over-zealous and power-bent public officers.

It would be ironic if the administrative and nonjudicial hearing procedures were in their course to follow, at least in part, the long trail hewn by the law, back to the traditional protective rules which were spurned as anachronistic and cumbersome.

The law is a living, growing organism, giving strength to and gaining strength from other dynamic forces in the world. It will be interesting, in this connection, to follow the growing impact of psychiatry upon the judicial process. The degree of acceptance by the law may parallel the degree of general, public acceptance of the validity and soundness of psychiatric findings.

Judges still open the door gingerly and peer skeptically through the crack at this aggressive infant science. Expert testimony may be received in certain courts to determine initially whether a witness possesses the minimal faculties and understanding required to stamp him as competent to testify. The test has been stated to be, does the witness understand what he is saying, and does he understand the obligation of an oath?

Medical testimony is received when a party's mental condition bears directly upon the contested issues on trial—such as the capacity of a testator to draw a will. But there is no such unanimity when psychiatry is enlisted to discredit the ordinary sworn witness. Some judges fear that if one side may introduce such expert testimony to discredit the witness, the other side may also produce its expert to contradict him and sustain the normality of the witness. If this should be done with a number of witnesses, the collateral and bewildering issues might engulf the main issues and confuse the jury. The trial would also be prolonged without limit.

There are strong pressures to lift the bars to psychiatric testimony—at least for the purpose of attacking the credibility of a witness. Wigmore, for example, urges that "no judge should ever let a sex-offense charge go to the jury unless the female complainant's social history and mental make-up have been examined and testified to by a qualified physician." He quotes a letter of Dr. Karl A. Menninger, the noted psychiatrist, in support of this recommendation.

Dr. Menninger wrote:

"Every girl who enters a plausible but unproved story of rape should be required to have a psychiatric examination. . . . The reason I think that rape in particular belongs in this category is one well known to psychologists, namely, that fantasies of being raped are exceedingly common in women, indeed, one may almost say that they are probably universal. By this I mean that most women, if we may judge from our clinical experience, entertain more or less consciously at one time or another fleeting fantasies or fears that they are being or will be attacked by a man. Of course, the normal woman who has such a fantasy does not confuse it with reality, but it is so easy for some neurotic individuals to translate their fantasies into actual belief and memory falsifications that I think a safeguard should certainly be placed upon this type of criminal charge."

The two recent and widely publicized trials of Alger Hiss for perjury illustrate the judicial pangs which accompany the growth of every rule of evidence. The defense produced an eminent psychiatrist who had not examined Whittaker Chambers, the key witness for the prosecution. He had, however, observed and studied him in the courtroom all the time he testified. The judge upon the first trial would not allow the testimony of this psychiatrist. Upon the second trial, under similar circumstances, another judge permitted him to testify concerning Chambers' alleged abnormalities.

The second judge allowed this testimony upon the theory that Chambers' credibility was one of the major issues upon which the jury would pass. It is the jury's exclusive function to determine the credibility of witnesses. He held that the "existence of insanity or mental derangement is admissible for the purpose of discrediting a witness."

Very illuminating on the process of judicial acceptance of scientific procedures is a sentence in the memorandum filed by the second judge in explanation of his decision. Commenting on a state court case which on the surface appeared to hold contrary to his ruling, he said: "This was in 1921—before the value of psychiatry had been recognized."

It matters not how well defined and unambiguous the applicable rules of law may be, there is always uncertainty as to the outcome of a trial. So long as facts are pitted against facts, the result is unpredictable. There are too many variables, including the personality, experience, intelligence, integrity, prejudices, and other characteristics of the human beings who shape its course—the lawyers, jurors, judges, and witnesses. There is unprovable perjury and coloration of evidence.

The evidence will strike certain judges or jurors one way, others another way. An able lawyer will present the same evidence in a more favorable light than a poor one.

Some rules of law will be accepted by jurors. Others will be rejected. Some rules will be understood. Others will be misunderstood.

We have come a long way since the blood feud and trial by ordeal. But to the man of the future our concepts of a fair trial may seem as benighted and primitive as the trial by ordeal now seems to us. Only a rash man would dare predict how far we shall go in the future. This much can be said. If the social and physical sciences fulfill their promise, and when the fruits of those sciences are accepted by the courts, the elements of fraud and chance in the trial of an issue will be materially reduced. There will be few surprises, and a trial will truly be a medium through which a party can assert the rights vouched to him under the law.

* VIII *

The Judge's Role in a Trial

THE MOST MODEST of judges at times thinks that he can try a case better than one or both of the lawyers before him. He may be correct in his professional appraisal. But the likelihood is that if he exchanged places with the lawyer, if he went down into the arena to try the case and if the lawyer went up on the bench, the judge would execute few of the brilliant thrusts which he had conceived while on the bench.

For the judge is perched up on a vantage spot overlooking the arena, aloof physically and emotionally from its turmoil and distractions. He keeps his finger on the pulse of the case, makes notes on the chart, and is concerned only with its healthy progress.

The lawyer, on the other hand, is concerned naturally with the outcome of the case. Victory may mean retaining this client and securing others; defeat may mean loss of the client and diminution of professional prestige. The amount of his fee may hang on the result. If he is emnloyed on a contingent basis he may be left without a fee.

He is worried about whether the important witness subpoenaed at the last minute will be friendly or hostile, or whether he will show up at all; whether the judge will grasp the point he made in the brief he labored over until late last night, or brush it off with the same off-handedness that made him lose face with his client the day before. Does the judge like briefs, or is he one of the few judges who scorns them? Will his gem of a secretary leave because he insisted that she break a date in order to type the brief?

How long can he hold in court the witnesses who are clamoring to be called so that they may return to their jobs? Can he explain to them that he does not control the length of his adversary's cross-examination? Should he put in all of his evidence on his direct case, or gamble and hold back part for rebuttal, after the defendant has introduced his evidence, to buttress his contentions near the close of the case? How liberal is the judge in receiving rebuttal evidence?

Dare he ask the judge to adjourn court a little early in the afternoon, so that he can take care of that important real estate title closing he had scheduled for today? How will his wife react when he tells her he'll not be home for dinner tonight, and that she'll have to entertain his relatives without him; that he has to look up law on some unexpected arguments raised by his adversary? Should he review the plaintiff's foreman's testimony with him once more tonight before putting him on the stand?

And lastly, he has heartburn from that sandwich he gulped down at lunch today, because he spent almost all the lunch hour answering the telephone messages left for him at the office. He hopes his duodenal ulcer won't kick up again.

Is it any wonder that a judge will consider the issues in a case with a clearer head than a lawyer operating under such pressures? I daresay the same would hold true if the judge and lawyer changed positions.

A judge will interfere rarely with a lawyer's handling of a case. There are exceptions, of course. There are exhibitionists and judges who are unable to shed their habits of advocacy. Lawyers dread appearing before one judge who was an able trial counsel before he ascended the bench. Now he will not yield the central role to a lawyer at any stage of the trial.

On cross-examination a lawyer appearing before this judge may lay a foundation carefully for a critical question or series of questions. By patient questioning, the purpose of which is unknown to the witness, he mines every avenue of escape from the insupportable position into which he is luring him.

The lawyer's tactics are apparent to the judge, who had employed the same technique with great skill during his career at the bar. The judge waits, poised, until the lawyer approaches his climactic questions. Then the judge darts in for the kill; he takes over the questioning, and often demolition, of the witness. But sometimes the judge, not knowing into what deeper involvements the lawyer was ensnaring the witness, injects himself prematurely and permits the prey to scuttle to safety.

Fortunately, few judges indulge in this type of behavior. But few judges veer to the other extreme, and desire to be "coldly sublime, intolerably just."

Even the old English judges, variously portrayed as models of aloofness and austerity, were known to relax the barrier between bench and bar. A story is told of the great English judge, Lord Kenyon. A young lawyer was reading the terms of a conveyance in his courtroom. When he came to the word "enough," he pronounced it "enow."

Lord Kenyon stopped him, saying, "Call it 'enuff.' All words ending in *ough* must be pronounced *uff*, as rough, tough, and the like."

The young man continued to read. When he came to the word "plough" he hesitated, then pronounced it "pluff."

Lord Kenyon shook with merriment, and then said, "Young man, I sit corrected."

There is another story of Lord Camden, who was Chief Justice of England several generations ago. He was staying with Lord Dacre, in Essex. One day he took a walk in company with another guest, a gentleman who was very absent-minded. They reached the top of a near-by hill where stood the parish stocks.

The Chief Justice was curious to experience for himself the punishment he had so often meted out, and persuaded his companion to open the stocks and fasten him inside. After this was accomplished his absent-minded companion continued his walk, and not until he had returned to Lord Dacre's did he remember that he had left the Chief Justice in an unjudicial position.

Meanwhile, the novelty of the stocks wore off. Lord Camden tried to get out and found he could not extricate himself. He asked a countryman who was passing by to release him, but that worthy merely grinned and walked on, saying, "No! no! old gentleman, you wasn't set there for nothing." Finally, some servants dispatched by Lord Dacre rescued him.

Sometime later the Lord Chief Justice was presiding at the trial of a lawsuit for false imprisonment, brought against a magistrate by a man whom he had sentenced to the stocks. The counsel for the defendant magistrate tried to make light of the case, arguing that everybody knew that sitting in the stocks was no punishment at all.

Lord Camden beckoned to the defendant's lawyer and, leaning over the bench, whispered, "Brother, were you ever in the stocks?"

"Really, my lord, never," answered the lawyer.

"Well, I have been," said the Chief Justice. "And I can assure you it is not the trifle you represent it."

I hope to convey a judge's informal and often warm kinship with the bar. The longer a judge is on the bench, generally the warmer and mellower will become his relations with the bar. Of course, if a judge sours with age, the rapport between him and lawyers will deteriorate. This will be the fault of the judge. He can always receive back from the bar more than he gives to it.

Lawyers are very generous in their appraisal and treatment of the judiciary. Most lawyers, without the slightest hint of truckling, extend to most judges a great measure of respect and deference. Part of this goes with the office, because most lawyers revere the law, and the judge is its oracle. Part of this respect must be earned by the judge in action. A lawyer rejoices when he finds character, perception, and erudition in a judge, because then the judge ornaments the profession of which the lawyer is so proud. And for the same reasons a judge, also a member of the legal profession, rejoices in recognizing such traits in a lawyer.

But no matter how amiable he may be, a judge must at times become stern. Judge Learned Hand recently had occasion to say: "Justice can be as readily destroyed by the flaccidity of the judge as by his tyranny; impartial trials need a firm hand as much as a constant determination to give each one his due."

A judge occupies a unique position in relation to lawyers. In one aspect he is their fellow craftsman, pooling with them a great community of interests, experiences, and viewpoints. In another aspect he is walled off, something like a priest.

He proceeds ponderously amid trappings and intonings on a legislative and professional grant of powers seldom given to human beings. In his courtroom he has greater powers than the President. A bystander may with impunity hurl an epithet at the President. Should anyone so address a judge in the courtroom, he has the power to fine or imprison him for contempt of court. People rise when he enters. Lawyers are deferential, laymen timorous. It is this dual personality which makes the judge at one time both familiar and distant to lawyers.

Most of the judges with whom I have talked like trial work best. They are not dealing with facts sterilized by reduction to affidavit and memorandum form. They are hearing a re-enactment of chunks of life from the lips of witnesses. They are brought into intimate contact with their brethren of the bar, the lawyers.

But there are some judges who prefer the calm of the library to the comparative strife of the trial. A trial judge must rule quickly and decisively on important problems which may later embroil and divide the members of an appellate court for months. He must be resourceful and keen in the handling of excited men and potentially explosive situations. Some judges lack the temperament and background to perform happily in such a climate.

Or, they have no appetite for the trial judge's participation in the fact-finding function—either in collaboration with a jury or in a nonjury case. There is some basis for judges' flinching from acting as triers of the facts. I have posed a question to myself, based on the following case:

A large bank sued upon a note which had been executed by a

small merchant. The note had fallen due about eight years before suit was commenced. The merchant had died, and his widow, as executrix of his estate, was made the defendant. The manager of the branch bank which handled the loan had been friendly with the deceased merchant. The latter had maintained a moderate line of credit with the bank for many years, and the manager may have carelessly agreed to keep the loan open without renewing the note in writing from time to time. The widow interposed a defense to the effect that the claim was outlawed by the statute of limitations.

It is perfectly true that a lawsuit to recover upon a promissory note must be brought, in New York, within six years after the note becomes due and payable. Otherwise, the suit will be outlawed by what is known as the statute of limitations, on the theory that the defense would be hard put to procure evidence to defeat the claim after so long a time had elapsed.

But there are certain ways in which the statute of limitations may be prevented from running, so that the time to sue will be extended beyond the six-year period. One is by the maker of the note acknowledging the debt in writing. In such a case the slate is wiped clean and the statute of limitations begins to operate again from the date of such an acknowledgment of the debt.

In this case the bank relied upon a letter it had received from the deceased merchant during his lifetime, less than six years before the lawsuit was started. The bank contended this letter defeated the defense of the statute of limitations. The letter undoubtedly acknowledged the debt; but it also contained language which could have been interpreted as expressing an intention to pay an entirely different note from the one on which the lawsuit was based. The decedent had made a number of notes payable to the bank. All had been paid, except the one in suit. In view of the ambiguity, I submitted the question of the applicability of the letter to the jury. It promptly decided in favor of the widow against the large bank, and returned a defendant's verdict.

Now, let us reverse the positions of the parties. Suppose it was the widow who was suing the bank upon a note, and it was the bank which similarly pleaded the defense of the statute of limitations. The widow relied upon a similar letter from the bank to her husband, and the bank too claimed that the letter referred to another note, which had been paid. Would a jury interpret the letter under such circumstances as it did in the trial before me—in favor of the bank and against the widow? I have serious doubts. Would a judge construe the same letter differently, upon reading it in the two different settings? I wonder.

A major reason for a trial judge's concern about his decisions in nonjury proceedings is that an appellate court will rarely disturb his determination of the facts. This stamps the trial judge's findings with a disturbing finality.

The finding of the facts, which entails the acceptance of the sound, and the rejection of the unsound, evidence, and the final packaging of the remaining ingredients at the end of the trial court production line, are almost exclusively the function of the trial judge or jury. The package may be labeled judgment for plaintiff or defendant.

Seldom may an appellate court change or reject such findings. It may decide that on the facts as found in the trial court, the law was misapplied or misunderstood, so that the verdict or decision went in favor of the wrong party. In that event they may say, "We've looked into the package and think you've put the wrong label on it. We won't disturb the contents of your package, but we're going to change the label so that it will read in favor of the other party."

The appellate court may also decide that the trial judge admitted improper evidence or excluded proper evidence, or that he instructed the jury erroneously. Then it may reverse the verdict or decision, and send the case back to be tried anew. It then says in effect to the trial court, "We have examined the ingredients of your package, and find that it contains certain harmful substances." Or, "We find that you left out certain ingredients which, in the public interest, we feel should have been included to ensure the purity of your product. We are therefore returning your package, and directing that you process it once more, in accordance with the formula we are now giving you."

Lawyers and judges, notably appellate courts—which do not themselves observe the witnesses—emphasize the importance of observing the demeanor of witnesses during a trial. The witness stand is elevated so that the person testifying may be exposed to critical gaze. The significance attached to a witness's mien and bearing may have had its psychological and historical origin in the searching scrutiny our ancient forebears trained upon oath-takers—looking for some Divine manifestation in the event they were lying.

I believe this emphasis is somewhat exaggerated. I distrust my own surface reactions to a witness's demeanor. He is seldom at ease; an adaptable knave will often accommodate himself more readily to the rigid and unnatural climate of the courtroom than will an honest man. One judge's impression of an open countenance may be another's impression of a shifty look. The most depraved character I ever prosecuted had the beatific expression of a choirboy.

The perplexing problems of law and policy that come to an appellate judge—a judge who hears appeals from the mandates of other courts—carry their own travail. The responsibility for decisions that may have widespread and even national impact is not a light one. But to him the parties might well be anonymous; faces and voices, the demeanor of the witness on the stand, the clash and fire of men and women in the intensity of combat, cannot be preserved in a printed record of a trial.

The approach of an appellate judge to a case is accordingly somewhat statesmanlike in its detachment. The blood, sweat, and tears of litigation have been wrung out in the trial court. If the case involves an appeal from a conviction of murder, the appellate judge decides, of course, whether the defendant was given a fair trial. But the framework of his decision also embraces a consideration of whether such a trial would be fair to all future defendants placed in a position similar to that of the accused in the case on appeal. The trial judge's primary concern, however, is that the particular parties before him be afforded a fair trial.

Of course, no judge is pleased when an appellate court holds that he decided incorrectly. But seasoned trial judges seldom take such reversals to heart. New and inexperienced judges sometimes place great stock in their so-called "batting averages." They do not realize that the incidence of reversals or affirmances plays a small part in the appraisal of their caliber by the bar or their colleagues on the bench. For many years, one of the most esteemed judges on our bench had close to the highest average of reversals. There were two reasons for this. First, because of his ability many difficult and involved matters were assigned to him. Second, he did not fear to pioneer in thoughtful decisions which extended the boundaries of existing law.

Perhaps the earlier reflections and anecdotes in this book may put some flesh on a few skeletal statistics of the trial work in my court. Without a glimpse behind the bench, these figures would be meaningless.

In the most recent year for which official court figures have been published, the twenty-nine judges in my court disposed of a little less than two thousand defended cases in which proof was completed. This represents an average of sixty-nine cases per judge in which trials were completed. Over five thousand cases were settled before or during trial, in the calendar and trial parts. Over four thousand cases were disposed of in the pretrial parts. Of course, no more than two-thirds of the judges are assigned to the trial of cases in any given month; the rest are assigned to motion parts, appellate and pretrial work, and other court activities.

It must be appreciated that this volume of completed trials was not turned out on a judicial conveyer belt, operated by anonymous judges in indistinguishable black robes. Each case represented an incident out of the life of the community itself, pulsating with drama, tragedy, or comic relief. No two cases were alike. Each was important to the parties concerned.

Nor can the importance of the litigation to the parties be measured in terms of the amount of money involved. In fact, sometimes the size of the verdict is misleading as to either the gravity or the difficulty of the issues in a lawsuit. Such a case was tried recently before one of my associates.

The plaintiff, an alleged expert on trunks and luggage, sued the estate of a deceased woman who for some years prior to her death had been an elderly recluse. The plaintiff ran a small luggage shop in the neighborhood of her home. Upon her death he had been called in to open her trunks, which were tightly locked. He had succeeded in opening them, and had asked and been paid five dollars an hour for his services.

About a month later the executors decided that they had not located all of the assets of the estate. Someone who had known the old lady suggested that they look for secret compartments in her trunks. The executors called in the plaintiff again, to make such an examination.

After some search he discovered a secret drawer in one trunk, containing half a million dollars in United States currency. He claimed five per cent, or twenty-five thousand dollars, as the reasonable value of his expert services. It was the plaintiff's contention that this trunk was specially made for the deceased woman, and that he was one of the few experts in the world who could have detected the secret drawer. The executors refused to pay, and he brought suit for twenty-five thousand dollars.

During the course of the trial the defendants offered to settle for a few thousand dollars. The offer was spurned. The case went to a jury which returned a verdict of twelve dollars and fifty cents, on the basis of two and one-half hours required for the plaintiff's services, at the rate of five dollars an hour. Unfortunately for the plaintiff, the executors were able to produce a thirty-year-old catalogue of a well-known trunk manufacturer. It displayed the identical type of trunk which the plaintiff had opened, secret drawer and all. The old lady's trunk, it developed, was a well-known stock job, manufactured originally for use by actors on the road.

The case had taken several days to try. There were novel questions of law involved, in ruling on the testimony and on the preparation of the charge, which required the judge to do considerable research. Certainly all of this was not reflected in the amount of the verdict.

Almost always a judge must rule instantaneously when objection is made to a question during a jury trial, or when a motion is made to dismiss the complaint or to direct judgment. Twelve jurors may not be left dangling while a judge makes up his mind. In a nonjury case a puzzled judge can instruct the lawyers to present some other line of testimony, so that he may study and meditate the problem overnight. At the end of the case he can reserve decision and take weeks, if necessary, to rule on motions.

Yet, despite the greater relaxation, the lessened judicial effort, the administrative economies and the saving of time in the trial of nonjury cases, most of the judges I know would rather conduct jury trials—that is, except for equity trials, which will be touched upon later. One of the reasons may be the greater responsibility involved in deciding facts as well as law. I believe, however, that it is mainly a matter of legal aesthetics. Once more excepting equity trials, to lawyer and judge a trial can have form and beauty only if it is tried before the traditional couplet of judge and jury.

* IX *

The Judge without a Jury

JUDGES are called upon to do much more fact finding than is generally realized. There is a common assumption that a party is entitled to a trial by jury in every kind of case, or at least in all important cases. This is not so. There are many types of cases, some of great significance to parties and the community, in which there is no right to a trial by jury.

In New York a defendant is entitled to a jury trial when he is indicted by a grand jury and charged with a felony, and also in certain civil cases. Felonies, such as grand larceny, robbery, murder, manslaughter, rape, arson, etc., are regarded as the more serious crimes. But there are crimes called misdemeanors—such as petit larceny, unlawful entry, malicious mischief, and many others—which may be tried before a judge or judges without a jury. In New York a defendant may be convicted of a misdemeanor and sentenced to an indeterminate term in prison for a period up to three years. And he has no absolute right to trial by jury. The federal constitution assures trial by jury in many civil and in all criminal cases which are tried in the federal courts.

There is a vast area of litigation which is tried before a judge without a jury. These are known as equity cases.

Our equity system was born hundreds of years ago out of the shortcomings of that remarkable potpourri of case decisions ground out by the courts of England, which are today hailed proudly as the common law. The early judges probably had the same aspirations and the same bedevilments as do the judges of today. They sought to impart uniformity, certainty, and predictability to the law; and they tried to do so by following the decisions in cases previously decided by themselves, their contemporaries, and their predecessor judges. In so doing, they bound themselves to the wheel of the very precedents they established. The law became rigid and unyielding, and proved incapable of coping with the demands of a developing and more complex social order.

When the common law proved too harsh or inadequate, a disappointed suitor who could gain the ear of the king laid his plight before his sovereign. He appealed to the king's conscience. Since the king was the supreme lawmaker and judicial officer, he could mold the law to do justice in the particular case. The king turned these complaints over to his chancellor, who was considered the keeper of the king's conscience.

In time the inadequacies of the common law channeled so much business to the chancellors that separate Chancery Courts were established. These were the early courts of equity, designed to give some stretch, some elasticity, to the rigidity of the other courts.

With the passage of time it was inevitable that the chancellors themselves should strive for certainty and regularity in their decisions, and that legal practitioners, in aid of their cause, should quote to them earlier decisions. Equity has itself hardened into a system of well-established rules, but has still retained a fascinating capacity for expanding to function in a world of ever-changing social and economic complexities.

The Court of Chancery functioned as a separate court until 1873, when the courts of England were consolidated and given both law and equity powers. A few states still maintain separate courts of equity. In New York and other states, the two systems of law and their distinctive forms and procedure have been merged in the same courts. But in all courts, the fundamental differences between the rights and remedies under each system still exist.

A major deficiency of the common law courts was that their power was confined largely to the giving of money damages. This sometimes affords inadequate relief, especially when given to redress a wrong after the harm has been done. But equity will, under the proper circumstances, act to prevent the injury.

A court of equity commands a defendant personally to do something or to refrain from doing something. This is something which the common law courts can seldom do.

A classic textbook illustration is the remedy afforded a landlord against a tenant who is cutting down trees on the landlord's property. At common law the landlord would have to wait until the trees were cut down and then seek relief through a money judgment. In equity the tenant may be restrained by court direction.

There are many cases in which a court of law, as distinguished from one of equity, recognizes a right but is powerless to enforce it. If you contracted to buy a house, the legal title would remain in the seller until he executed and delivered a deed to you. If he refused to do so, the only remedy offered under the common law would be a right to sue for damages. This is not always a satisfactory substitute for the house, if you needed and wanted that particular house. In equity, however, the seller could be directed to convey the house to you, under the equitable doctrine of specific performance.

Then there are actions to reform contracts or written instruments, when signed under mistaken impression as to the contents, so as to reflect the true intentions of the parties; or actions to rescind contracts, to disaffirm them altogether. There are suits to remove a cloud on title. Equity will grant relief under certain circumstances against infringement of trade-marks, unfair competition, and disclosure of trade secrets and inventions obtained through fraud or breach of trust.

Foreclosure actions and the administration of trusts and receiverships lie in the equity courts. These courts also take jurisdiction in the field of domestic relations—divorce, annulment and separation actions—although such cases were unknown to common law or chancery. Sometimes the judge calls in a jury, or a party demands a jury, to try a specific issue, such as the alleged adultery. But the ultimate decree on the entire case is rendered by the judge—after the jury has rendered its verdict on what is called the "framed issue."

Equity may enjoin parties from action by issuing an injunction. Sometimes a temporary injunction is sought for temporary relief so that a party is not left helpless during the period before the case will be reached for trial.

Recently such a motion for temporary relief was argued before me. The Howard Johnson Company, operating a large chain of restaurants which are distinctive in appearance, charged that the defendant had deliberately imitated its name and the style of its restaurants. As a result, it claimed the public was confused and deceived into patronizing the defendant's restaurant. It was clear from photographs attached to the motion papers that the defendant had adopted and displayed the name of Johnson on his signs, although his own name was entirely different. The defendant had also used the plaintiff's distinctive style of lettering and certain slogans which had been made familiar to the public through extensive use and advertising by the plaintiff.

The imitation was so clear and flagrant that I granted immediate relief and directed that the more glaringly similar features be altered. This was enough to remove confusion from the minds of potential patrons and yet the structural changes involved would not be so extensive as to put the defendant out of business.

Temporary relief of such a nature is granted sparingly. Whenever there is no element of urgency, the courts prefer to determine such issues upon a trial, rather than upon motion papers.

Equity lawsuits, in traditional adherence to the practice of the early English Chancellors, are still tried by a judge without a jury. These nonjury cases form a large and significant portion of a trial judge's labors.

Here a different style of advocacy prevails. It is not that the substance of the case is presented in diminished or augmented form. It is something like the difference in adult conversation when children are in the room and when they are out of earshot. Not that jurors are regarded as immature, but they neither talk nor comprehend the implications of legal language. More caution is used, more technicalities invoked, in a jury trial. Judge and lawyers guard their tongues within the hearing of a jury. When questions of law are to be argued, the jury is usually excused. An expression by judge or lawyer having a set meaning to the legal fraternity might convey quite another meaning to a layman.

Such a misunderstanding occurred in the trial of a lawsuit upon a promissory note. Every obligation, to be enforcible, must have a consideration. In this case the consideration—the *quid pro quo* with which the plaintiff had parted in exchange for the defendant's promise to pay—was a sum of money equal to the face amount of the note.

The plaintiff's lawyer asked him, "Did you give the defendant any consideration on this note?"

"Consideration!" snorted the plaintiff. "I couldn't have given my own brother greater consideration. I let him stall me for two years, until I needed the money and had to get tough."

There is also a difference in the treatment of evidentiary facts and factual argument before a judge and before a jury. A trial lawyer, in communicating inferences and conclusions to a judge, is dealing with one mind—and, moreover, with a mind trained for a lifetime to think and weigh values in the same manner as the lawyer. In reaching toward a jury a lawyer is dealing with twelve different minds. Twelve minds operating in a fashion unknown to the lawyer, and trained in diverse fields. Twelve personalities of which he knows very little.

So, if the professionals never relax their guard in the presence of the jury, it is not because they are in any sense patronizing, or because they regard jurors as inferior creatures. Lawyers and judge simply cannot take the chance that a stray expression or phrase be misinterpreted by a single juror.

Almost always the personality, the professional history, the capacity of the judge is known to trial lawyers. In trying a case before him they know how deeply they need to press any phase before the judge will grasp and possibly accept their contention. They know how extensively or moderately they need to examine or cross-examine witnesses. In fact, in a nonjury trial a judge will not hesitate to let a lawyer know that he has pursued a subject far enough.

Sometimes a witness has made a written statement at variance with his testimony at the trial. The cross-examining lawyer will produce the statement with a flourish, have the witness identify it, and mark it in evidence. He will read it to the jury, rolling his eyes meaningly and emphasizing the passages which conflict with testimony.

Then, not content, he will ask the witness, "Was your recollection of this incident better or worse two years ago, when you signed this paper, than it is today?"

If the lawyer asked this question in a nonjury case, the judge would say, "Please, counselor. We haven't a jury." Implicit in this plea would be the unspoken suggestion, "Spare me this. I've read the statement and am fully aware of the discrepancies." Or, "I used to pull this question on witnesses when I tried cases thirty years ago."

Most nonequity cases are tried before a jury. Many times, however, lawyers do not file a jury demand. Sometimes this is done designedly, sometimes through neglect, sometimes to save the amount of the jury fee.

The jury fee in our court is twelve dollars. The fee for filing a note of issue—which places a case upon the calendar—is twenty-five dollars. Adding another three-dollar clerk's fee, the cost of placing a jury case on the calendar is forty dollars.

A judge sitting in a nonjury case will not, cannot, by virtue of his conditioning, reject those rules of law which, we suspect, jurors sometimes refuse to accept. They may be as unpalatable, as archaic to the judge personally as they are to the jury. He is well aware that had a jury been demanded it might decide the case differently. His heart may be wrenched by the plight of the plaintiff. Yet, however racked he may be by the process, he must decide the case on the law as it exists. Judges must constantly fight against the temptation to yield to the luxury of legislating the law for the particular case. And so we have the bugbear of all juridical systems—occasional inconsistencies in the application of the law.

Every trial judge in the State of New York, in the trial of accident cases, has had to steel himself at times in applying the rule of contributory negligence. This rule provides that a plaintiff cannot recover if the slightest degree of negligence on his part contributed to the accident.

A case was tried before me involving the death of a man in his thirties, who was survived by a widow and three small children. For some reason the lawyer representing his estate did not demand a jury.

The evidence disclosed that the defendant was driving his car at an excessive rate of speed, that he had passed another car dangerously close to a curve, and that as he entered the curve his left wheels were on the wrong side of the white line bisecting the road. His car collided with that being driven by the decedent, in the opposite direction. The latter suffered internal injuries which resulted in his death in a hospital two days later. Unquestionably, the defendant had operated his automobile negligently.

The decedent was a man who had been employed at a moderate salary and it was unlikely that he had made adequate provisions for his wife and three young children.

The defendant was represented by an insurance company which, I learned later, carried liability insurance on his car in an ample amount. The defendant's lawyer proved that the decedent had been to a bachelor party tendered a fellow employee on the evening of the accident. He had had a few drinks. From a state trooper's testimony, and that of the driver of a car behind the decedent's, I was convinced that he too was straddling the white line. The conclusion was inescapable that the decedent had been as much to blame as the defendant, and that his negligence had contributed to the occurrence of the accident; that if he had been driving carefully the accident might well have been avoided.

Under the circumstances I had no alternative but to decide in favor of the defendant. Had I found in favor of the plaintiff, who was the widow acting as administratrix, I would have given her a verdict of sixty thousand to seventy thousand dollars. It was no comfort to me to feel that a jury might have found in her favor or given her half that amount as a compromise verdict. Rendering a decision for the defendant was a distressing judicial duty.

In a nonjury trial the layers of evidence piled on for jury consumption are absent, and the muscles of the case fairly ripple before the eyes of the judge. Lawyers and judges enjoy particularly the trial of equity cases. Both sides want an orderly, craftsmanlike record, so that the issues can be presented squarely on appeal. From the short history of equity jurisprudence which I have given, it is evident that equity cases usually pose more challenging and absorbing problems than does the law side of the court.

Some of the most delightful and nourishing communions I have established with members of the bar have taken place in the relaxed atmosphere of the trial of equity cases. I recall one such episode in the course of a suit brought on behalf of the Horace Mann-Lincoln School against Teachers College of Columbia University. The plaintiffs sought to restrain the college from cutting the school off from any share in the income of a six-million-dollar trust fund set up by the General Education Committee of the Rockefeller Foundation, and administered by the college.

My verdict would depend upon a construction, an interpretation, of certain provisions in the trust agreement. Both sides were represented by batteries of competent, courteous, and distinguished counsel. Among the plaintiffs' lawyers was Professor Austin Scott of Harvard University, perhaps the foremost authority on the law of trusts in this country, a teacher revered and beloved for his scholarship, integrity, and personal warmth by two generations of lawyers whom he has taught at Harvard. *Scott on Trusts* is the most respected and most quoted book on the subject. Professor Scott had been retained to argue the inevitable questions on the law of trusts, on behalf of the plaintiffs.

Soon after the commencement of the trial such a question arose. Professor Scott argued it, as expected, ably and comprehensively. His adversary got to his feet. There was a twinkle in his eye.

"I shall rest my position," he said, "on a statement from what I regard as the most authoritative voice on trust law in this country. May I read a quotation from the leading book on the subject —*Scott on Trusts*?"

He proceeded to read a few paragraphs which appeared to support his viewpoint and refute the argument just made by Scott.

Scott replied, wryly, "Would that mine enemy had written a book! I suppose it will come back to plague me throughout the trial. I'll admit that the bald statement, as quoted, appears to refute my argument. But it must be read in conjunction with other sections." And he referred me to other sections of the book.

These exchanges went on, in the most amiable spirit, throughout the trial. It is impossible to try a case with close questions involving the law of trusts without constant recourse to Professor Scott's book. The defendant's attorneys made the most of statements in his book which they deemed helpful to their cause. They referred me to other portions of the book which modified or amplified such statements. All counsel felt serene in the knowledge that I would not accept any statement at face value when torn from the context of the book. Incidentally, chief counsel for the defendant had been a student of Professor Scott, and he confided to me later that he revered him.

The usual little tricks which lawyers are taught to spread before juries are seldom used in a nonjury trial. In fact, the books which undertake to teach a lawyer how to try a case seem to confine themselves to jury trials. I have skimmed through the latest one, a most entertaining volume. Nowhere do I find any suggestions for the trial of an equity case.

A most difficult type of case to try without a jury is one involving the domestic relations of husband and wife. The usual litigation wounds are chafed raw by the parties' proximity, intervention of relatives, emotional strains, and other factors.

The bitter hatred which the parties hold for each other seems to infect their lawyers. The most decorous of lawyers snap and snarl at one another. Lawyers who ordinarily submit very restrained papers drain their vocabulary of vituperation when dictating affidavits in a matrimonial action. Attorneys capable of drawing the most subtle distinctions see only blacks and whites in such litigation.

Finally, of all nonjury trials, judges dread most the so-called custody proceedings. These concern the custody of a child or children, brought on by writ of habeas corpus. Usually one parent seeks to wrest custody from the other, on the ground that the respondent is not a fit person to rear the child. Very often neither parent is a fit custodian. Sometimes a judge must reluctantly override the legal presumption that, all other factors equal, the mother is the better custodian. Most judges feel that these, as a class, are the most heart-rending, and at times frustrating, decisions they are called upon to make.

This is the one type of case in which judges are most likely to get off their haunches, roll up their sleeves, forget about laissez-faire theories of judicial aloofness, and take over the handling of the case. There are good reasons for these impulses. The subject matter of the litigation is not the property interests or the personal feelings of the parties. The persons most directly affected are the children for whose custody the parties are vying. Children are not represented by lawyers, and are often the hapless pawns of their parents' blind hatred toward each other. Therefore, in a custody proceeding the dominant concern of the court is not with the feelings or convenience of parents but with the best interests of the children.

I remember the most difficult decision I have ever been called upon to make in my ten years on the bench. It was all the more troubling because I knew my decision would be conclusive. The law was clear and the decision hinged on my appraisal of the character and personality of a young woman who sought the custody of her infant child.

She and her husband had turned the child over to an authorized, highly regarded child adoption agency and signed an unconditional surrender agreement. Within two weeks the infant was given to the prospective adoptive parents—a stable, prosperous, happily married couple. Six months later, after much vacillation, the petitioner demanded the return of her baby.

Space does not permit a detailed review of all of the factors that went into the ultimate decision. It was very close. The law holds that the decisive consideration is the welfare of the child. But, as I wrote in my opinion, "So important is the status of a natural parent, that in determining the best interests of the child, it may counterbalance, even outweigh, superior material and cultural advantages which may be afforded by adoptive parents. . . . For experience teaches that a mother's love is one factor which will endure: possibly endure after other claimed material advantages and emotional attachments may have proven transient."

The scales were finally tipped in favor of the adoptive parents and against the natural mother by some impressive psychiatric testimony. The purport of the medical testimony was that the petitioner was a constitutional psychopath with abnormal emotionality.

And yet the final responsibility was mine and could not be shunted off on psychiatrists. I concluded my opinion with the following, which may give some glimmering of the torments wringing the decision-making process:

"But the hard core of this problem eludes an exclusively legal approach and determination. A sense of serenity with the solution is achieved only when it is realized that by giving her child over to an agency, on terms of presumptive finality, the petitioner clearly affected her moral claim to the child. And such is the public policy, as indicated above, that her moral claim is synonymous with her legal claim, and the moral values are one with the legal values involved.

"For what is this moral claim of a mother to her child? On what does it rest? What is it which makes motherhood so precious a boon that society chooses to leave a child even with the most poverty-ridden and ignorant of mothers rather than give him over to even the wealthiest and most cultivated of foster parents? What is expected of a mother which is of such incalculable worth as to outweigh all else in the world?

"What except a fullness of love for the child; a totality of dedication to it, an all-embracing consecration that knows no wavering, no swerving. This is a mother's gift, for which, society holds, a child may well count all the world well lost.

"And it is in just this that the petitioner is found wanting. She is a person of intelligence and socially acceptable character. She is in my opinion a person no more unstable than a multitude of other persons. But she gave up her child of her own free will, to implement a reconstruction of her personal life; not after her last dollar had been spent and her last resource drained, but with a sizable sum at her disposal. Regretting her action thereafter, for five months she nevertheless time and again faltered in her resolution. Her letters reveal repeated periods in which she envisaged with equanimity a future without this child. Such conduct does not reflect the attributes required in law and in morals to regain custody of a child in a proceeding of this nature.

"With the well-being of the infant paramount and uppermost in my mind, and despite my deep sympathy for the well-intentioned petitioner, I am constrained to direct that the child remain in his present custody."

* X *

Lawyer and Judge—Coprofessionals

I APPRECIATE that many laymen do not share the high regard in which bench and bar hold one another. The following caricature of lawyers and judges, drawn by Swift in *Gulliver's Travels,* has brought chuckles from generations of laymen.

"I said there was a Society of Men among us, bred up from their Youth in the Art of proving by Words multiplied for the Purpose, that White is Black, and Black is White, according as they are paid. To this Society all the rest of the People are Slaves. For Example: If my Neighbour hath a mind to my Cow, he hires a Lawyer to prove that he ought to have my Cow from me. I must then hire another to defend my Right; it being against all Rules of Law that any Man should be allowed to speak for himself. Now in this Case, I who am the right Owner lie under two great Disadvantages. First, my Lawyer being practised almost from his Cradle in defending Falsehood, is quite out of his Element when he would be an Advocate for Justice, which as an Office unnatural, he always attempts with great Awkwardness, if not with Ill-will. The second Disadvantage is, that my Lawyer must proceed with great Caution: Or else he will be reprimanded by the Judges, and abhorred by his Brethren, as one that would lessen the Practice of the Law. . . .

"Now, your Honour is to know, that these Judges are Persons appointed to decide all Controversies of Property, as well as for the Trial of Criminals; and picked out from the most dextrous Lawyers, who are grown old or lazy: And having been biassed all their Lives against Truth and Equity, are under such a fatal Necessity of favouring Fraud, Perjury, and Oppression, that I have known several of them refuse a large Bribe from the Side where Justice lay, rather than injure the Faculty, by doing any thing unbecoming their Nature or their Office."

On the other hand, I once heard Harrison Tweed, then president of the Association of the Bar of the City of New York, make the following statement in the course of some informal remarks:

"I have a high opinion of lawyers. With all their faults, they stack up well against those in every other occupation or profession. They are better to work with or play with or fight with or drink with than most other varieties of mankind."

Most judges will warmly endorse this statement, although lawyers will continue to vex them at times, just as judges will irritate lawyers at times. Possibly the greatest source of annoyance to a judge are the endless oral arguments and bulky briefs and pleadings. I believe Arthur Train once said that lawyers are "as tautological as cuckoo clocks."

But judges are pretty good-humored about this tendency. They realize that long-windedness is an occupational disease from which many judges themselves are not free. And so they bear this cross with greater equanimity than did Thomas Egerton four centuries ago, when he was Lord Keeper of the Great Seal in Elizabeth's reign.

It is related that a hapless litigant named Richard Mylward filed a replication, a legal pleading, which contained six-score sheets. The Lord Keeper estimated that sixteen sheets would have sufficed. He ordered that

"the Warden of the Fleet shall take the said Richard Mylward into his custody, and shall bring him into Westminster Hall on Saturday about ten of the clock in the forenoon, and then and there shall cut in a hole in the myddest of the same engrossed Replication, which is delivered unto him for that purpose, and put the said Richard's head through the same hole, and so let the same Replication hang about his shoulders with the written side outward, and then, the same so hanging, shall lead the same Richard, bareheaded and barefaced, round about Westminster Hall whilst the courts are sitting, and show him at the bar of every of the three Courts within the Hall, and then shall take him back again to the Fleet and keep him prisoner until he shall have paid £10 to her Majesty for a fine, and 20 nobles to the defendant for his costs in respect of the aforesaid abuse, which fine and costs are now adjudged and imposed upon him by this Court for the abuse aforesaid."

Despite the severity of the punishment imposed, it was probably less galling to a lawyer's spirit than a crushing remark made from the bench by Sir George Jessel, while presiding in the English Court of Appeal. Jessel, who was known for his kindliness to the younger practitioners, never failed to deflate pomposity among the older members of the bar. It was one of these, known for his verbosity, who was to feel the keen edge of Jessel's wit.

The lawyer was relating to the Court of Appeal what had transpired at the trial in the court below, and, after quoting interminably from the testimony, he said: "At this point, the trial court stopped me."

"A moment, sir," said Jessel. "It would be of great benefit to me and their Lordships if you would explain how this was done."

Centuries ago a learned antiquary observed that, in his time, "an acre of land could not pass without almost an acre of parchment."

I find that lawyers generally can be the most long-winded and yet the most close-mouthed of all human beings. These seemingly opposed traits are a natural result of a lawyer's training and experience. Both his silence and his verbosity are disciplined and conscious, and are conceived to protect his clients' interests. Analyze the argument of the average lawyer. You will note an absence of impulsive, wandering, and unconsidered statements, which will distinguish his wordiness from garrulity.

When addressing a judge or jury, a lawyer is seldom given any indication as to whether a point has found lodgment in the mind or minds of his audience. He cannot know whether his listeners will reject the argument he considers so significant, or whether they will be swayed by one of the points he considers unimportant. A daring spirit may stake his case on a bold presentation of only one or two contentions, scorning to dilute them by additional but minor propositions. However, no matter how inclined most lawyers may be thus to back their own judgment, they will be fearful of assuming such a risk on behalf of clients, and they will assert every argument they can possibly bring to bear.

For similar reasons, whether advancing few or many thoughts, lawyers will repeat and restate them. Dr. Samuel Johnson, a layman, appreciated this clearly enough. "This," he told Boswell, "you must enlarge on, when speaking to the Committee. You must not argue there, as if you were arguing in the schools (University); close reasoning will not fix their attention; you must say the same thing over and over again, in different words. If you say it but once, they miss it in a moment of inattention. It is unjust, Sir, to censure lawyers for multiplying words when they argue; it is often *necessary* for them to multiply words."

A similar prolixity characterizes documents drawn by lawyers. There are few legal documents which could not be abridged without loss of meaning or legal significance; but one must remember that the lawbooks cite many instances in which the failure to include a necessary word in a writing has proved costly to a litigant. A lawyer, steeped in this history, will try to be as inclusive as possible when he is drafting a document. If there is to be a choice between repetition or omission, he is far more likely to choose the former, with full knowledge that a literary stylist might not approve. He is simply, and understandably, playing it safe.

It was because laymen drawing their own documents were not so cautious or skilled that the barristers in the English Inns of Court sang this little ditty:

Now this festive occasion our spirit unbends,
Let us never forget the profession's best friends,
So we'll send the wine 'round and a nice bumper fill,
To the jolly testator who makes his own will.

Lawyers, when trying a case, keep hammering and reiterating on the theory that they can take no chance of their evidence's eluding a single juror. This insistence breeds a common fault among trial lawyers—of overtrying a case. Many a case has been lost because perceptive jurors have become disgusted with or suspicious of a lawyer's burdensome repetition of evidence and argument.

And yet experienced lawyers know there is little that can be taken for granted in a jury trial. A common oversight is the failure to produce, or to account for the failure to produce, every witness who could give material testimony. If ten railroad employees witnessed an accident, the railroad's lawyer may call only four to the witness stand, since the testimony of the remaining six would be similar and repetitious.

The omission may be dangerous. In summation the opposing attorney may pound the rail in front of the jury box and ask why these witnesses were not produced. He may shout that they were in the control of his adversary and were kept away because they would hurt his case. Experienced lawyers, fearful of leaving this opening but also apprehensive of incurring the jury's displeasure by introducing repetitious and boring testimony, may resort to several expedients.

"I have four more witnesses who will testify to substantially the same facts as the preceding three," they might say loudly. "I wonder if my adversary, to save the court and jury the time and hardship of listening to them, will make this concession, that if called, they will testify to the same effect as the other three witnesses, without, of course, conceding the truth of their testimony?"

Or they might say, "I have several more witnesses who will testify to the same purport as the last two. If Your Honor thinks this phase of the case has been developed sufficiently, I won't call them."

Most judges will tell the lawyer he is trying the case, and should exercise his own discretion. But he will have at least established some basis for explaining to the jury, if it becomes necessary, his failure to call the witness.

The danger of overtrying a case is not only that it wearies court and jury, but that an unexpected and harmful morsel of testimony may be unnecessarily introduced.

I recall a case in which the plaintiff had been employed as advertising manager by a corporation which operated a large chain of retail stores. He was suing for unlawful discharge. The defendant called its president, general manager, and several advertising agency executives, who testified to the incompetency of the plaintiff. Not content with that, the defendant also called its department heads to testify to their dissatisfaction with the plaintiff's exploitation of their department's merchandise. One of them, a rather comely woman about forty years of age, was cross-examined as follows:

LAWYER: You say you became so dissatisfied with the plaintiff's services that you complained to the general manager?
WITNESS: Yes, sir.
LAWYER: When was that?
WITNESS: Oh, some time in June, 1948.
LAWYER: Now, prior to that time, had you ever gone out with the plaintiff?
WITNESS: What do you mean by that?
LAWYER: Had you ever gone socially with him—to the theatre, dinner, cocktail lounges?
WITNESS: Yes, a few times.
LAWYER: How few?
WITNESS: I don't remember.
LAWYER: I'm not suggesting anything improper, madam. You were divorced and the plaintiff was single. Isn't that so?
WITNESS: Yes.
LAWYER: How long before June, 1948, did you first go out with the plaintiff?
WITNESS: Maybe a year—year and a half.
LAWYER: And when was the last time you went out with him?
WITNESS: Oh, in the spring.
LAWYER: Of 1948?

WITNESS: Yes.

LAWYER: Would you say you went socially with him once a week during that time?

WITNESS: Oh, I don't know.

LAWYER: Once a month?

WITNESS: More than that.

LAWYER: During that time did you find his services satisfactory—I mean as advertising manager, not as an escort?

WITNESS: I guess so.

LAWYER: When did you first find fault with his services?

WITNESS: A little while before I complained to the manager.

LAWYER: That was after he stopped going out with you?

WITNESS: The two had no relationship.

LAWYER: I'm sure of that. One last question: When was the plaintiff married?

WITNESS: I don't know.

LAWYER: Wasn't that also a short time before you complained?

WITNESS: I don't know.

LAWYER: And, of course, the fact that he married also had no relationship to your complaint?

There was no answer.

The plaintiff recovered a large verdict. It is possible that this witness lost the case for the defendant. And there was no necessity for calling her as a witness.

A lawyer is sometimes cast in the role of father confessor to a client, who will confide to him secrets not known to the client's family or intimate friends. Because the nature of the professional relationship invites such confidences, the law has stamped these disclosures as confidential communications which may not be revealed by the lawyer without the consent of the client.

It may be because of this conditioning, but if it suits a lawyer's, or his client's, purpose to remain mute, he will be a veritable Sphinx. If he possesses information bearing on the case, which is unknown to his adversary, wild horses cannot drag it from him. Until the opportune moment arrives during the trial, no matter what the provocation, he will not breathe a hint of it. He will not even divulge any part of it at a pretrial conference, when a judge is trying to shake down the facts and wring concessions from both sides.

Sometimes these tactics backfire. Many years ago an associate of mine on the district attorney's staff was prosecuting a young thug who was charged with clubbing a haberdasher and making off with the contents of the cash register. When arrested, he had told the detectives that at the time of the holdup he had been visiting his married sister, who lived many miles from where the haberdashery was located.

Despite his youth, the defendant had a record of several arrests and convictions. He exerted a bad influence on the young people of the neighborhood, and the prosecutor was anxious to secure a conviction. But the haberdasher had been so frightened that his identification of the defendant as his assailant was somewhat tentative. It therefore was important to smash the anticipated alibi.

A witness read of the arrest and came forward. He was a schoolteacher who had formerly taught the defendant. He stated that a few minutes after the holdup had taken place, he had met the defendant, hurrying breathlessly, just two blocks from the haberdashery store. To make conversation he had asked him what had brought him to that neighborhood. The defendant had answered that he was visiting a friend.

The prosecutor was in a good strategical position. He could use the teacher as a witness on the State's direct case, as his testimony would place the defendant in the vicinity of the scene of the crime shortly after its occurrence. Or, he could save him for rebuttal, that is, hold him back until the defendant had offered proof in support of his anticipated alibi, and then place him on the stand to prove that the accused was miles away from his sister's home, and near the haberdashery shop.

At that time the law did not authorize the district attorney to pin a defendant down as to the details of his alibi by requiring him to furnish a bill of particulars in advance of trial. The prosecutor feared that if he disclosed the teacher's testimony on his direct case, the defendant might change his alibi or concoct a defense to meet the situation. So he bound everyone to secrecy and decided to hold his star witness for rebuttal.

At the trial only the haberdasher and a detective testified on the State's direct case. The defendant's attorney cross-examined the haberdasher vigorously and effectively on his identification of the accused. All he asked of the detective was that he repeat the defendant's assertion that he had been with his sister.

The prosecution rested. The jury was excused and the defendant's lawyer made an eloquent plea to dismiss the indictment, on the ground that the defendant had not been identified adequately. The judge denied the motion.

Then, to the consternation of the prosecutor, the defendant's lawyer rested, without calling a witness. He knew nothing of the surprise witness, but he feared to submit his client to cross-examination on his criminal record. The judge refused to permit the assistant district attorney to reopen his case, since he had withheld the witness designedly.

Upon summation the defendant's lawyer stressed the shaky identification and the youth of his client. He couched the statement to the police officer as though it were proof that the defendant was at his sister's home, and he asked what proof the State had presented to disprove it. He secured a verdict of acquittal. The prosecutor had outwitted himself.

Lawyers and judges share a great, common tradition. Most lawyers are not mercenaries who will enlist in any cause to earn fees. Alexander Cockburn said: "The weapon of the advocate is the sword of the warrior, not the dagger of the assassin."

Some will always be found to spring to the defense of any worthy cause, no matter how unremunerative or unpopular, and no matter what risk to personal fortune or reputation is involved. And judges, without flinching, will time and again deliver unpopular decisions in the teeth of a storm of contrary public or official opinion, when reason and conscience so dictate.

The insistence of the learned, opinionated, stubborn Sir Edward Coke that Acts of Parliament and King alike were subject to the common law of the land is an illuminating example of the independence of the judiciary. To the claim of King James I that his prerogative derived from the Divine right and was therefore above the law, Coke, in 1608, quoted from the great Bracton that "the King is subject not to men, but to God and the law"; and similarly, in Bonham's Case, decided in 1610, Coke laid down the principle which is the fountainhead of the modern doctrine of judicial review of the constitutionality of legislation. He stated that an Act of Parliament is subordinate to the common law of the land.

Instances of intrepid independence by members of the bar also abound. The great Lord Erskine frequently defied royal displeasure with political dissenters by supplying them with brilliant and eloquent defense to criminal charges. When he undertook the defense of the avowed atheist, Thomas Paine, Erskine demonstrated that he was no more to be cowed by popular than by royal pressures.

Nor has the American bar, from its earliest days, lacked for courageous and independent advocates. Outstanding is the case of John Peter Zenger, which Gouverneur Morris termed "the morning star of the American Revolution."

Zenger was a New York printer whose publications were critical of the administration of the Colonial Governor of New York. In 1734 he published a journal which censured the Governor's conduct, and he was promptly indicted for libel. Zenger engaged two local lawyers of good standing, James Alexander and William Smith. In the exercise of their professional duties and with complete propriety, they sought to challenge the jurisdiction of the court. Both were disbarred for presuming to represent their client in this fashion.

Andrew Hamilton of Philadelphia, a leader of the Colonial bar, came forward to defend Zenger. He was aged and infirm; the journey to New York was an arduous one and he could anticipate a strenuous ordeal in the trial. Nevertheless, he accepted. Charles and Mary Beard in their volume *The Rise of American Civilization* thus describe this historic defense of freedom of the press:

"The trial which followed proved to be a dramatic episode as well as a defeat for the king's representative. An able attorney, Andrew Hamilton, brought up from Philadelphia to plead for the printer after local lawyers had been cowed into submission, conducted the case with a grand flourish, making the issue 'the cause of liberty.' Moved by his argument and imbued no doubt with popular sympathies, the jury defied the judge, and amid general rejoicing gave the imprisoned editor his liberty."

It is heart-warming to participate, as lawyer or judge, in a contested proceeding in which counsel and judge have mutual respect and liking for one another. The judge does not expect the lawyers to prejudice by one jot the rights of their clients by subservience to the judge's whims or desires. But he knows that to save the court time and the adversary expense and trouble, lawyers will concede what can ultimately be proved; that they will oppose each other vigorously but fairly; that each lawyer will present the facts and argue the aspect of the case most favorable to his client, but not distort evidence so as to mislead the jury or court.

The lawyers in turn know that the judge may err, but that if so he will be honestly mistaken and afford them a fair record for appeal. They know that in conference they may tell him facts off the record, and that their confidence will not be violated. They know that they may come to him with any of the myriad difficulties which beset counsel and that the judge will accommodate himself to any situation which does not retard the court's functions substantially, nor prejudice an adversary. This co-operation is freely given and received.

This case illustrates how a wise lawyer may save the parties and the court great trouble and expense. Cornelia Otis Skinner, the actress and writer, had brought suit against the Paramount Pictures Corporation for a large sum of money. Upon reading the complaint it was evident that the outcome of the trial hinged upon my interpretation of a clause in the contract between the parties. Upon reflection, I was of the opinion that this clause could not be construed to mean what the plaintiff's lawyer contended it meant. I was convinced that no matter what evidence Miss Skinner submitted, I would be required, as a matter of law, to dismiss her case.

I so informed counsel, and suggested, to save at least a week of trial, that the plaintiff's lawyer place on the record what is known as an offer of proof.

Both lawyers, sensible and intelligent men, agreed, although only the consent of the party offering the proof was needed. The plaintiff's lawyer dictated to the court reporter a synopsis of the evidence he proposed to introduce during the trial. This constituted his offer of proof. Of necessity, it included the clause in the contract which I believed defeated the claim.

I ruled that, even accepting such proof as the fact, Miss Skinner still had no case under the contract, and I dismissed the complaint. The rights of the parties were fully protected. She could appeal my decision, and rely upon the offer of proof as completely as though it were actual proof presented from the lips of witnesses. If my ruling proved correct, everyone would be saved the wear, tear, and expense of several days of grueling litigation. If I were wrong, the parties could still have their trial.

I recall a case in which an attorney did not have the foresight to make an offer of proof; he thereby suffered great discomfiture and put his client to considerable unnecessary expense. It was in an action for breach of contract. At about 3 P.M., after a day of trial, the attorney for the plaintiff beckoned to his opponent, and both approached the bench.

"With the exception of a witness who's flying in from California, that's my case, Judge," he said. "He's due to arrive tonight, and I'll have him in court first thing tomorrow morning."

"I don't think he's made out a case as yet," said the other lawyer.

"I know that," said the plaintiff's lawyer. "This man from California is my star witness. He'll prove my case."

I recessed court until the next morning. As promised, the California witness took the stand. After some preliminary questioning, the plaintiff's attorney brought his testimony down to a conference the witness had held with the plaintiff. After he had testified to the substance of the conversation, the defendant's lawyer rose.

"I move to strike out the entire answer. It's not binding on the defendant."

I granted the motion. For half an hour the plaintiff's lawyer struggled to introduce testimony of this and subsequent conversations. Upon each question the objection was sustained or the answer stricken out. Finally the attorney gave up and I was compelled to dismiss the case. After a transcontinental trip the witness had not been permitted to answer a single question bearing on the issues of the case.

The plaintiff's lawyer should have known that, viewed most favorably to his side, it was still highly questionable whether the witness's testimony was admissible. Had he made an offer of proof, he could have avoided the unnecessary expenditures of time, trouble, and expense and preserved his client's rights. My ruling would have left him in no worse position than he was in after producing the California witness.

It is uncommon but it happens that some maverick will mistake a judge's courtesy for weakness, and try aggressively to take advantage. He will be set down in short order—usually to the unconcealed delight of his fellows at the bar.

Lawyers are advocates and the value of their arguments to the judge is tempered, not improperly, by their partisanship. Witness the common spectacle of two honest and competent lawyers advancing flatly irreconcilable viewpoints. Seldom is this because of legal skulduggery. It is simply a product of difference in approach.

Once out of court, most lawyers "do as adversaries do in law, strive mightily but eat and drink as friends."

The following tribute to lawyers, delivered in 1930 by then Chief Judge of the New York Court of Appeals Benjamin N. Cardozo, has just as much validity today as it had then.

"When I meditate upon these things, the enthusiasms of forensic efforts, the fire that goes into them, the meaning of defeat or victory, not merely to the pocket of the advocate, but still more to his pride, his repute and his sense of duty done, I think with mounting wonder of the spirit of fraternal fellowship that animates the profession even now—the good temper, the humor, the acceptance of fortune fair or foul as all in the day's work. Especially I am impressed with the kindness and generosity of the Bar in its relation to the bench. 'We take our pleasure sadly,' says an English essayist, writing of his countrymen, 'but we take our troubles with a smile.' Perhaps that is not a bad summary of the spirit of the Bar. We judges are doing things all the time that must disappoint you sorely. We are handing down decisions in closely balanced cases where the patient and careful work for months and even years of conscientious members of the Bar is shattered over night. If one were to consider such a situation in the abstract, without knowledge of the facts, one might suppose that the result would be a chronic state of irritation and hostility between two contending camps. Nothing of the kind! If we do the day's work with a reasonable measure of intelligence and devotion, we are rewarded by friendship which is really more than friendship—by a friendship so tinged with emotion that we can only describe it as affection. I can speak for one judge at least in saying that it evokes in his heart an affectionate response."

This affinity between bench and bar sometimes asserts itself in odd ways. Once a long and involved equity case was on trial before me. There were several defendants, each of whom was represented by a different lawyer. One defendant's attorney was able and experienced, but he belabored every point so interminably that the trial was consuming twice as much time as had been estimated. He did not pursue this course as a trial tactic or to take unfair advantage. He simply did not believe a point or a fact had lodged until it had been repeated *ad nauseam*. And being single-minded and conscientious, he would not heed the implorings of the other lawyers in the case to abbreviate his examinations.

Finally, to speed the proceedings, I was driven to nudging him with remarks from the bench each time I thought he had exhausted a line of examination and was beginning to cover the same ground all over again. This is done frequently by judges; and it is taken in good part by the bar, provided the judge does not barb his remarks with sarcasm or abuse. In this case I simply told the lawyer he had asked the questions before. Sometimes he desisted and went on to another line. If he appeared uncertain, I would reassure him by referring to my notes.

One day, shortly before we recessed for lunch, a boy of about fourteen entered the courtroom. He shyly half waved to this lawyer, and the latter beamed back at him. They strongly resembled each other, and it was evident they were father and son. Up to this point I had been interrupting the lawyer with some frequency—and possibly with some show of impatience.

I soon declared a recess for lunch. As I was leaving the courtroom I saw the lawyer throw an arm around the boy's shoulder, and the lad responded with equal affection. When we resumed the trial, the father led his son to the bench and introduced him to me. The boy was on his Easter vacation and had come downtown to have lunch with his father and observe the trial.

Of course, seated as I was in the direct path of the boy's proud gaze, I could not interrupt his father. I dared not even interpose a suggestion. As a result, he devoted the entire afternoon to plodding through the tedious cross-examination of a witness upon matters that had been thoroughly raked and reraked by the other defendants' counsel as well as by himself. All the while I sat with what I hoped would impress a boy of fourteen as an expression of rapt and reverent admiration for his father's prowess.

To the bar as an entity, by a species of guild acceptance, almost every judge is learned, upright, and wise. Custom has dropped a veil of approbation between judge and the outside world, which will be pierced only by his dishonesty or corruption.

Lawyers in bar association positions will oppose the designation or nomination for judgeship of a man whom they regard as unfitted for the position. This they will do fearlessly, although they know the risks involved in courting the displeasure of a possible future judge. But, if that man has served a term adequately, the bar will press for his renomination without reservation. Maybe this policy pays communal dividends by prodding a judge into justifying his public reputation. Many inconspicuous lawyers have developed into fine judges.

There is one disadvantage in these attitudes. A judge may go to his grave not knowing whether he was good, bad, or indifferent. How will a judge learn of his true merits? Surely, no matter how intimate their relationship may be, no lawyer will say, "Hope you don't misunderstand, old man, but I think that last opinion of yours stinks." Nor will a colleague be so indelicate as to hint at such a thing.

* XI *

The Lawyer's Role in the Trial

WE OFTEN HEAR the old-timers wail that the day of the great trial lawyer is gone, that the present crop is a pretty poor one. This contention impresses me as too difficult to prove or disprove. It is like attempting to establish that Joe Louis was a better fighter than John L. Sullivan. They never fought each other. Nor did John W. Davis and Daniel Webster ever meet in a courtroom contest. A judge can shed no light on this controversy, unless his tenure spans two generations. Even then his rheumy eyes might look too reverentially upon the past.

There is still a great deal of grandeur about a good trial lawyer. Not the kind of grandeur identified popularly with thunderous declamations or rolling rhetoric, but the kind that clothes the person of a good surgeon, who derives his satisfaction, strengthens his assurance, from the respect accorded him by his fellow professionals. Large audiences do not applaud his deft skill. But fearful patients, relatives, and friends look to him with confidence bordering on reverence, accepting his advice, certain that if an unexpected contingency arises he will cope with it.

And so it is with a trial lawyer worthy of the name. In England the barrister who heads the battery of trial counsel is appropriately called the leader. An attorney in the trial of a case should be a leader in fact—a leader not only of his assistants or juniors but of his client as well. The client must place his case in the hands of his lawyer as unreservedly as a patient places himself in the hands of his surgeon.

The philosophy of the trial lawyer has changed radically, and I believe for the better, since the generation in which Judge Joe Baldwin gave the following advice to young lawyers: "If you have a strong case in law—talk to the judge—if you have a strong case in fact, talk to the jury. If you have no case in law or fact, talk to the wild elements and bellow like a bull."

At one time most young men were first attracted to the law by the drama and adventure of the trial. This may hold true today; but if so, most of them end up as office lawyers who rarely enter a courtroom.

For one thing, the growing emphasis on pretrial procedures is eliminating much of the element of surprise which made the trial a game of chance, and put a premium on the lawyer's adroitness. Now many more cases are won by thorough, painstaking preparation than by brilliant coups in the courtroom.

An excellent and comprehensive report on prelegal education, recently made by Chief Justice Arthur T. Vanderbilt of New Jersey, reveals that today there is no single, compelling reason influencing most young men to study law. In a survey sponsored by the American Bar Association and Carnegie Foundation, questionnaires were circulated in 1949 in eighty-one law schools.

To the question, "At what age did you decide to study law?" twelve per cent answered that it was before they were fifteen years old; thirty-eight percent, between their fifteenth and nineteenth years; thirty-six per cent, between their twentieth and twenty-fourth years; and thirteen per cent, when they were twenty-five years old or more.

When asked, "What caused you to study law?" thirty-nine per cent answered general interest; eleven per cent, for business background; ten per cent, due to family and friends' influence; and only four per cent were animated by a desire to aid society.

Thirty per cent of the students polled replied that they had observed the trial of ten or more cases; forty-eight per cent had seen the trial of five or more cases; eighteen per cent had never observed the trial of a single case.

This is the age of specialization in the law. Litigation as a specialty does not promise for young lawyers the meaningful employment or the economic advantages which it once possessed. The traditional branches of the law no longer attract their quondam quotas of brains and leadership from the universities. New and fertile pastures have formed in the wake of the economic and social changes of the past two decades. Many of the best minds now gravitate to what they regard as the most significant, or perhaps the most profitable, fields—the various forms of administrative law. Many undergraduates shape their studies with a view to practicing tax law or labor law. Also, some prefer to co-operate in shaping affirmatively the course of events, rather than later recording those events in the minutes of court proceedings; in other words, they prefer to make history instead of debating it.

The day of the general practitioner who could with equal facility draw a will, close a title, or try a case is waning—at least in urban centers. I daresay most lawyers in large cities do not in the course of a year try a single case. For the occasional litigation which trickles into their offices, they seek trial counsel.

William Miller, in an illuminating article in the *Yale Law Journal,* traces the developing dependency of large commercial enterprise upon day-by-day legal servicing. "This impelled them," he states,

". . . as the strictness of the law increased, to have growing recourse to private legal advice in the making of day to day business decisions. The demand for such advice, indeed, became so great that the best paid metropolitan lawyers almost without exception after 1900 made business counseling the focus of their work, at the expense of traditional advocacy; and many lawyers yielded to the blandishments of the corporations to become house counsel and even regular business executives themselves.

"These twin tendencies—the growing routinization of business politics and the growing representation of lawyers in business management—are largely twentieth-century developments."

But there is most satisfying and challenging work to be done in the trial courts. And, despite the inroads made by arbitration forums, there is still remunerative work to be had in the courts.

Judges often have to work hardest in guiding through the maze of a trial young lawyers who were at the top of their classes in law school. They have learned their lessons well—in legal principles, but not in advocacy or resourcefulness. They have been trained better to argue appeals than to try cases.

In a routine, run-of-the-mill assault case, I witnessed honest, imaginative, and daring advocacy which paid dividends. The lawyer was then an inconspicuous member of the trial staff of a large casualty insurance company. He has since made rapid and deserved strides in his profession.

The trial took place during the recent war. The plaintiff was a soldier in uniform; this was a circumstance which did not make the defendant's prospects any brighter.

In his opening statement to the jury, the plaintiff's lawyer stated that his client and some friends had visited a dime-a-dance hall maintained by the defendant on Broadway, in midtown Manhattan. It employed scores of hostesses. The male patrons would buy tickets at ten cents apiece, and each ticket entitled the customer to one dance with the hostess of his choice. Two large bands alternated to furnish continuous dance music.

The plaintiff's lawyer went on to say that, without provocation, a bouncer employed by the defendant had struck the plaintiff and fractured his jaw.

The defendant's lawyer waived his opening statement.

The testimony introduced by the plaintiff bore out his lawyer's outline of the case. The defendant's lawyer contented himself with asking only a few questions of the plaintiff on cross-examination.

"Did this bouncer speak with you before he struck you?" he asked.

"All he said was, 'You can't dance close on this floor,' and then, bang, he hits me on the jaw!" the plaintiff answered.

"Before that, had he spoken with you or cautioned you in any manner?"

"No, sir."

"Did you know the bouncer? Had you ever met him before?"

"No, sir."

"Did the young lady, the hostess, with whom you were dancing, know this bouncer, as far as you know?"

A moment's pause. "Not as far as I know."

"There were hundreds of other men, many in uniform, on this dance floor at the time you were struck?"

"Yes."

The questioner waited a few seconds, to emphasize his next question.

"Do you know why this bouncer chose to strike you, a perfect stranger, out of the hundreds of men on that floor?"

"No."

The bouncer was the only witness called by the defendant. He looked the part; he was a big, hulking man with fists like hams.

According to the bouncer, he had cautioned the plaintiff several times against dancing improperly with the hostesses and finally warned him that he would be put off the floor at the next infraction. A little later he saw the plaintiff, out of the corner of his eye, rush toward him with fist upraised, as though to strike him. He extended his hand, palm out, to ward him off. The plaintiff ran into his palm and fractured his jaw.

This, of course, was an incredible story. I was curious to observe how the defense attorney, who had never appeared in my courtroom before, would handle so preposterous a tale in his summation to the jury.

Without heat he quietly analyzed the testimony of the plaintiff. He asked the jury to conclude with him that it was highly unlikely that the plaintiff should be singled out for assault in such unexplained manner.

"Not," he added, "that I expect you to believe the testimony of my client's bouncer. I personally consider his story fantastic. In preparing the case I tried to elicit the truth from him, but he stuck to this story. As a lawyer, my problem therefore was either to keep him off the stand or let him testify to an occurrence I cannot ask you to believe. It wasn't much of a choice, but I thought seeing and hearing him would be more helpful to you."

Then he went on to tell the jurors how fortunate he considered himself in having a jury of New York City residents to render a verdict in this case. They were intelligent, perceptive, and above all things, fair and unprejudiced. In this cosmopolitan city, for example, it was customary for baseball fans to applaud the exploits of visiting players—a rare phenomenon in most other cities. The jurors were citizens of the world, and as such, above petty biases or other unworthy considerations.

"And as fair, worldly, and experienced men and women," he concluded, "I address only one question to you. Do you know of anyone who ever got a bust in the jaw in this city who did not ask for it? I submit, ladies and gentlemen, neither side has presented the true facts. But I am sure the plaintiff received just what he was asking for."

The jury brought in a verdict for the defendant, in a case which at the outset had given every indication of resulting in a substantial verdict for the plaintiff. They may have sensed a third set of facts not proved by either side, constituting provocation for the assault.

The defendant's lawyer violated some of the petty rules of advocacy venerated by the bar. He did not object when his adversary used the opprobrious word "bouncer." In fact, he adopted it himself throughout the trial. The average lawyer would have sprung to his feet with an objection, which the judge would have sustained. To what avail? The bouncer himself was in court, and the nature of his duties was explained in detail.

Few lawyers would have had the courage to take the risk of rejecting the testimony of their only witness, or the imagination and psychological insight to ask the jury to draw an inference not based on the evidence submitted by either side. And, very gratifying to a judge, he made a thoroughly honest presentation of his case. He did not distort or tamper with the evidence itself. He asked the jury to draw an inference which was not unreasonable, from evidence he frankly characterized as unbelievable.

But blasphemously, he had asked a "why" question. He had asked the plaintiff whether he knew of any reason why the bouncer should single him out for assault.

Now the handbooks and articles on How To Try a Case are unanimous in shrieking the perils and pitfalls of asking "why" questions. The most devastating comment one lawyer can make to another as to a colleague's inexperience and ignorance is to say he asked a witness "why" on cross-examination.

True, such a question often "opens the door" to the admission of damaging testimony which otherwise would be inadmissible: hearsay statements made by a third party, workings of the witness's mind, etc. The plaintiff in this case, for example, might have answered that he had heard he had been dancing with the bouncer's girl, or that he resembled an enemy of the bouncer. The defendant's lawyer, however, was representing a desperate cause. He took a calculated risk in asking the question. But he did so only after he had established that the bouncer did not know either the plaintiff or the hostess; the plaintiff was therefore precluded from assigning a grudge or jealousy as reason for the assault, the motive which would most readily come to mind.

Sometimes a lawyer must choose one of two risky courses. A decision which often confronts a lawyer for the defendant in a criminal case is whether to have his client take the stand, if he has been convicted previously of a crime or crimes. All lawyers consult with their clients when faced with such a decision. The clients usually respond, "You're my lawyer. What do you recommend?"

Some lawyers answer, "I've explained the risks you'll run either way. You can decide as well as I, and since your liberty is at stake I'd rather have you assume the responsibility."

The client is much less distraught when his lawyer says, "I've given the problem a good deal of thought. In my judgment you should take the stand." Or, "You can't afford to take the stand."

This lawyer is asserting the leadership for which he has been retained. Still, so great an advocate as Sir Edward Marshall Hall often required his client to make the ultimate decision—and in writing.

It sometimes requires iron nerves to scorn minor objections, concede what must be proved, and withhold fire until the opponent reaches the nerve center of the case. The client tugs apprehensively at his lawyer's coat sleeve as evidence, superficially damaging, rolls in unopposed. The lawyer senses the unspoken rebuke: "I hired you to battle for my interests, not to lay down without putting up a fight." And yet the lawyer must possess the moral courage to continue his apparently indifferent course.

Lawyers who lack the stamina and perception to do this often assist the prosecution immeasurably in criminal cases, particularly in prosecutions for criminally receiving stolen goods. In such cases the State must prove, first, that the goods were in fact stolen—by some person whose identity may be known or unknown. Second, and this is the crux of the case, that the defendant acquired them with knowledge that they were stolen.

The establishment of the original larceny is merely foundation proof, although, of course, essential proof. Proof of the larceny alone, without proof of the felonious receipt of the goods by the defendant, cannot sustain a conviction.

When I was an assistant district attorney a certain lawyer was very successful in representing and acquitting defendants accused of crime. He was very aggressive and alert, and he fought the assistant district attorneys with the tenacity of a bulldog. Defendants recommended him to one another as "a lawyer who gives you a real run for your money."

Another lawyer also appeared frequently and successfully in the criminal courts in those days. He was a more intelligent, although less vigorous advocate. Throughout the early part of a trial, in which he defended a man accused of receiving stolen goods, he sat by, seemingly indifferent, while one of my associates presented proof of the burglarizing of a loft and the removal of a large quantity of silks. His client was a wholesale silk merchant.

The thieves had not been caught. The victim of the burglary identified certain merchandise found at the defendant's place of business; the prosecutor also relied upon what he regarded as an unsatisfactory explanation by the defendant of the source of this merchandise.

The defendant's attorney did not interpose an objection until the complaining witness endeavored to identify the silks. The fierceness of his objections at that time was probably respected by the jury because he had been so pleasant and seemingly fair up to this point. Some of the identifying testimony was barred. The remainder was evidently rejected by the jury upon the defense attorney's final argument that the silks were standard goods, manufactured by a large mill, and that pencil markings, upon which the alleged identification was based, were not satisfactorily shown to have been made by the complainant's employees. The defendant was acquitted.

The first lawyer I have mentioned was counsel for the defense in a case which was to follow this trial, in the same courtroom. During the recess which followed the verdict of acquittal, he buttonholed the other lawyer in the corridor outside the courtroom.

"Jack," he said, "I'm lucky in every kind of case except receiving stolen goods. I've lost the last four I've tried. How did you get that fellow off?"

Jack pondered a moment.

"You're a competitor of mine, Jim," he said, "and I shouldn't be giving away any trade secrets. But you're a good guy and the reason's obvious.

"Your idea of trying a case is to fight the D.A. every inch of the way. You know your law, you throw every objection in the book at the People's case—whether the evidence hurts your client or not. That's effective strategy in most cases—but not in the average receiving case.

"We know the prosecution can always prove the larceny. We can make it tougher for them to prove it, make them bring extra witnesses, and drag out the trial. What is the result? Most of the trial is devoted to a bitter fight as to whether the goods were actually stolen. After a lot of delaying actions by you, the prosecution proves the larceny right up to the hilt—double in spades.

"By this time, because of your resistance, the jury is confused as to what is the real issue in the case—whether a larceny has occurred, which never should have been in doubt, or whether the defendant knowingly bought the stolen goods. When the prosecution finally satisfies them that the goods were stolen, it has gone a long way toward satisfying them that your client is guilty. No matter how clearly the judge's charge may instruct them that the larceny is just a technical foundation to be proved before really commencing the trial of your client, the jurors have already made up their minds."

There is a maxim that a lawyer must not prejudge his client's cause and should accord him the benefit of every presumption of righteousness. It would appear to permit a conscientious lawyer to anesthetize his qualms about the merits of a case and accept a fee. The unscrupulous lawyer, of course, needs no such device to square his conduct with his conscience.

For generations this ethical concept has been hotly assailed and staunchly defended by lawyers and philosophers. Its defense rests largely on the proposition that no one can know that a person is guilty, or his claim baseless, until it has been so proved and declared by verdict. Dr. Johnson has been quoted persuasively in this vein.

"I asked him," said Boswell, "whether, as a moralist, he did not think that the practice of the law, in some degree, hurt the nice feeling of honesty."

JOHNSON: "Why no, sir, if you act properly. You are not to deceive your clients with false representations of your opinion: you are not to tell lies to a judge.

BOSWELL: "But what do you think of supporting a cause which you know to be bad?

JOHNSON: "Sir, you do not know it to be good or bad till the judge determines it. I have said that you are to state facts fairly; so that your thinking, or what you call knowing, a cause to be bad, must be from reasoning, must be from your supposing your arguments to be weak and inconclusive. But, sir, that is not enough. An argument which does not convince yourself, may convince the judge to whom you urge it; and if it does convince him, why, then, sir, you are wrong, and he is right. It is his business to judge; and you are not to be confident in your own opinion that a cause is bad, but to say all you can for your client, and then hear the judge's opinion.

BOSWELL: "But, sir, does not affecting a warmth when you have no warmth, and appearing to be clearly of one opinion, when you are in reality of another opinion, does not such dissimulation impair one's honesty? Is there not some danger that a lawyer may put on the same mask in common life, in the intercourse with his friends?

JOHNSON: "Why no, sir. Everybody knows you are paid for affecting warmth for your client; and it is, therefore, properly no dissimulation; the moment you come from the bar you resume your usual behaviour. Sir, a man will no more carry the artifice of the bar into the common intercourse of society, than a man who is paid for tumbling upon his hands will continue to tumble upon his hands, when he should walk on his feet."

Sometimes a lawyer becomes certain that his client is guilty or his claim or defense fraudulent. This certainty may come during the first consultation, or after the case has been prepared for trial. Or it may be admitted to the lawyer by the client, who still expects the lawyer to represent him and assert the justice of his cause. Conversations like the following take place occasionally in prosecutors' offices throughout the country.

DEFENDANT'S LAWYER: What's the best plea I can get for my man, JIM?

PROSECUTOR: He'll have to plead to the indictment—grand larceny in the first degree. We've got him dead to rights. Identification, possession of the proceeds, everything.

LAWYER: There's no percentage in pleading to the indictment. He's a two-time loser [meaning he has been convicted twice previously for felonies] and he'd have to get the limit under the law. You'll just force me to go to trial.

PROSECUTOR: Okay with me. He's guilty as hell.

LAWYER: Sure, I know that. He's admitted it to me, because I never let my clients kid me. And I wouldn't kid you. But if you force me to trial, there's always an outside chance a miracle will happen and he'll get off.

What happens if the case does go to trial? The lawyer is an officer of the court; he is sworn to serve faithfully that important arm of government. The very maintenance of a civilized and ordered society rests upon the effective functioning of the courts. If the lawyer helps a man whom he knows to be guilty to escape, or if he helps defeat a just claim, to that extent he imperils the structure of society. True, he owes a duty to his client. Query, does the state command a superior allegiance when there is a conflict between the two duties? In practice, the conflict will never arise if a lawyer does not lend himself knowingly to the presentation of perjury.

No such conflict exists when a lawyer honestly believes his client to be innocent or in the right, or when he entertains doubt of his guilt. A party is then entitled to the best legal representations he can procure. If there is room for doubt, that doubt should be resolved by court decree and not be prejudged by lawyers.

The fascinating ethical facets of the concept that a lawyer may not prejudge the justice of his client's case have caused it to be debated with a sound and fury out of all proportion to its limited employment or importance in actual practice. Practical considerations and vanity inhibit lawyers with easy scruples from taking on many cases in which they know their clients to be in the wrong. In most of these cases the prospects for success are very slim. It's bad business for a trial lawyer to suffer defeat in court. The barometer of his prestige and prosperity rises with favorable results and drops with adverse ones. So lawyers are very chary of going to trial with losing cases.

An exception must be noted for those apparently lost causes in which a great principle is involved. Clarence Darrow, in undertaking the defense of Scopes in the famous "monkey" trial, knew it would be well-nigh impossible to convince a jury of Fundamentalist Tennesseans of his client's innocence. Nevertheless, he undertook a defense which held no prospect of success.

A factor which tends to deter unethical conduct is a lively fear of disciplinary action. The bar has a tendency to devour its young. Frequently young, inexperienced lawyers, who have succumbed to a single temptation, are suspended or disbarred. Little distinction is drawn between mature and immature lawyers.

Many lawyers have lost their licenses for too energetic solicitation of business—except, perhaps, when it's done in the better clubs.

There are a few lawyers, a tiny segment of the bar, who will lend themselves to a distortion of the facts—suborn perjury, to put it bluntly—in order to win cases. Henry Clay said, "It would not be thought very just or wise to arraign the honorable profession of law and physic because the one produces the pettifogger and the other the quack."

More and more the majority of lawyers are growing to look upon a trial as a sober, orderly search for the truth, and less and less as a combat. Most lawyers are happy to have it this way. They can engage in their profession and secure for clients their just due, with dignity, honor, and personal satisfaction.

Credit must also be given to this same majority of lawyers for the fact that so much potential litigation dies a-borning in their offices. I daresay that the possible lawsuits which lawyers discourage clients from launching exceed in number those which find their way into the courts. Lawyers, well aware of the heartaches, hazards, and disappointments of litigation, dissuade many irate clients from bringing suit, or they arrange satisfactory compromises.

I know of no child prodigies among trial lawyers. A certain

The defendant's attorney moved to set aside the verdict as excessive. I granted the motion but with the reservation that the verdict would be permitted to stand if the plaintiff consented that it be reduced to twelve thousand dollars. The plaintiff consented and the verdict was reduced accordingly.

A few months later I met one of the jurors who had sat on both the first and second cases.

"The injuries were about the same in both cases," I said. "How did you reconcile five thousand in one and twenty thousand in the other?"

"Why, Judge," he answered, "the first case was very close. The plaintiff had only a little the better of it and the accident could have happened if any one of us was driving the defendant's car. But in the second case there was no excuse for what that drunken son-of-a-gun did." He looked up at me and said confidently, "Surely, there's all the difference in the world between these two cases."

"Not as far as the size of your verdict was concerned," I said. "Once you decided in favor of either plaintiff, the same rules applied in each case. You couldn't penalize the defendant, or add extra damages in one case, and compromise or cut down the verdict in the other, because of the manner in which the accident occurred."

If I had pressed him further, as I have done at times with other jurors in similar circumstances, he probably would have squirmed out an assurance that the jurors had followed my instructions and given me some lame justification of the verdict. Sometimes, jurors will follow a judge's charge on the law only if it squares with their own notions of justice. Otherwise, they will apply their own particular home brew of the law to reach what they consider a just or sensible result.

I had charged both juries explicitly and in great detail as to what should be the measure of damages if they found in favor of the plaintiff. Technically, this was correct and unassailable. These cases were tried during the first year I was on the bench. Since then I have learned to anticipate such entirely human jury reactions. Whenever the facts hold out a temptation to veer to either extreme in assessing damages, I add a pointed and an explicit note of warning. Nevertheless juries will sometimes substitute their own notions of justice. And the size of the verdict will vary in ratio to the jury's sense of outrage at the manner in which the accident occurred.

There is no blinking the fact that there are times when jurors will not apply the law to the facts as inexorably as will a judge. If the second case had been tried before me without a jury, if I had been judge of the facts as well as the law, I would have rendered a much smaller verdict. I—or any judge, for that matter, with judicially conditioned reflexes—would have rejected the impulse the jury obeyed, to translate into swollen damages its sense of outrage at the way the defendant drove his car.

By the same reasoning, if I had found in favor of the plaintiff in the first case, I would have given him a larger verdict. But, according to my notes, I would have found for the defendant in that case. It was very close. Both drivers tried to beat the light in that accident, and I would have felt constrained to find the plaintiff guilty of contributory negligence.

It is sometimes said that if juries accepted literally the court's instructions on the rule of contributory negligence, they would return few plaintiffs' verdicts in accident cases. The argument goes that juries listen devoutly to this portion of the charge, understand it fully, then file out and apportion the damages according to the relative or comparative fault of the parties; that they weigh the plaintiff's negligence and the defendant's negligence, and adjust the figures until a balance is struck. It so happens that in the admiralty courts and in certain states, liability and damages are measured by a somewhat similar standard. This is known as the rule of comparative negligence. But it is definitely not the law in New York and can become the law only through legislative change. Perhaps the jurors applied this rule in the first case; perhaps they avoided finding in favor of the defendant and arrived at a low compromise figure.

I have no way of knowing, and without such knowledge I cannot accuse the jury of flouting the law. If they found the plaintiff free from contributory negligence and found the defendant negligent, then, despite my view of the case, they applied the law correctly, particularly since it was in their sole province to decide upon the facts. And therein lies the weakness of this criticism of the jury system. No judge or any other critic knows what facts a jury finds from the evidence. All I or any other judge can say is that we disagree with a verdict—and that usually has no more force than any other person's opinion, since the jurors are the exclusive judges of the facts.

From conversations with jurors after the rendition of a verdict, we are morally, if not legally, certain that they sometimes disregard portions of the judge's charge. But we have no valid basis on which to estimate the frequency or infrequency of this practice.

Dean Pound has termed this well-known propensity "jury lawlessness." In effect, every time jurors disregard the laws, such as the prevailing law of contributory negligence, and make law specially for the case, such as a species of the law of comparative negligence, they are legislating within the jury room. This theory is given serious consideration by lawyers in their preparations and calculations for trial or settlement. In evaluating cases lawyers are governed not only by the law on the books but by the law in practice. I am certain that the second fractured leg case could have been settled, before trial, for at least three times as much as the first.

I suspect also that lawyers, legislators, and judges give oblique recognition to the fact that there is a jury law which at times overrules statute law. It is well known that in New York jurors have applied a form of comparative negligence. One asks, why not make honest men and women of these jurors by enacting a comparative negligence statute? Why do lawyers, judges, and legislators preserve the anomaly of one law in theory and a different one in practice?

Perhaps no pressures are exerted by the community for law reform because each jury reforms the law anyway to conform to community notions in each particular case. There is no appreciable gap between the community conscience and the law as it is actually enforced by juries.

Dean Green, in *Judge and Jury,* has made the following acute observation:

"Seemingly, juries saw only the parties before them, and placed the risk where they thought it could best be borne. The judges had been interested in principles; juries were interested in doing justice between the parties. The judges evolved a nice scheme for determining responsibility, the juries gave verdicts which wrecked the scheme. Juries held their ground here until legal theory could catch up with the new order of things which had emerged under the very eyes of the judges without most of them noticing it."

I cannot join in a criticism leveled frequently at our jury system: that the emotional content of juries is much higher than that of judges—and too high to permit of sound verdicts. The verdicts resulting from jury lawmaking are sometimes dramatic and startling, because they vary so drastically from the verdicts indicated by a strict application of the law. The tendency is to attribute these variations to emotional susceptibility and sentimentality, and not to a conscious desire to reject a law which the jury regards as unfair and impractical.

The average jury may contain members whose reason sometimes yields to their emotions. But as a jury, as an entity, it seldom succumbs to such influences. At least, I find little evidence of it in the trial of civil cases.

Jurors may be lawless, but they are not irrational. They may not realize all of the influences and forces which affect their decisions; but then, neither does a judge. I believe jurors do require that a law square with their ideas of morality and fair play.

John Dryden touched on this in verse:

The man who laugh'd but once, to see an ass
Mumbling to make the cross-grain'd thistles pass;
Might laugh again, to see a jury chaw
The prickles of an unpalatable law.

The critics who urge elimination of the jury seldom extend this recommendation to criminal trials. One compelling reason is that the jury institution in criminal cases is traditionally associated with the protection of the civil liberties of the individual.

Yet the tendency to emotion-laden verdicts would appear to be stronger in criminal cases than in civil cases. Loss of freedom would impress jurors as being much more devastating than loss of dollars. Still, many prosecuting officers boast a conviction average in excess of eighty per cent and even ninety per cent of the cases tried. Surely, in rendering many of those verdicts of conviction jurors had to steel themselves against their apprehensions of the misery that would flow from their verdicts—often upon the innocent family of the accused. It may be that the basic standards of morality written into our criminal law conform closely to the standards of the man in the street.

It is curious that the "lawlessness" of juries should be the focal point of modern criticism of the jury system, since it was just such "lawlessness" which in earlier times made the jury, in the words of Blackstone, "the grand bulwark of every Englishman's liberties." It was jury "lawlessness" when seventeenth-century English jurors disregarded repressive legislation and acquitted of charges of sedition and libel men whose only crime was political dissent.

A major argument of those who would eliminate juries is that a trained and experienced judge, unlike most jurors, will hew to the line of the relevant and not be led astray by the extraneous. This argument I believe to be valid without agreeing with the suggested remedy.

An experienced judge is a disciplined sifter of the facts. He is, nevertheless, just an expert in his field. An automobile mechanic is an expert in another field. I drive my car and hear all sorts of rattles, creaks, and squeaks. I don't know whether they come from the vitals underneath the hood, where they would be material and relevant, or whether they come from the door and windows, where they would be irrelevant and immaterial. So I take the car to an expert—an automobile mechanic. His trained ear sorts out the noises more surely than does mine. The trained ear of the judge

sorts out admissible and inadmissible evidence, with comparable expertness. And, of course, both experts will be wrong at times.

In reserve, if it affords any comfort to litigants, resides the limited power of the court to correct jury excesses. It is not uncommon, as indicated earlier in this chapter, for a judge to set aside or reduce a verdict which he regards as excessive. A judge may also set aside a verdict in a civil case which is contrary to the weight of the evidence.

Of course, a judge will direct the verdict for either party and take the case out of the hands of the jury when it becomes evident that there are no facts in dispute and that only questions of law are involved. The court will also nullify a jury verdict which is palpably based on a mistaken notion of the law. Such a verdict was returned before me recently.

The plaintiff had been struck by a taxicab. He sued the corporation which owned the cab involved in the accident. He also sued and joined the driver as a defendant.

The driver, concededly employed by the corporation to operate the cab, had been clearly negligent. The plaintiff had suffered a fractured kneecap. The only theory upon which the corporation could be liable was that its employee, the driver, had been negligent. Both defendants, corporate and individual, were linked together in a form of Siamese-twin liability. If a verdict were returned against the corporation, it followed that a verdict in the same amount must be returned against the negligent driver.

The jury foreman reported an astonishing verdict of eighty-five hundred dollars in favor of the plaintiff against the corporation, and only twelve hundred dollars against the taxi driver. The verdict was inconsistent. I conferred with both lawyers, who were anxious to dispose of the case and avoid a retrial. With their consent, I instructed the jury that the same fractured patella, suffered by the same plaintiff, could not possibly be worth eighty-five hundred dollars against a corporation and twelve hundred dollars against an individual. I also charged them that if they found that the driver had not been negligent, they were required to find in favor of the corporate defendant.

The jurors retired and returned again, with a verdict of eighty-five hundred dollars against both defendants. After they had been discharged, I called the foreman to the bench and asked him how they had arrived at the first verdict.

"We felt the driver couldn't afford to pay as much as the corporation," he explained.

I had suspected as much. Fortunately, the court is not powerless to act in such a situation.

There is a certain inscrutability about the general verdict of a jury. Often defying external analysis, it cannot be shrugged off as an emotional distortion of fact and law. On the rare occasions when the veil is lifted from the deliberations, one may ascertain whether the consideration given all factors was deep and not superficial, practical and not whimsical. For example, we know that often, in fixing damages, a jury will estimate the lawyer's fee and include it in the verdict. Although it is not a proper item of damage legally, the jurors know that practically it is an item that must be paid. A jury's verdict is sometimes an amalgam of a shrewd appraisal of the facts squared with community values.

In the past five centuries the entire concept of the function of jurors has been revolutionized. A few hundred years ago a jury was supposed to reflect the community's knowledge of the facts of the matters in issue, and of the guilt or innocence of the accused. A civic-minded, conscientious juror was expected to make inquiries among trustworthy neighbors concerning the case to be tried well in advance of trial; he would thus come to court fortified to render his verdict. From a group of neighbors presumably knowing something about the subject matter of the case, and chosen to act upon that knowledge, the jury evolved into a group presumably having no knowledge of the case and prepared to form an opinion on only the evidence presented in court. In fact, so extreme has been the swing that knowledge of the facts gained other than from the evidence might disqualify a juror today.

Today, we are concerned that jurors gather all information about the case in the courtroom, from testimony and evidence in the record. We do not permit the juror to gather his facts where he will. We do not trust his ability to discard the inappropriate evidence. So we exclude irrelevant and immaterial evidence, which may tend to confuse him and divert him from the real issues. And we exclude incompetent evidence because he may accept dross for gold.

During my first year on the bench a case was tried before me in which the plaintiff sued for injuries she had sustained from a fall down a flight of steps in a tenement house. She claimed that the stairs were littered with rubbish; also, that they were in total darkness. The defendant contended that the steps were free of any debris, and that there was a window at a landing near where she fell which afforded ample light during the daytime. The accident occurred at 4 P.M.

On the second day of the trial one of the jurors raised his hand and said he would like to ask a question of the plaintiff.

"What is your question?" I asked.

"I would like to know what kind of a day it was—the day of the accident. Was it clear, rainy, or what?"

I recalled the plaintiff to the witness stand and directed her to answer the question.

"It was a clear day," she said.

"Then there should have been plenty of light at four o'clock," argued the juror.

"What makes you say that?" I asked.

"I went to this building after court adjourned yesterday," he said. "It was after five o'clock but there was still plenty of light to see the steps."

I granted the defendant's motion for a mistrial, and discharged the jury. Thereafter, whenever there was the slightest chance of a recurrence of such an incident, I would admonish the jury not to visit the scene of the accident at any time during the trial.

On the surface it might appear that this juror displayed unusual initiative and perception. But there are many dangers in such unregulated excursions. He may have visited the premises during a different season than the one in which the accident occurred, and when the days were longer. The windows may have been remodeled after the accident. If the stairways happened to be clean when he saw them, he might be inclined to believe they were clean on the day of the accident—and conversely if they were covered with rubbish.

I believe that the fears that jurors are led away from the main issues by trivia and irrelevancies are largely unfounded, although it will happen in an occasional case—particularly with a substandard jury. Juries are excellent, good, bad, and indifferent—just like judges.

But generally the judge will so conduct the trial that only evidence bearing properly upon the issues will be submitted to the jury. He presides over a conveyer belt transmitting factual material to the minds of the jurors. Before the belt reaches its destination he will extract any defective materials. It is a problem in administration. The problem is not only to rule out hearsay and self-serving declarations, but to control lawyers so that they will not offer the jury forbidden tidbits within the framework of improper questions.

Preoccupation with the sterilization of the data fed to jurors has resulted in many of our trial rules for the admission and exclusion of evidence—rules which, if they err, err on the side of repression rather than full disclosure. It is, therefore, not surprising that a discernible correlation exists between the elaborate evidentiary rules developed in Anglo-American jurisprudence and the preeminence of the jury system in that same jurisprudence.

The thinking of a judge who reviews steadily a passing parade of varied cases may become grooved. He may not bring to each case the eager, fresh consideration of a juror. From long experience, his attitude toward certain types of witnesses and certain types of cases may understandably have become frozen. The judge will have to admonish himself constantly in order to do justice in the particular case before him. Conceivably, if our attitudes have frozen hard, we may be unfair to an honest claimant in some cases. One is hard put to choose between the initial skepticism of judges and the initial gullibility of jurors.

A judge may know from hearing him testify frequently, and

from the hearsay process of comparing notes with other judges, that a certain doctor's testimony will always be weighted heavily in favor of the side that retains him. He may know from similar sources that another doctor will always testify with complete honesty. If a prospective juror knew or had similar knowledge about a party or a key witness, one of the lawyers would see to it that he would be challenged and excused from serving in the case. But a judge may not be disqualified for such reasons. This, of course, is knowledge acquired outside the evidence in a particular case. It is not available to the jury, which may be more impressed by the testimony of the charlatan than by that of the ethical physician.

It would be desirable, and dramatic, to expose the knave while he is on the witness stand. But the judge may not convey his inbred suspicion to the jury. Experience has proved that in the long run it is better to contain the evidence within well-defined rules, even if injustice occasionally follows in an individual case. An astute opposing lawyer, however, could convey some of his misgivings to the jury by cross-examining the doctor as to how many times he appears in court yearly, how many examinations he has conducted in the past for the other side's lawyer, whether he generally testifies for plaintiffs or defendants, whether he was brought into the case by the lawyer, his charges for court appearances, etc.

There are lawyers whom judges have grown to distrust, and who must document every assertion they make before a judge will accept it. There is the overwhelming majority of lawyers, whose word will be accepted without question by judges.

When cases are tried by a judge without a jury, he must be on guard lest his previously formed opinion about a familiar expert witness or lawyer prejudice his deliberations in the individual case.

Judges, like jurors, have their strengths and weaknesses in comprehending and appraising testimony. They are much better qualified than most jurors to understand commercial transactions. Bills of lading, negotiable instruments, debentures, voting trust agreements, invoices are all familiar words to judges. They have heard of them for a mature lifetime—as practicing lawyers and sitting judges. Such terms might be so much Greek to housewives, mechanics, shopkeepers, and others inexperienced in commercial usages.

On the other hand, there are areas of litigation in which a judge has to grope to follow the evidence. Some judges have little mechanical aptitude or understanding. They have great difficulty in coping with a case involving problems of engineering, construction, chemical processes, manufacturing processes, patents, and the like. The average jury will often contain a few members whose grasp of these problems will be better than that of the judge.

The recent proliferation of administrative agencies in American law may, at least in part, be attributed to the recognized difficulties of judges as well as juries in understanding the complex factual situations which arise in such fields.

Then, just like jurors, I suppose judges labor under psychological blocks. I am not qualified to discuss their nature, how effectively they are offset by conditioning, and to what extent, if at all, they distort the fact-finding and decision-making process. When I was a practicing attorney I recall that the bar employed rough psychology in seeking or avoiding assignments before certain judges. Lawyers representing wives in matrimonial matters shunned a judge who had borne a heavy domestic cross for many years. And lawyers representing husbands avoided a judge who had a reputation as a ladies' man. Some judges were labeled "plaintiffs' judges." Presumably their sympathies were drawn to plaintiffs in accident cases. Other judges were labeled "defendants' judges," particularly if they had represented casualty insurance companies before ascending the bench. I suspect that upon investigation these alleged prejudices would prove to be greatly exaggerated.

But if psychological or emotional blocks do tend to cloud one's judgment in deciding litigated issues, less damage will be done if they affect jurors. Except for rare occasions, where prejudice is communal, they will cancel out one another's prejudices and obsessions, as it is most unlikely that all twelve jurors will suffer the same blocks. The very efforts of opposing lawyers to select jurors with leanings and sympathies toward their contending clients help to stabilize a jury.

There is no doubt that both time and money could be saved by the elimination of juries. The judge has to sit through every stage of the case in any event. If he is better qualified to render a verdict, the jurors are just so much expensive surplus. Their period of service represents a loss of manpower to the national economy and some consequent dislocation of industry. They represent also a more direct cost to the government: jury fees. From the time they are summoned to the time of their discharge they engage a good part of the courts' facilities and of the courts' personnel—judges, clerks, and bailiffs.

Without juries, there would be no prolonged conditioning of jurors under guise of inquiring into their qualifications. The flourishes and devices which lawyers so fondly believe impress jurors would be abandoned before judges. So would evidence of dubious materiality. For some reason most trial lawyers believe that a jury will smile favorably upon their clients if they put on a good show. In other words, reward them for the entertainment. They also believe conversely that such histrionics annoy a judge—an unquestionably sound belief.

Concessions as to inevitable proof are given freely in a nonjury case. There is no doubt that the elimination of the jury would speed the judicial processes. The decisive question is: How would it affect the administration of justice? And, correlative to that question, would it weaken public confidence in the administration of justice? If so, the most substantial economies in time and money would not justify the change.

There can be no compromise with the quality of justice in a democracy. If in fact the jury serves a useful purpose, it must be preserved at any cost. But if in fact the jury is neither affirmatively helpful nor harmful, or if the factors involved are too nebulous to permit of an assured answer, then it might still be desirable as a matter of public policy to preserve the system because of the reverence in which it is held by the public.

It must be repeated that the jury system has always drawn

nourishment as the defender of the individual against tyranny and oppression. Those who cherish it in that role are willing to yield a bit on its efficacy as a truth finder and still maintain it to be an essential pillar of good government. Of course, they cannot concede any great margin of inefficiency, because a system which is not geared to search out the truth with a reasonable measure of competency and consistency is a poor protector of the weak and oppressed.

But this has been a dominant consideration in the development of the jury. While there have been ignoble passages in its history, there have also been glorious and stirring episodes.

An early and significant victory in the struggle to gain independence and dignity for the jury as a juridical body was won in the trial of William Penn and William Mead. They were charged with the crime of unlawful assembly and preaching to great crowds of people in the streets of London. Their trial—if it can be termed such—was held in September, 1670, before the justices of the Old Bailey. These justices comprised the Mayor, Recorder, and several aldermen.

One Thomas Vere was foreman of the jury. One of the jurors was Edward Bushel, a man well known for his fiery spirit and independence.

After a farcical trial, by our standards, the jury retired. In one and a half hours eight jurors returned, and reported that they were agreed, but that the remaining four were not in accord and remained above. The court sent an officer to fetch the intransigent four, one of whom was Bushel. When they were brought into the courtroom the Recorder berated Bushel in strong language as the instigator of the opposition to a verdict of guilty. The justices made no secret of their fervent desire for a conviction.

The jury retired once more. When they returned the following colloquy took place:

Clerk: Look upon the prisoners at the bar; how say you? Is William Penn guilty of the matter whereof he stands indicted in manner and form, or not guilty?

Foreman: Guilty of speaking in Gracious-street.
Court: Is that all?
Foreman: That is all I have in commission.
Recorder: You had as good say nothing.
Mayor: Was it not an unlawful assembly? You mean he was speaking to a tumult of people there?
Foreman: My lord, this was all I had in commission.

This, as the Recorder observed, was the equivalent of no verdict. Several of the jurors seemed ready to yield to the threats and suggestions of the justices. Bushel stoutly contested this tendency, and reminded his fellow jurors of what had transpired in the jury room. The jury retired a third time, but returned with the same statement as to Penn and a verdict of not guilty as to Mead. They were denounced violently by the justices.

The Mayor at one point said to a juror, "Starve then, and hold your principles."

The chronicler of the trial notes that the jury was retired for the night, "without meat, drink, fire, or any other accommodation. They had not so much as a chamber-pot, though desired."

The next day there were a number of similar exchanges between court and jury, in the same violent vein.

At one point the Recorder fulminated:

"Till now I never understood the reason of the policy and prudence of the Spaniards in suffering the Inquisition among them. And certainly it will never be well with us, till something like the Spanish Inquisition be in England."

Once more the jury was detained for the night, without accommodations. The next morning, the following has been recorded:

Clerk: How say you? Is William Penn guilty, etc. or not guilty?
Foreman: Not guilty.
Clerk: Then hearken to your verdict. You say that William Penn is not guilty in manner and form, as he stands indicted; you say that William Mead is not guilty in manner and form, as he stands indicted; and so you say all.
Jury: Yes, we do so.

RECORDER: I am sorry, gentlemen, you have followed your own judgments and opinions, rather than the good and wholesome advice which was given you. God keep my life out of your hands; but for this the court fines you forty marks a man, and imprisonment till paid.

The jurors were haled to Newgate, as prisoners, for nonpayment of the fines. Six hours later they obtained their freedom on a writ of habeas corpus. Sparked by Bushel, they later sued several of the justices for illegal arrest. Bushel's Case established the right of jurors to render a verdict consonant with their reason and conscience, and ended the practice of fining jurors. Judges now "may try to open the eyes of jurors, but not to lead them by the nose."

The historical association of the growth of freedom of expression and the jury system in England, particularly in the seventeenth to nineteenth centuries, is clear. Again and again during that period efforts to inflict criminal punishment for the expression of criticism, dissent, or unorthodoxy foundered upon the rock of a jury which was inspired and courageous enough to sustain freedom of belief, speech, and press. In this country, because of that association, the right to a jury trial was a major tenet in our early concept of freedom.

It is very difficult to take an unqualified position in the controversy between those who would abolish and those who would retain the jury system. Certainly, it has many infirmities, but it also retains a good deal of vigor. I experience no great embarrassment or difficulty in meshing my functions with those of jurors, and I even derive stimulation from their collaboration.

Intrinsically, jury trials are unquestionably more expensive, more protracted, and more apt to be blown off their course by irrelevancies, emotions, and professional guile than trials before judges only. On the other hand, the jury can offer a composite shrewdness, general and specific knowledge, and balanced community thinking, to supplement the expert and experienced leadership of the judge. This is the team conceived by our Anglo-American jurisprudence as best qualified to find the truth in litigation.

It is a long way from the tribal chase upon mere accusation, and should not be discarded lightly.

In any event, I would oppose immediate and radical surgery on the jury system. It is not so diseased as to require drastic measures, and it has a certain therapeutic value for the parties. To many litigants their day in court means only trial by a jury of their peers.

Even before the adoption of the Bill of Rights, the United States Constitution provided for the right to trial by jury in federal criminal cases. As Hamilton put it in *Federalist* Paper No. 83:

"The friends and adversaries of the plan of the convention, if they agree in nothing else, concur at least in the value they set upon the trial by jury; or if there is any difference between them it consists in this: the former regard it as a valuable safeguard to liberty; the latter represent it as the very palladium of free government. For my own part, the more the operation of the institution has fallen under my observation, the more reason I have discovered for holding it in high estimation; and it would be altogether superfluous to examine to what extent it deserves to be esteemed useful or essential in a representative republic, or how much more merit it may be entitled to, as a defence against the oppressions of an hereditary monarch, than as a barrier to the tyranny of popular magistrates in a popular government."

Whatever one may think of contemporary jury legislation, there is no doubt it has at times proved beneficial in the past. A legal writer has made an astute observation in these words:

"The passive effect of the jury system can be enormous. Persistent acquittals of prisoners have done more to soften the barbarities of the English penal code than all the pronouncements of all the judges. . . . Judges sitting by themselves are liable to drift from reality, and they would probably be the first to admit it." (J. A. Pugh, "Notes on the English Jury System," 1927 *Scots Law Times Notes* 49.)

It is curious that most defenses of the jury system take the form of fervid, flowery exaltations of jurors as the paladins of justice and democracy. The great Lord Erskine had emblazoned on his heraldic shield the motto "Trial by Jury." Mr. Justice Holmes found the jury "specially inspired for the discovery of truth." A tribute which I believe still conveys most articulately the sentiments of the public generally was delivered by Joseph H. Choate in 1903. He was then possibly the foremost trial lawyer in the country, and therefore had good reason to cherish the jury system. He said in part:

"The truth is that the jury system is so fixed as an essential part of our political institutions; it has proved itself to be such an invaluable security for the enjoyment of liberty and property for so many centuries; it is so justly appreciated as the best and perhaps the only known means of admitting the people to a share in maintaining their wholesome interest in the administration of justice; it is such an indispensable factor in educating them in their personal and civil rights; it affords such a school and education in the law to the profession itself, and is so imbedded in our constitutions, which declare that it shall remain forever inviolate, requiring an amendment to alter it—that there may be no substantial ground for fear that any of us will live to see the people consent to give it up."

* XIII *

Jurors Are Nobody's Fools

ONE JURY verdict which has intrigued and perplexed me greatly occurred in a libel case.

In all but one of the libel cases tried before me the juries found for the defendants—either a newspaper or magazine. In reaching each of these defendants' verdicts the juries rejected a variety of tugs the other way, not the least of which was the coupling of poor plaintiff and rich defendant corporation. For whatever that concurrence is worth, I was in complete accord with these verdicts. But to this day I cannot reconcile one verdict with the facts.

Some years ago the following headline appeared upon the front page of one of New York's most widely read newspapers:

"DOCTOR TWICE
PRONOUNCES ACTRESS DEAD
POLICE REVIVE HER"

The headline conveys most of the story. An actress out of work was found submerged in an overflowing bathtub in her apartment. She had taken an overdose of sleeping pills. The plaintiff was a physician whose office was across the street from the actress's apartment.

According to the newspaper account, he was called in by the police, examined her, and pronounced her dead. He was urged to examine her again, after fifteen minutes of first-aid treatment had been administered by the police. He did so again and stated she was dead. Then, the story went on, the police emergency squad applied a pulmotor and revived her.

This, if untrue, constituted libel per se, because it affected the plaintiff in the practice of his profession. There would then be no need to prove specific items of damages, as presumably his reputation was so impaired that he should be allowed general damages.

The doctor made out a strong case in support of his contention that he never declared her dead. In fact, he stated that on his first examination he had detected a flutter of life and so advised the police. He testified that he remained in the apartment two hours, administering injections and other restorative measures. He took credit for reviving her.

Oddly enough, most of the policemen present in the apartment agreed with the plaintiff, although the article had praised the police squad. The newspaper's reporter testified that he had been given the story, as subsequently printed, by a policeman at the door of the apartment, and that he hurriedly telephoned it in to the city desk, to meet a deadline.

The doctor proved that this story gained wide circulation among his patients and professional colleagues, and that he was the object of derision for a long time. It was discussed freely at his local medical society meetings. No doubt it caused him great mental anguish, impairment of reputation, and loss of practice. He communicated the alleged error to the newspaper and asked for a retraction. This was refused.

The jury retired and returned in about two hours with a verdict of one thousand dollars for the plaintiff. I could not reconcile what seemed to me to be so paltry an amount with the damage done to the plaintiff's reputation. I personally had thought the evidence favored the plaintiff's version of the case. However, there was testimony, although weak, which if believed would have justified a verdict for the defendant. If the jury had found in favor of the defendant I would have been surprised, but not inclined to quarrel with the verdict. Implicit in the jury's verdict was a finding that the published front-page story was untrue—and yet it assessed damages at only one thousand dollars.

During the following week I addressed this question to four of the jurors, who also served in subsequent trials before me: "How did you arrive at the figure of one thousand dollars in fixing the damages suffered by the plaintiff?" I received four different answers.

One said, "I was sure the newspaper story was untrue. I was well impressed by the doctor, who seemed to know his business and who gave up an entire morning to save this woman's life without thought of a fee. But I also believed the reporter when he said that the story he phoned in was the one given to him by the cop at the door. I never realized what pressures those fellows work under to make their deadlines. You can't expect them to check and double-check every story. In fact, I would have been inclined to find for the newspaper, if it had not refused to publish a retraction. As it was, when the amount was worked down to a thousand dollars, I thought that was about the right figure. Besides, I figured the important thing from the doctor's viewpoint was to win a verdict—the rest was secondary."

A second juror echoed the last reason given by the first juror. "I was for the plaintiff from the start, and wanted to give him much more money. Three or four were not sure the story was untrue and said they would hold out against a big verdict. So I figured a disagreement would do the doctor no good. The important thing for him was to clear his reputation and the amount of the verdict didn't matter so much."

A third said, "You charged us about the plaintiff having to sustain the burden of proof. Well, some of the cops testified he said she was dead, and some testified he didn't. I was pretty much up in the air, and didn't vote one way or the other. Then the figure got down as low as one thousand dollars. Someone said that wouldn't hurt the newspaper much and it would help out the plaintiff in his profession. So I went along."

A fourth juror answered, "I was for the plaintiff all along, and I thought a thousand dollars was the right amount. I didn't swallow all that eyewash about how his practice was ruined. His feelings were hurt and a few patients and doctors ribbed him. Any verdict in his favor would set him right again. That's not worth big dough. It's not as if he fractured an arm."

To him, and evidently to most of the jurors, a fractured reputation was not worth as much as a fractured limb!

Noteworthy is the shrewdness with which each juror perceived that the principal aim of the plaintiff would be for a favorable verdict; and that the amount was of subsidiary importance. It is significant that the plaintiff would not permit his lawyer to make a motion to set aside the verdict as inadequate. He felt that he had won vindication, and was content to let it go at that.

If I had found a verdict in favor of the plaintiff in that case it would have been many times the amount awarded by the jury. This disturbed me, as I had to grant there was a certain validity to the reasons advanced by the jurors I had questioned. And they had been adopted, to some extent, by the doctor in refusing to move to disturb the verdict. I wondered whether my judgment was influenced by the reverence in which I have always held the medical profession.

So I discussed the verdict with a number of judges. Their reactions in no way differed from mine. I decided there was probably a vast gulf between the attitudes of judges—and probably all professionals—and of laymen, toward the monetary worth of a reputation. A professional, and particularly a judge in the public eye, prizes his reputation for integrity and competence as his very breath of life. Leaving satisfactions of the spirit aside, it is his stock in trade. Destroy a professional person's reputation and you render useless his inventory, his machinery, his every asset. I fear that nonprofessional jurors did not comprehend the value of his professional reputation to a doctor. But as a judge, I must entertain the reservation that possibly the jury's assessment of pecuniary damages was more authentic than mine.

As the judge charged with administering the jury system in the county courthouse, every few months I ask the jury clerk to select eight or ten jurors at random and send them to my chambers. For an hour or more I discuss informally with them our mutual problems. They speak with anonymity, as I do not know their names and make no effort to identify them.

I must confess that most of the recommendations revolve about the physical facilities in the courthouse, or the lack of them. They suggest, among other things, soap and paper towels in washrooms, rubber foam cushions for the hard benches, airing the assembly rooms out during lunch, staggering hours of service, and the like. These are all important considerations. We give heed to them and endeavor in every way possible to make jury service as dignified, pleasant, and rewarding as possible. But at times jurors also make penetrating comments on the conduct of trials and the behavior of lawyers and judges.

From these informal conferences, and from my observations as a trial judge, I have formed an image of the composite juror. He, or she, regards jury duty as both a privilege and a nuisance. Once drawn for duty, however, he generally serves cheerfully and with a sense of dedication to duty. A juror resents as wasted the time he must spend in the assembly room awaiting impaneling. He seldom resents the time he devotes to actual service in the trial of a case.

Judges are aware of the hardships imposed upon jurors who are impressed into service, particularly those with small incomes. In New York an employer is under no compulsion to pay the difference between jury fees and wages to an employee engaged in jury service, although some employer-union contracts now remedy this hardship. Judges must therefore lend a sympathetic ear to wage earners who show they are in debt, facing unusual expenditures, or who for other reasons need every penny of their salary potential; and it is seldom that a meritorious appeal for deferment is refused. Another class of persons who are generally granted long deferments are those conducting what are known as one-man businesses—small tailor shops, stationery shops, hand laundries, and the like. If they are compelled to serve, they would in most instances be required to close their shops.

There is another factor calling for leniency in acting upon such pleas. A juror beset by grave financial worries is not likely to give the calm and considered appraisal of the evidence and law which litigants are entitled to receive from jurors.

I have never encountered a situation such as confronted Mr. Justice Stareleigh in the selection of the jury for the trial of Mr. Pickwick's case. It is thus described by Charles Dickens:

"The gentleman in black then proceeded to press into the special jury, two of the common jury-men; and a greengrocer and a chemist were caught directly.

" 'Answer to your names, gentlemen, that you may be sworn,' said the gentleman in black. 'Richard Upwitch.'

" 'Here,' said the green-grocer.

" 'Thomas Groffin.'

" 'Here,' said the chemist.

" 'Take the book, gentlemen. You shall well and truly try—'

" 'I beg this court's pardon,' said the chemist, who was a tall, thin, yellow-visaged man, 'but I hope this court will excuse my attendance.'

" 'On what grounds, sir?' said Mr. Justice Stareleigh.

" 'I have no assistant, my Lord,' said the chemist.

" 'I can't help that, sir,' replied Mr. Justice Stareleigh. 'You should hire one.'

" 'I can't afford it, my Lord,' rejoined the chemist.

" 'Then you ought to be able to afford it, sir,' said the judge, reddening; for Mr. Justice Stareleigh's temper bordered on the irritable, and brooked not contradiction.

" 'I know I *ought* to do, if I got on as well as I deserved, but I don't, my Lord,' answered the chemist.

" 'Swear the gentleman,' said the judge, peremptorily.

"The officer had got no further than the 'You shall well and truly try,' when he was again interrupted by the chemist.

" 'I am to be sworn, my Lord, am I?' said the chemist.

" 'Certainly, sir,' replied the testy little judge.

" 'Very well, my Lord,' replied the chemist, in a resigned manner. 'Then there'll be murder before this trial's over; that's all. Swear me, if you please, sir'; and sworn the chemist was, before the judge could find words to utter.

" 'I merely wanted to observe, my Lord,' said the chemist, taking his seat with great deliberation, 'that I've left nobody but an errand-boy in my shop. He is a very nice boy, my Lord, but he is not acquainted with drugs; and I know that the prevailing impression on his mind is, that Epsom salts means oxalic acid; and syrup of senna, laudanum. That's all, my Lord.' With this, the tall chemist composed himself into a comfortable attitude, and, assuming a pleasant expression of countenance, appeared to have prepared himself for the worst."

It is sometimes difficult to make jurors understand that in a large court such as ours, in which twenty jury trials may at one time be in different stages of progress, a sizable reservoir of jurors must be held in reserve throughout most of the court day. Cases collapse or are settled unexpectedly, and the judges in those parts send for panels of jurors to try the cases held in reserve. The jury clerks keep in touch with the various trial parts hourly. They are able to anticipate the need for jurors in a part where a trial is about to end. But they cannot anticipate the sudden termination of a trial.

When a juror has sunk his teeth into a trial, he will see the job through no matter what personal sacrifices or inconveniences he must suffer. When evening approaches, and a jury is deadlocked, the members do not rush through a makeshift verdict in order to go home. The court attendants are given a variety of messages to deliver. "Call my husband at this number—tell him I'll be home late and to take the children to a restaurant for dinner"; "Call Mr. Blank and tell him we'll have to postpone our conference until tomorrow afternoon"; and so on.

The sympathies of jurors are alerted to the side which they feel is getting an unfair deal. At these conferences in my chambers, jurors offered many comments on the unfair trial tactics of counsel, or even of a judge. One juror complained of the unfair manner in which the defendant's lawyer, and at times the judge, "rode" an inexperienced young lawyer representing the plaintiff in an accident case. I had this juror describe the plaintiff's lawyer in detail, and was able to identify him. I then dismissed the criticism with a cryptic "You can sometimes be misled by outward appearances in a trial."

In this instance the juror, and no doubt his fellow jurors, received just the impression of this lawyer which juries had been receiving for more than twenty years. Slight in build, with a boyish face, he appears to be a tremulous, inexperienced stripling in court. He does nothing to remove that impression. He is, however, one of the most successful trial counsel in negligence cases in the city. Scores of lawyers retain him to try their accident cases. Although he appears to be a youth in his twenties, he is at least forty-five years of age.

Clients of this perennial juvenile benefit greatly from his callow appearance. He is extremely deferential and most diffident. He shrinks back, affrighted, when his adversary, bursting with impotent rage, bellows his objections.

As a result, the jury obtains the impression which the jurors complained of at the conference. This young, inexperienced lawyer is getting a "ride." The big boys are playing rough with the little fellow. The jurors often express their resentment by giving the plaintiff a large verdict.

Judges in most courts do not characterize the evidence; they are careful to give no hint of their opinion of a case by words or demeanor. In their charges, particularly in marshaling the evidence, they try to present all aspects of the case impartially. Judges know that juries watch them carefully to get a clue as to the judge's impression of the case, and that jurors are usually influenced by such an impression, if they believe they have distilled it from a judge's remarks and demeanor. This is because jurors usually have great respect for the experience, acumen, and, most of all, the fairness of judges.

Sometimes a judge forfeits the respect of a jury. He may do this by taking sides during the trial, or by lashing out intemperately, albeit impartially, at everybody. Or a jury may gain an erroneous impression that a judge is unfair. In either event, the jury's sympathies are enlisted on the side of the underdog. Their partisan consideration of the case sometimes gains that party an undeserved victory.

So pronounced is this jury reaction that "judge-baiting" has become a recognized, although frowned upon, trial technique. It is employed by a few lawyers only, before excitable judges with low boiling points. Such a lawyer, if he has a weak case before such a judge, will set out deliberately to provoke the latter's ire. After he has exposed his breast to a number of fiery judicial bolts, he may gain the sympathy of the jury for himself and his client.

When I was an assistant district attorney assigned to the Court of General Sessions where felony criminal cases are tried, one of its nine judges was an honest, courageous, learned, but hopelessly irascible man. His denunciations and sarcastic thrusts were almost always leveled at defense counsel, because generally he would be aroused by what he deemed to be defendant's perjury or expedients to circumvent justice.

We prosecutors dreaded bringing our cases before him. Not only did we undergo an emotional ordeal, but we could rarely secure convictions. The juries expressed their resentment of his antics by returning verdicts for the harried defendants.

If a jury convicted, an appellate court was likely to reverse and order a new trial. A member of the district attorney's staff once tabulated the record on appeal in one of this judge's cases; the judge had asked more questions than counsel on both sides combined!

In those days a panel of jurors was assigned to serve exclusively for one month in each of the nine parts of the court. This was a very dangerous procedure. The jurors attended before the same judge for a month. Cases were prosecuted by the same two or three assistant district attorneys. In a short time the jury would be resentful of a judge like the one I have described, and retaliated by going counter to what he appeared to desire. Or, in most parts of the court, jurors would develop something akin to a "crush" on the judge and look for hints as to what he thought of the merits of the case.

Furthermore, a very dangerous form of camaraderie would develop between jurors and prosecutors. When not actually serving in a case, jurors would chat with the prosecutors, exchange cigarettes and views. After a while some unthinking jurors, from an excess of personal loyalty, would come to regard themselves as allies of their friends the prosecutors.

One judge would condition a jury during the first week of the term by paternal and benevolent lectures. At the termination of each case he would discuss it with the jury, then compliment or criticize, as required in his judgment. After a week, a jury would rise to his lifted eyebrow as responsively as a trained seal rises to a lifted pointer.

Fortunately, there were then and are now very few judges who feel a psychological urge to dominate a jury. Most judges are more than content to let the jury perform its role unhampered and uncontrolled. Many are happy to relegate to juries the fact-finding functions, which are generally more difficult than those of interpreting the law. The average judge desires only that there be a fair and full presentation of the available evidence.

As I've already pointed out, lawyers must be careful lest they outrage a jury's code of sportsmanship, or the consequences will be devastating.

During my first few months on the bench, an accident case was tried before me in which the plaintiff was a middle-aged woman. She testified to the happening of the accident and her injuries. She was cross-examined vigorously and at length by the attorney for the defendant, a young lawyer employed by an insurance company.

"One last question," he said, after a moment's hesitation. "According to this hospital record, you gave a history of syphilis some twenty years ago. Is that true?"

The poor woman lowered her head and nodded.

The plaintiff had suffered a fractured tibia in the accident. Her lawyer brought out through both her doctor and the defendant's doctor that there was no relationship medically between this injury and the venereal condition. Upon summation he made great capital of this fact, and commented upon the gratuitous injection of this mortifying and irrelevant testimony into the case. The jury retired and brought in a verdict for the plaintiff in an amount at least fifty per cent higher than her injuries would warrant normally.

I have since heard similar evidence introduced three times. In two of these cases there was some medical connection between the injuries allegedly resulting from the accident and the venereal condition. Nevertheless, in each case the jury returned a swollen verdict for the plaintiff.

Most experienced negligence lawyers have learned from bitter experience not to use such evidence. They might try to trap the plaintiff into bringing it out. Or they might simply introduce a hospital record into evidence and make no comment on the entry indicating a history of venereal disease, in the hope that some juror will examine the record in the jury room and discover the item.

On the other hand, and despite Hollywood, jurors can dismiss coldly the wiles and charms of the fair sex, when they sense that these are exerted to corrupt their judgment. A beautiful young lady once testified before a jury and me in support of her husband's version of an oral agreement. After taking the oath she coiled herself into the witness chair and crossed her legs in rigorous adherence to the style dictated by tradition: generous display of hose, just the hint of white thigh. Since time immemorial Dame Fashion, in the person of legal historians and movie directors, has decreed this position for ladies accused of murdering their husbands or lovers, and for jilted beauties suing rich brokers.

As the young lady adjusted herself in the witness chair one of the jurors cupped his mouth and leaned to one side. In a sibilant whisper intended only for his fellow jurors' ears, but audible throughout the courtroom, he said, "They call that cheesecake!"

The entire jury tittered. I, of course, gave no indication of having heard the remark. The young lady flushed and, clearly tipped off balance psychologically, made a very poor witness. Her husband lost his case.

Jurors have told me time and again that they dislike bullyragging of witnesses, shouting, and such displays. Unless a cross-examiner has reason to believe he can demolish a witness, he will impress the jury more by assailing the testimony rather than the witness personally. Jurors do not like to hear witnesses accused lightly or undeservedly of perjury.

They also cannot understand why a lawyer standing within a few feet of them must shout at the top of his lungs during summation. If he did that in their living rooms, they say, they would consider him a boor.

Once Leo Durocher, the baseball manager, agreeing that a certain ball player was a nice guy, quickly added, "But nice guys don't win ball games." My experience is that nice guys do win lawsuits.

One criticism of the jury system can be dismissed very quickly: that some jurors accept bribes. In one of the local district Municipal Courts of New York a band of professional jurors did manage to be assigned for service in that court with great frequency. They had a leader who would strike bargains with litigants for verdicts, give his instructions, and his cohorts would usually deliver. It later developed he had a code of ethics which he followed scrupulously. He never made a deal with both parties to a lawsuit. Furthermore, once he had made his arrangements with one party, he would never cancel them and switch allegiances, even though, as sometimes happened, the other party made a higher offer.

This ring was smashed and there has been no recurrence of such conditions in that or any other court in New York. True, there may be rare instances of bribery of individual jurors, just as there are rare instances of bribery of individual judges. But the slightest ingenuity in the mechanics of selecting and assigning jurors can prevent the development of any pattern for corrupting them.

In our court, for example, there is no way of knowing in advance which twelve jurors out of a panel of several hundred will be assigned to a particular part and accepted for service in a particular case. Once a jury is in a box, overtures of course could be made to individual jurors. But that is a very hazardous undertaking.

The jury system must be manned by knowledgeable jurors. The credit items must be transferred to the debit column, unless the jurors are an intelligent and earnest cross section of the community. A litigant entitled to trial by a jury of his peers should not be required to submit his liberty and property to twelve dolts. They should at the least comprehend and follow the issues—whether in criminal, commercial, negligence, or any other type of litigation. Many of them should have the experience to weigh values, the shrewdness to penetrate falsehood, and the character to withstand blandishments.

In our court, during the past two years, we have made some progress in raising the caliber of the average jurors. If we continue to make this progress and expand into an educational program, I am confident most criticism of the jury system, in our court at least, will be stilled.

The main problem will be to condition jurors to decide "according to the evidence," as their oath reads; to change laws by their votes on Election Day, not in the jury room. I am sure most jurors are unaware of this propensity, and that intelligent discussion will go far to eliminate it.

What can be done about training jurors so that they can hold down their positions on the team with competence?

Theoretically, the courts should be able to turn to the educators and say, "Look here, we've been hearing a lot of talk about educating our youth for citizenship. What function of citizenship is more important than intelligent, courageous, and honest jury service?"

As a practical matter, however, our jury system might well founder before such an educational program would make an impression upon our population. It is, therefore, a job in education which the courts themselves must undertake.

Jurors are generally summoned to serve a two-week term. For the first few days they should go to school in the courthouse. A juror need take such a course only once in a lifetime.

The instructors should be employed on a permanent basis. There would be no point in setting forth a full curriculum in this chapter.

It could, however, include the structure of the court, its various parts and functions. The jurors should be cautioned, in terms of the law, against harboring prejudice because of a party's race, creed, color, or national origin. The democratic beginnings and concepts of the jury system should be stressed.

The function of the pleadings should be illustrated, from actual samples. The major rules of evidence and those most commonly resorted to should be explained. Similar study should be made of those portions of a judge's charge which are fixed and mandatory, such as burden of proof, preponderance of evidence, etc.

The jurors should be taught the rudiments of the law specially applicable to the types of cases which will be presented to them most frequently, such as accident and breach of contract. What constitutes negligence, actual and constructive notice, measure of damages, and similar aspects of such cases would be explained.

A short history of the development of the jury system should be given. It would help orient the juror as to the necessity and importance of his functions. If he is critical or cynical about these functions it will pose him the problem of suggesting a better medium for safeguarding his personal and property rights and ascertaining the truth without fear or favor. He will derive a sense of dignity in the performance of duties rooted in the traditions of centuries, and a sense of inspiration from the stirring and courageous achievements of the past. The instructors can collaborate with the jury officials in striking off the rolls persons who are clearly incompetent to serve. For example, morons, persons who are physically incapacitated or who suffer aberrations which prevent them from serving adequately, should be disqualified.

Jurors should be afforded physical facilities which will make their service as comfortable as possible. Their waiting periods, when not engaged in trials, should be made less irksome than they now are in most jurisdictions.

Chief Judge Laws, of the United States District Court for the District of Columbia, thus described model juror accommodations during the recent dedication of the new Federal Courthouse in his district:

". . . in this new building we have provided for him a luxurious waiting room, one comparable to those in club quarters. We have provided parking for his automobile, which is no small item. We have provided for him during the necessarily enforced periods of his idleness, which no court system has been able to work out a means to prevent, a private, soundproof room, where he can bring his secretary or his associates and carry on business uninterruptedly, perhaps for hours in the day, until he is called as juror to serve in a specific case. We have provided for him a message center, where a message can be delivered to him by an officer of the court at any time. We have provided for him private sleeping quarters, where he can spend in comfort the overnight sessions which jurors oftentimes are compelled to hold."

I believe jurors should be paid adequately for their services. There is a school of thought which holds that if the jury fees are made high they will attract an undesirable type of juror. This is a danger only if the enforcement of jury service is lax.

Formal or higher education will not necessarily prepare a juror for his duties. An alert day laborer may be a more valuable and perspicacious juror than a sluggish college professor or business executive. But all must be educated to an awakened and understanding interest in the scope and importance of their jobs as jurors. They must be trained for the particular job on hand. The incompetents must be weeded out and the remaining eligibles groomed to serve intelligently, expertly, and cheerfully.

* XIV *

Drama in the Courtroom

THERE ARE rarely episodes in a courtroom which would appear dramatic to a nonprofessional—that is, dramatic in a florid or theatrical sense. To the lay observer, watching lawyers go about their business in the average courtroom is about as exciting as watching chemists poking about a laboratory. Both professions best perform their functions of finding the truth in a dispassionate atmosphere.

Occasionally, a trial contains elements of great public interest. The courtroom is crowded, spectators queue up in corridors, the press is represented, the air is charged with emotion and crackling with excitement.

There is no doubt that such a setting heightens the dramatic possibilities of what otherwise might be a drab trial. Lawyers, witnesses, sometimes even judges, act up to the situation. Sex is an unfailing ingredient to attract the public interest in a trial—whether it be a divorce action or murder prosecution.

But generally a courtroom functions in a subdued and, to many, a boring key. While trials are still private contests among parties, passions have usually cooled and tempers subsided by the time the case is reached for trial. Trials seldom retain the aspect of a bitter-end grudge fight—that is, except in matrimonial litigation, in which the waiting period before trial seems to fan the flames of acrimony. In most other cases it apparently operates as a cooling-off period.

There are few outbursts by lawyers or clients in court. Some of those eruptions, I suspect, are not outlets for pent-up emotions but designed to impress jury or judge. Most lawyers and judges seek to perform their duties with detached competency. The procedure is dignified, the setting is somber. It is all so heavily formalized that it discourages sensationalism.

Times change. Books and plays become dated within the short span of one generation. The wail of "Fireman, save my child!" that once sent excited shivers down the spines of theatre audiences would now excite only cries of derision. The realism that has invaded the arts and so many areas of contemporary living has not by-passed the courts. They have shucked most of their former mid-Victorian rhetoric. Even judges' opinions are becoming more prosaic and less Olympian.

Lawyers realize they must sell their wares—as factual claims—to a jury; and the less flowery the presentation, the better the chances of success. The evidence that would have provided a good show a generation ago has little entertainment value today. But this is due only in part to a change in the critical tastes of the community.

Jurors are now more serious in the performance of their duties and are impatient with exhibitionism. One reason may be that the ordinary and extraordinary processes of government have become an intimate concern of most persons. Wars and depressions have sobered people. Today government enters directly into home and business to collect taxes, provide social security, draft members of the family for war, and to ration commodities. As one of the important arms of government, the courts receive the earnest and intense consideration now accorded all governmental agencies.

The summation—closing statement of counsel to the jury—and cross-examination are most likely to furnish the dramatic features of a trial. On rare occasions a lawyer will guide his own witness through an unexpected and startling disclosure. Ordinarily he will do this when the facts are known to the other side, and he wishes to blunt the effect of the inevitable cross-examination on that subject. I have heard a lawyer commence the direct examination of his client as follows:

LAWYER: Have you ever been convicted of a crime?
CLIENT: Yes, sir.
LAWYER: What crime?
CLIENT: Rape.
LAWYER: Now, how long ago were you convicted?
CLIENT: Over twenty-five years ago, sir.
LAWYER: And how old were you at the time?
CLIENT: I was barely seventeen years old.
LAWYER: How old was the girl in the case?
CLIENT: She was seventeen, too.
LAWYER: Were you convicted of what is known as statutory rape?
CLIENT: What do you mean by that, sir?
LAWYER: That is where no force or violence is used in subduing the female. When the female complainant is under eighteen years of age, the law presumes she is incapable of giving her consent. Even if she should be the aggressor, the male having intercourse with her, in the eyes of the law, is guilty of statutory rape.
CLIENT: Then I pleaded guilty to statutory rape.
LAWYER: Did you go to jail?
CLIENT: No, sir. I received a suspended sentence.
LAWYER: Did the girl make the complaint against you?
CLIENT: No, sir. Her father did. He had unexpectedly come upon us.
LAWYER: Did the girl admit to the judge that she had had relations with other boys before this?
CLIENT: Yes, sir.
OPPOSING LAWYER: I move to strike that out.
COURT: Strike it out. The jury will disregard it.

LAWYER: Are you married?
CLIENT: Yes, sir; and I have three children.
LAWYER: Does your wife know of this conviction?
CLIENT: Of course.
OPPOSING LAWYER: Move to strike it out.
COURT: Strike it out. I think you should now get down to the issues in this case, counselor.

Had opposing counsel objected, it is unlikely that the examining lawyer would have been given such latitude on direct examination of his own witness. But he could have later developed much of the testimony on redirect examination, and he would have at least deflected the force of the cross-examination by first bringing out the fact of the conviction. It is possible that, instead of impairing his credibility, his attorney's treatment of the earlier conviction served to gain the sympathy of the jury for the witness. It returned a verdict in his favor.

If you were sitting as a juror today, with what feelings would you listen to this closing summation from a case that was tried in 1875? This gem is cited as a masterpiece of eloquence in a respected volume entitled *Modern Jury Trials*, by Judge J. W. Donovan.

One May Stephens, a widow, was drowned in a cistern, leaving two small children, both under fourteen. She had several insurance policies. One of the insurance companies refused to pay, asserting among other reasons that the deceased widow had insured heavily because she intended to commit suicide and that she suffered from secret diseases which had not been revealed to the company. A guardian was appointed for the children and he commenced suit in the Superior Court of Detroit for five thousand dollars—the face amount of the policy.

After the evidence had been presented, the plaintiff's lawyer pleaded with the jury as follows:

"Oh, what a monstrous absurdity! Experts chosen for learning, skill and experience, baffled by a poor, weak widow, who is seeking to impose upon the world by a fraud. She had a little money. She was coaxed to invest it for her child—her bright-eyed boy, for her little girl, fast budding into womanhood. She did. She went too far. She was over-persuaded. These men, pleading in her ear, telling the stories of profits, singing their siren songs, that, like the mermaids in the legends of old, which lured the returning seamen from their well-filled boats to tie up the ships and follow the sweet songs until far away from home, in the mountains and forests, they were lost, to die alone in hunger and delirium. It is said that ever afterwards travelers took warning, as they passed, and put wax in their ears to shut out the music of the allurers as they passed. This may be a lesson in our day, for only wax could shut out the pleading appeals to join this coaxing company. . . . Oh, what a picture is here to behold! Two little orphans battling with a giant corporation! A money power, backed by the bondholders and directors. How it rouses our impulses to witness the contest!

"That mother, the object of this bereavement, is gone. Her lips are dumb; her voice is hushed—low in the silent grave. No whisper can come back to say: 'I slipped. I fell. I was misguided. I did all; I risked all for you! for you, my children, my own! For you, my little ones.'

"She has gone. She has whispered the last good night and gone! The secrets of her death are locked up till the judgement day. There they are sacred; there they will remain secure.

"Oh! I can see her now; it is early twilight, it is winter, the snow is falling fast and slippery; whitening the little plank walk to the cistern. She has company, she hurries down the walk, catching up a pail, leaving the hook hanging over the curbing, bending low she slips, falls, the water covers her, no one hears, she is drowned! It is an accident; and I almost hear her say, as she looks down to you, to this upright judge, this honest jury: 'Gentlemen, you may cheat my children, if you will, but spare them the burden of dishonor; the money will be a poor pittance at the most to that priceless character that my innocent children should inherit.' . . . And my little clients (here the speaker laid one hand on each of the client's shoulders and amid the hushed silence of rapt attention, said), my little clients, may God bless you! I have done my best to make your names an honor to our state!"

Of course, the jury returned a verdict in favor of the plaintiff. The summation was a shrewdly calculated appeal to the emotions and prejudices of the jurors.

I submitted an outline of the facts in this case and a copy of the summation to one of the best trial lawyers in the City of New York. On the identical facts, I asked him if he would prepare a summation for a contemporary jury. He tried hard, but finally gave up and confessed he could not recast it in more effective form. He said he would not dare deliver a summation today in so flowery a style, but that he could not prepare a more effective one in modern idiom.

The successful trial lawyer does not ask a jury to reward him for his individual brilliance. He tries to present himself as the neutral instrument through which the irrepressible facts assert themselves, although he may have devoted half the night to shaping his summation so as to convey that impression.

I remember a case which was tried by that master craftsman, the late Max D. Steuer. Steuer never ranted, never shouted, never implored the heavens. He got his dramatic effects—and very effective ones—by voice shadings. He would commence a summation by barely speaking above a whisper. The jurors would shift to the edges of their chairs and strain their ears, in order to hear him. A pause would be freighted with more significance than the wildest gesticulations of another lawyer. When he raised his voice to an ordinary, conversational pitch, his audience would be stirred more visibly than by orators who made the courtroom rafters ring.

In this case Steuer had been addressing the jury in such restrained fashion for over an hour. He came to a discussion of an account book which he asserted contained fraudulent entries. He opened the book, pointed to several entries on different pages, and reviewed certain auditors' testimony. Then he closed the book, with an indescribable look of disgust on his face. He grasped it abruptly in both hands, raised it above his head and brought it down sharply on the rail in front of the jury box.

The effect was electric! The crack of the impact burst on our ears like a clap of thunder. No tirade could have execrated those entries as effectively as did that gesture. And then, after a short pause, he continued his argument in his usual soft tones.

Even in the good old days extravagant courtroom assertions occasionally boomeranged. The following incident is related in Grant's *Law and Lawyers,* an English book published over one hundred years ago:

"On the Norfolk circuit, the famous Jack Lee was retained for the plaintiff in an action for breach of promise of marriage; when the brief was brought him, he inquired whether the lady for whose injury—spretaeque injuria formae—he was to seek redress was good-looking. 'Very handsome, indeed, sir!' was the assurance of Helen's attorney. 'Then, sir,' replied Lee, 'I beg you will request her to be in court, and in a place where she can be seen.' The attorney promised compliance; and the lady, in accordance with Lee's wishes, took her seat in a conspicuous place. Lee, in addressing the jury, did not fail to insist with great warmth on the 'abominable cruelty' which had been exercised towards 'the lovely and confiding female' before them, and did not sit down until he had succeeded in working up their feelings to the desired point. The counsel on the other side, however, speedily broke the spell with which Lee had enchanted the jury, by observing that his learned friend in describing the graces and beauty of the plaintiff had not mentioned the fact—that the lady had a *wooden leg*! The court was convulsed with laughter, while Lee, who was ignorant of this circumstance, looked aghast; and the jury, ashamed of the influence that mere eloquence had had upon them, returned a verdict for the defendant."

It is difficult to separate present and past trial techniques because one may not speculate as to where the apocryphal tales end and the valid ones begin. Wellman, for example, a most respected writer, in his book *Gentlemen of the Jury,* states that this story, which I now quote, was told him by a justice of the Iowa Supreme Court before whom the case was tried.

"A railroad company was being sued for personal injury. The experts for the plaintiff contended that as a result of the injury the plaintiff was a confirmed and hopeless victim of neurasthenia (nervous prostration), and their evidence tended to show that one so afflicted had deteriorated mentally and would rapidly decline. A rather pitiful picture was painted. On cross-examination the attorney for the railroad developed from the expert doctor that the main ground for his opinion that the plaintiff was suffering with neurasthenia was the fact that he appeared to suffer no pain when pricked with a pin on the top of his head, and that this test was quite conclusive proof of neurasthenia.

"The lawyer for the defendant was an ex-judge, a man somewhat advanced in years and exceedingly resourceful. Incidentally, he was as bereft of hair as the oft cited billiard ball. When it came time to argue the case to the jury he proceeded to expound the facts with clearness and vigor for a considerable length of time and finally approached the subject of neurasthenia.

"After paying his respects to the learned experts for the plaintiff he took up the subject of the final test in the examination the experts had made of the plaintiff. He assured the jury of his great personal regret, and in fact his surprise and astonishment, at the discovery the examination of these learned men had disclosed, namely, that one who did not experience pain by the prick of a pin on the top of the head was a neurasthenic and rapidly progressing to complete mental decline. He assured the jury that he felt he was a man of reasonable physical vigor and had always supposed he was still possessed of his normal mental faculties, but to his great distress he now discovered he himself was a hopeless neurasthenic and would demonstrate to the jury that he had no business trying lawsuits, but should be preparing himself rapidly to meet his Maker.

"Thereupon he turned back the lapel of his coat and extracted a good sized needle which he promptly stuck in the top of his head. He kept this up until he had some ten or twelve needles sticking in the top of his bald head and looked like an animated pin cushion. He finished his argument and, needless to say, a verdict was returned in favor of the defendant. He confided to the judge in later years that the last needle got outside the area of the cocaine which his physician had hypodermically injected into his scalp just before he began his argument, and almost unmasked the hoax. As Judge Faville said to me, 'If I could picture to you the scene of this venerable old war horse prancing up and down before that jury with his bald head bristling full of needles and haranguing them at the top of his voice, I should be very happy indeed.' "

Presumably this incident occurred a generation ago. One wonders whether Judge Faville was pulling the venerable Wellman's leg. Aside from the incredible features of the story, the lawyer stooping to such a trick would be subject to disbarment. Yet I have seen this story repeated in another book. In time I suppose it will attain some currency, and a flavor of authenticity.

But there is nothing apocryphal about the fact that the patient, temperate manner also appears to be most effective on cross-examination. A surrounding movement is usually more successful than a frontal attack, and a rapier is more decisive than a flail. Steuer would spend hours on cross-examination, softly leading a witness into an inextricable position. First, he would cause the witness to take a firm stand on this position. Then he would block all possible exits by having the still unsuspecting witness reject and eliminate every explanation for the position, except the explanation that supported Steuer's contentions. When the encircling action was completed, Steuer would move savagely to the attack.

Other lawyers probe quietly for a vulnerable spot in the testimony. When they believe they have found it, then they sink their teeth in it and try to shake the truth out of the witness.

Another reason for using these moderate styles of cross-examination is that they entail less danger of evoking jury sympathy for the witness. Jurors, as laymen, feel a certain kinship for another layman being harassed by a lawyer. If the cross-examination causes the witness to modify or change his testimony, or demolishes or seriously challenges his credibility, it will not offend the jury—no matter how strenuous the questioning. A trial is still regarded as a private fight, and a party's lawyer as justified in displaying antagonism. If a witness, however, is treated roughly and emerges unscathed, the jury may feel he was abused unnecessarily, and resent the lawyer's harshness. Therefore, a lawyer will seldom displease a jury if he generates his righteous heat and indignation only if and only when he has reached the climactic point where he is ready, with some reason, to dispute the assertions of the witness.

I once heard the cross-examination of a witness which reminded me of the story of the G.I. who in civilian life had acquired great proficiency in the use of the straight razor as a lethal weapon. In charging the enemy he discarded his rifle and whipped out his trusty razor. A German infantryman came at him with fixed bayonet. The doughboy merely flicked his wrist, and the razor blade gleamed in the sunlight.

"Ach, you missed me," cried the German.

"Oh, yeah," drawled the doughboy. "Just wait till you try to turn your head."

In the case I have in mind the witness left the stand completely unaware of the fact that in the course of a short cross-examination he had irretrievably lost his case. He had been examined quietly, and without heat. Only the professionals in the courtroom—the lawyers and myself—were aware of the cross-examiner's objective, and were intently following his questions.

This was a lawsuit brought by a stockholder against a nationally known corporation manufacturing radios and television sets. The plaintiff sought damages as a result of an allegedly false and fraudulent financial statement published by the corporation. In his complaint he asserted that he was induced by the representations in this statement to purchase some shares of stock, and that they had dropped sharply in price because of the true financial condition of the company. In order to establish his case the plaintiff had to prove that in purchasing the stock he relied upon the allegedly false representations in the financial statement.

The plaintiff was a successful and self-made businessman. He was not unpleasantly aggressive and positive in manner, and the attorney for the defendant played skillfully upon those characteristics. He drew him out about the operation of his business, and elicited that he often backed his own judgment despite industry opinion to the contrary.

"Maybe you relied on your own judgment in your own business," said the lawyer, "but you didn't do so in buying this stock."

"Why not?" bridled the witness.

"Because you're not in the television business, and you knew nothing about the television business."

"I made quite a study of television and had great faith in its future."

"But that's not why you bought this stock," suggested the lawyer.

"It certainly was," affirmed the witness.

"I thought you bought it because you liked the figures in the financial statement; that you would have bought this stock if the company had sold washing machines or automobiles."

"Oh, no, counselor. As a matter of fact, even the published figures were not so hot. They showed the company operated at a loss, only not as large a loss as the books indicated."

"Wasn't it pretty foolhardy of you to invest money in a losing venture—especially in a strange business?"

"Can't you understand, counselor, once and for all, that I had and still have confidence in the future of television. It wasn't such a strange business to me. I'd studied it and was backing my judgment on its future. That was my reason for buying this stock."

This testimony, of course, combined with other evidence, precluded any finding that the plaintiff, in purchasing the stock, had relied upon the allegedly false representations in the financial statement. I directed judgment in favor of the defendant.

I cannot dispute Wigmore when he hails cross-examination, not trial by jury, as "the great and permanent contribution of the Anglo-American system of law to improved methods of trial-procedure," or as "the greatest legal engine ever invented for the discovery of truth." I must always add the mental reservation, however, "within the limiting boundaries of a judicial trial." Perhaps the true and the great value of cross-examination will be better appreciated if it is not sentimentalized as an infallible or even commonly effective weapon for the ascertainment of truth.

Startling disclosures have been wrung from the lips of reluctant witnesses by cross-examination. The witness will admit he has been lying or be cornered so that such a conclusion is irresistible. On the other hand, the unsuccessful cross-examination can't be detected for the very reason that there is no way of establishing absolutely that the witness was not telling the truth.

The main objectives of cross-examination have been held to be (1) to cause the witness to repudiate, change, or modify his testimony; (2) to cause him to testify to something favoring or helping the side of the cross-examiner; (3) to discredit the witness through his own testimony.

Most of the cross-examinations which are cited as proof of its efficacy, certainly most of the sensational examinations, fall within the first two categories. But it is my belief that year in and year out, in the generality of cases, the greatest value of cross-examination lies in its efficiency in the development of evidence affecting the credibility of witnesses. Seldom is a witness visibly shaken on his original narration of facts. Cross-examination, however, often brings out prosaic evidence, well known to the parties but unknown to the jury, which indicates possible bias, prejudice, or motivation for favoring the side which has called the witness.

In a case tried before me the plaintiff's most important witness was a chemist. He had a distinguished background, including the fact that he taught in a New York City university. There were two defendants in the case, represented by two different lawyers.

The first lawyer to cross-examine the witness had evidently studied diligently the technical aspects of the case. He sought to put this knowledge to use by cross-examining the chemist upon his expert findings. While he displayed an amazing grasp of chemistry for an amateur, he was no match for the witness in his own field. As a result he made a miserable mess of the cross-examination and only hammered home once again the plaintiff's major contentions.

The other lawyer, however, limited his examination to a few questions.

"You were not subpoenaed by the plaintiff, Doctor?" he asked, very respectfully.

"No, sir."

"As a matter of fact, you came to court voluntarily?"

"Yes, sir."

"Are you being paid for testifying, Doctor?"

"I am charging a fee for my professional opinion."

"Of course, Doctor, no offense meant. How much is that fee?"

"One thousand dollars, for my preliminary opinion and my appearance in court."

"Just one more question, Doctor. Do you know of Dr. Jones?"

"I know him well."

"Is he regarded, in professional circles, as a competent chemist?"

"He is an excellent man."

"Thank you, Doctor. That will be all."

This defendant produced Dr. Jones as its expert witness.

I have read stories of lawyers and barristers who have transfixed quailing witnesses with their piercing eyes, and cross-examined them with such devastating effect that they slunk from the stand, completely crushed. However, I have yet to see a lawyer demolish a witness by sheer force of personality or genius. Lawyers will sometimes destroy a witness's direct testimony, but usually by dint of exhaustive preparation and by securing admission of conflicting facts from which there is no escape.

A trial sometimes ends suddenly, usually because a lawyer realizes that he will fail to make out a case under the law and that to continue will merely delay the inevitable dismissal of his complaint. Rarely, in my experience, has a witness been destroyed so effectively that the case itself collapsed, then and there. In previous chapters I have related two cases in which that happened. In neither case was the witness annihilated by the individual brilliance of the lawyer.

Sometimes an inept or overaggressive lawyer will touch off testimony on cross-examination which will overthrow his entire case. Quoting Wigmore once more, " 'You can do anything,' said Wendell Phillips, 'with a bayonet—except sit upon it.' A lawyer can do anything with a cross-examination—if he is skillful enough not to impale his own cause upon it."

In a malpractice action tried before me the defendant was a physician who practiced in a poor neighborhood. The plaintiff's lawyer was not content with trying to prove that the defendant had been negligent in diagnosing and treating the plaintiff. He tried to arouse the jury's indignation by intimating that the defendant had also grossly overcharged the plaintiff.

The doctor's nurse, who had assisted him in his treatment of the plaintiff, testified in his behalf. Upon cross-examination the plaintiff's attorney questioned her closely and viciously upon the number of visits the doctor had made to the plaintiff's home and the number of times the plaintiff had visited the doctor's office. He openly questioned the genuineness of her office records and derided her protestations that each entry represented a visit. Then he shifted his questions to the fees paid by the plaintiff.

Sneeringly, he asked, "Even if all those visits were made, were they necessary, or was the doctor building up his fees?"

The witness gripped both sides of the chair so fiercely that the whites of her knuckles showed. She half raised herself, and then the storm broke.

"You've been poking fun at my doctor," she blazed, "and you're not fit to wipe his shoes. Have you any idea of how much good he does every day? Do you know that he won't let me send bills to more than half his patients, because they can't afford to pay? My doctor is a poor man. There's many a time, when the first of the month comes round, that I have trouble scraping together the rent for his office and his home. I'm ashamed to tell you how many months I only draw part of my pay, because there just isn't enough."

The lawyer gesticulated and shouted "I object!" and "Move to strike it all out, Your Honor!" but she continued.

"Do you think he and his family live in luxury? They live right in the same neighborhood—in a walk-up flat. My doctor and his wife and three kids. He's a wonderful doctor, and he could make a lot of money, if he wanted to. But he's devoting his whole life to helping these poor people."

After she had fully finished I recognized the clamoring, red-faced lawyer for the plaintiff. I granted his motion to strike her answer from the record, and gravely instructed the jurors to disregard it. From the celerity with which they later returned a verdict for the defendant, I doubt that they heeded my admonition.

This lawyer got just what he deserved—professionally and personally. He had no reason to expect that the nurse would admit that the visits were unnecessary or padded, nor had he any factual basis with which to challenge her expected denial. Besides, he conducted himself boorishly and unfairly, in a manner designed to antagonize the jury.

Good lawyers never expect miracles upon cross-examination, and they do not venture beyond the periphery of their preparation. They will examine purposefully and to the point. Poor lawyers will fish and flounder and carry on long and aimless examinations.

And lastly, an experienced and disciplined lawyer is never ashamed to relinquish his cross-examination with an undramatic but safe "No questions, Your Honor."

Settlements and Pretrial Conferences

LAST MONTH I read the papers in a very disturbing motion for a preference. This was an application to take a case out of its regular order and to schedule it for immediate trial. Cases are given a calendar number when certain papers are filed, and then move in regular numerical order toward trial.

The plaintiff in this case had been hit by an automobile about a year before and suffered serious injuries. Two months before the motion was made it was discovered that he was a victim of cancer in one of its most malignant forms. He had already lost so much weight and vigor that he could no longer walk. The doctor gave him only a few months to live. The case was two years away from trial, if it pursued its normal course on the calendar.

The only witnesses to the accident were the defendant and plaintiff. In support of his motion the plaintiff's lawyer contended that after the plaintiff's death he would be unable to prove his case. The defendant countered with the argument that the plaintiff's condition was such that he would be carried into the courtroom on a stretcher and testify from that position. Inevitably, asserted the defendant, the jury's sympathies would be aroused by the plaintiff's condition, to the prejudice of the defendant, even though it would be made clear that the accident was not the cause of the wasting disease which necessitated the plaintiff's using a stretcher.

The defendant's lawyer suggested that the plaintiff's deposition or examination be taken immediately at his home, and then read at the trial. The plaintiff's lawyer argued that this was a poor substitute for an appearance on the witness stand; furthermore, he could not thus anticipate and meet all the testimony which the defendant might later give at the trial.

My secretary invited both lawyers to my chambers. When they arrived, I told them I had not as yet decided how I would dispose of the motion. I suggested, in view of the uncertainties involved, and the unusual circumstances, that the plaintiff accept a little less than he thought his case was worth in settlement, and that the defendant's insurance company pay a little more than it thought the case merited.

In an hour, after several telephone calls, the case was settled. Both sides were pleased with the outcome. Perhaps the most beneficial result, although of no legal significance, was the fact that the plaintiff obtained some sorely needed cash to relieve his last days. I regarded this settlement as a very satisfying judicial achievement.

The legal purists, however, are inclined to look down their noses upon settlement efforts as one of the grosser judicial activities. No particular profundity or erudition is required, the judicial trappings are discarded, the judge descends from his ivory tower into the market place. During the negotiations the judge is pretty much on his own. He must command respect by dint of his character, experience, and skill. Some judges, and some lawyers who like to worship their judges from afar, are uncomfortable in such a setting.

It seems to me, on the other hand, that the settlement of cases is the most civilized activity in the courts. The courts have evolved as the most peaceful, least wasteful medium for resolving disputes. Trial by judge and jury has replaced trial by combat. A court trial is still strife, although no longer physical in nature. It represents an expenditure of time, energy, and money by a number of persons, toward an unpredictable result. Feelings are lacerated, reputations soiled, fortunes lost or gained, tensions and worries heightened. So even under our enlightened, modern system of jurisprudence, settlement is more peaceful than trial as a method of adjusting controversies.

Civilization itself can develop no faster than the procedures it produces within itself for nurturing and expanding the law which governs it. The first seeds of this law were sown when our primitive forebears came to realize the devastating effects of the blood feuds, and sought to ameliorate them. It may have had its beginning in an incident such as this improvised one.

Assume that Mog, while out hunting, saw a wild boar plunging through the brush. He hurled his spear and pierced the throat of an old man who had stepped into the path of the spear's flight. The dead man was the father of Gog, a mighty warrior of a neighboring clan. Gog's and Mog's clans had been very friendly up to this time, even uniting at times to repel common enemies.

Mog left the spear in his victim's throat and fled to the chief of his clan, to whom he reported the episode. The body was soon discovered, and the spear identified as belonging to Mog. Gog swore a mighty oath and called upon his chief to declare a blood feud with Mog's clan.

A blood feud was tantamount to a state of warfare between the two clans. It was the primitive formula for avenging a wrong to a member of the clan. Once the feud was initiated, members of each clan would attack one another on sight. This might continue until both clans were destroyed, or until they were so decimated that they would be easy prey for some marauding tribe.

Mog's chief sent a messenger to Gog's chief, with an invitation to confer. The latter accepted. Each flanked by a bodyguard, they sat under a spreading tree on the edge of the forest. This was a prefeud conference—object, to avoid a feud.

Mog's chief, after the preliminary amenities, said, "Your people and mine have at last found friendship. We own herds of cattle, we raise crops. Our young men are forgetting the paths of bloodshed and are pursuing the ways of peace. It is regrettable that an old man has died. But you and I should not permit blood to be spilled on that account."

"What do you propose?" asked Gog's chief.

"I propose to make a gift to your clan to express our sorrow at the death of this helpless old man."

"Gog's father was an elder of the clan, wise in council, and strong and swift. We valued him highly. He was not helpless and not very old."

"He was too old and feeble to hunt, or till the fields, or tend the flocks. Besides, Mog was not at fault. The old man leaped out from behind some bushes into the spear."

"How could so old and feeble a man leap? But everyone knows how poor a hunter Mog is. He is half blind and very careless."

"Mog is a careful hunter. In any event, he did not mean to kill the old man."

"Maybe not. But that does not restore him to his son Gog, who loved him dearly and grieves for him."

"What will assuage the grief of the son for this useless old man who has been a burden to him for many years?"

"I shall accept five pigs, three sheep, and two horses as a most inadequate substitute for the vengeance Gog could demand for the death of the wise, strong father who has guided and counseled him throughout his life."

"I shall give you two goats."

The other chief braced himself preparatory to rising. "I shall yield to Gog's demand for a blood feud," he said.

"Wait, wait. I shall give you two goats and one sheep."

"No, I shall stay no longer."

"Three goats, one sheep, and one pig."

"No goats. We have an abundance of goats. I shall give you one final demand. Two pigs, two sheep, and one horse."

"Two pigs and two sheep my poor, groaning people will give to you."

"Very well. Deliver them before sundown."

"It shall be done. And there will be no bloodshed?"

"There will be no bloodshed."

This is a classic example of a primitive settlement. Only indirectly were damages paid for the wrong. The transaction instead took the form of buying peace, of paying a price for the relinquishment of the vengeance that Gog's clan would wreak on Mog's clan —and incidentally upon itself—just as modern litigation takes its toll of plaintiff as well as defendant.

Max Radin, the legal philosopher, tells this whimsical story about an Amir of Afghanistan, who was approached by two of his subjects. They both laid claim to a field between their properties, and called upon the Amir to render justice. Each submitted testimony and documents in support of his claim.

The Amir heard each subject without interruption. He then asked one, "Have you a son?" The answer was "Yes."

He asked the other, "Have you a daughter?" Again the answer was in the affirmative.

Then the Amir said—or ruled, since he was an Oriental potentate—"Marry the young people to each other, and give them the field as a portion."

An Englishman who was present on an official mission inquired, "Suppose they had been unwilling, Your Highness? What would you have done?"

"In that case," replied the Amir, "I should have hanged them both and confiscated their lands."

Radin goes on to point out that the law may dispose of mutually contradictory claims in three ways. It may please one of the claimants and displease the other. This is generally the outcome of concluded litigation. Secondly, the law may attempt what the Amir accomplished, namely, to please both claimants to a less degree than either desired. Or, it may do what the Amir might have done—please neither, but increase the public treasury. The settlement process pleases each party to a less degree than he desires; but it may rescue one of them from a crippling experience.

My idea of a good settlement is one in which all parties leave the courthouse a little dissatisfied with the result, but completely satisfied with the judicial processes which brought it about. To achieve this consummation with fair consistency a judge must possess a blending of experience, skill, tact, and patience.

Some courts take the initiative in inaugurating settlement negotiations, by setting down cases for pretrial conference, in stated parts, at stated times, long before they will be reached for trial.

The main functions of these pretrial conferences are to secure agreement and concessions on facts that are not substantially in dispute, to simplify and narrow the issues, dispense with appearance of unnecessary witnesses, generally to remove unnecessary impediments to a shortened but fair and adequate trial, and to speed calendar progress by settling cases. It is a simple and informal court function, although attendance is required as rigorously as at a trial.

Without minimizing the undeniable importance of its other accomplishments, this chapter will deal only with the settlement aspects of the conference. The pretrial conference is a boon to lawyers and litigants because neither side has to make the initial settlement overtures, outside of court, with the accompanying implications of weakness. Both sides know that the judge will broach settlement, among other proposals.

Trial does hold forth the certainty of worry and the fear of outcome. No matter how convinced a client may be of the righteousness of his cause, his lawyer cannot guarantee him victory. Many lawyers fear or are disinclined to try cases. The modern general practitioner appears infrequently in court, and is therefore either rusty or inexperienced. Arbitration tribunals, workmen's compensation bureaus, and the numerous administrative agencies have siphoned off a good portion of the litigation formerly conducted in the courts. These lawyers are fearful lest they lose good clients through an inept performance in court—particularly if it should draw impatient or caustic comment from the bench.

Besides, it is generally unprofitable for a lawyer who is not a trial specialist to handle litigation. He can seldom be compensated adequately for the occasional case which he takes to court. Each visit to court, whether to argue a motion, await assignment to a trial part, or to try the case, means time away from his office. During this time he could be closing titles, advising corporate clients, or performing a myriad of fee-paying tasks.

The pretrial conference is of recent origin. Its use in this country, while expanding rapidly, has been limited, thus far, largely to the federal courts and courts in certain large cities—such as New York, Detroit, Cleveland, Los Angeles, Boston, and Miami. It has also met with success in England and Scotland.

There is a disposition to dismiss the many settlements effected during the conferences as a sort of by-product. As a practical matter, this sentiment is difficult to reconcile with the fact that in some courts as many as three cases out of four are settled in pretrial conference. A settlement does more than reduce the time consumed by trial; it eliminates the trial. It eliminates many intermediate motions which would otherwise be made. It also materially aids in the achievement of a major objective—a better trial of those cases which are not settled—by concentrating judicial notice upon fewer trials.

Arthur T. Vanderbilt, Chief Justice of the New Jersey Supreme Court, has written: "These settlements arise largely from the fact that for the first time each side sees his own case in the perspective of his adversary's case. Our trial judges do not use the pretrial conference to bludgeon settlements; that is not only undesirable, but it is quite unnecessary. The lawyers themselves, faced with the facts, have sense enough to know when a settlement is in order."

A typical pretrial conference in the Supreme Court, New York County, might go something like this:

The judge is seated behind a small, flat-top desk in a small, drab, robing room adjoining a courtroom. He wears a business suit—not a robe. The calendar of cases to be discussed that day is called in the outer courtroom, where the lawyers await their turns. In New York County the calendar is published each day for two weeks before the case is set down for conference. On any given day the calendar in a pretrial part will contain from twenty to forty cases.

The lawyer representing the estate of the person killed in an accident and the lawyer representing the defendant file into the robing room. They seat themselves in plain, wooden chairs at the desk, facing the judge.

JUDGE: Will you please outline your case—briefly?

PLAINTIFF'S ATTORNEY: My client was crossing Madison Avenue at Forty-eighth Street, when an automobile operated by the defendant at an excessive rate of speed struck him. His head hit the pavement, he suffered a fractured skull and died next day in the hospital. The traffic light was with my client.

JUDGE: How old was the decedent?

PLAINTIFF'S ATTORNEY: Well, he was no youngster, Your Honor.

JUDGE: How old was the decedent?

PLAINTIFF'S ATTORNEY: In his sixties, Judge.

DEFENDANT'S LAWYER: He was seventy-two, according to the hospital record.

JUDGE: Did he work?

PLAINTIFF'S LAWYER: He did some bookkeeping work for his son, who has a small factory. The old man had been in the same kind of business for many years, and his son valued his advice very much.

DEFENDANT'S LAWYER: We've investigated and found he hadn't worked or been in business for years, Judge. He lived with his son, who supported him. Maybe the son put the old man on the payroll to cheat Uncle Sam out of taxes.

JUDGE: Did he leave any other relatives?

PLAINTIFF'S LAWYER: Another son. He's a physician.

JUDGE: Did the sons contribute to his support?

PLAINTIFF'S LAWYER: Why no, Judge. This old man earned a small salary. He was very independent.

JUDGE: Well, is it at least fair to say that he did not contribute to his children's support?

PLAINTIFF'S LAWYER: (Reluctantly) Yes, Judge. But he was helpful around the house and factory.

The reason for this line of inquiry is that in an action for wrongful death the near relatives of the deceased may recover only what are called pecuniary damages: the dollar-and-cent value of the life of the deceased to them on the day he died. They may not recover for their anguished feelings or emotional traumas.

The same rule extends to the measure of damages for the death of a child. The jury may consider the future financial value of the child's earning capacity to his parents; also the cost of his upbringing to the point of self-sufficiency. But the mother cannot be compensated for the pillow drenched with tears every night, nor the father for the heavy heart he carries to work every morning. It is as cold and unsentimental as that. The norms are substantially similar to those discussed by Mog's and Gog's chieftains thousands of years ago: the age of the deceased, his life expectancy, his physical condition, economic status, and earning capacity at the time of his death, his dependents if any, the ages of his next of kin, and the monetary, material loss they suffered as a result of the decedent's death.

Obviously, in this case the measure of damages was low, since the deceased probably represented more of an economic burden than a benefit to his children. Satisfied that if the plaintiff prevailed the verdict would be moderate, the judge tried to find out whether the defendant was at fault.

JUDGE: (To defendant's lawyer) How does the liability shape up?

DEFENDANT'S LAWYER: There isn't any. He ran out from behind a parked car, right into the right front side of our car.

PLAINTIFF'S LAWYER: How fast could an old man of seventy-two run?

JUDGE: Where did the accident happen in relation to the crosswalk at Forty-eighth Street?

PLAINTIFF'S LAWYER: Just a short distance short of it.

DEFENDANT'S LAWYER: Short distance! The accident happened in the middle of the block. Here's the police blotter report, and that's what it says.

PLAINTIFF'S LAWYER: The cop wasn't a witness to the accident.

DEFENDANT'S LAWYER: But he got there before the ambulance came, while the old man was still lying on the pavement.

JUDGE: Shall we say that there is a sharp dispute as to liability—that it's anybody's ball game?

Defendant's Lawyer: Fair enough. Who can tell what a jury will do?

Judge: (To plaintiff's lawyer) How much are you asking in settlement of this case?

Plaintiff's Lawyer: I'd like to hear an offer.

Judge: It's customary for the plaintiff to state his demand first.

Plaintiff's Lawyer: All right, Judge. We'll take ten thousand dollars.

Judge: How much do you estimate a case like this could bring by way of verdict?

Plaintiff's Lawyer: Fifteen to twenty thousand.

Judge: No judge in this building would permit a verdict of that amount to stand.

Plaintiff's Lawyer: Could ten thousand dollars stand up, Judge?

Judge: Maybe. But you're not making allowance for the very real possibility that a jury may return a verdict for the defendant.

Plaintiff's Lawyer: What do you think the case is worth?

Judge: I'd rather not state at this time. (Turning to defendant's lawyer) Have you an offer?

Defendant's Lawyer: Judge, I won't hold anything back. The company authorized me to go to seven hundred and fifty dollars —tops.

The defendant was represented by a lawyer in the employ of the insurance company with which he carried liability insurance. This lawyer in effect stated he was offering the maximum figure fixed by the claims department, instead of bargaining by first offering something less.

Judge: Not enough. You fellows are so far apart that I'll have to take the bull by the horns and suggest a figure. I think this case should be settled in the area of two thousand to twenty-five hundred dollars.

Plaintiff's Lawyer: Oh, Judge, that's too little. I could never sell that to my clients.

JUDGE: You have a perfect right to disagree. Shall I remand the case for trial?

When a case is remanded it is placed on the calendar to await its turn for trial. When it is settled it is marked off the calendar and is out of the courts forever. Our experience is that over fifty per cent of the cases handled in the pretrial parts are settled in those parts; the remanded cases move toward trial and, en route, many are settled. The remainder, of course, are tried or dropped.

PLAINTIFF'S LAWYER: Well, will the insurance company pay twenty-five hundred? It's a pretty low price for this case.

DEFENDANT'S LAWYER: Will you take it?

PLAINTIFF'S LAWYER: I'll have to take it up with my clients.

DEFENDANT'S LAWYER: The top figure I have is seven hundred and fifty dollars, and I don't know whether I can get a nickel more. But I can't even discuss it with my claims department unless I submit a figure that will be accepted.

PLAINTIFF'S LAWYER: (After some hesitation) Very well, we'll take twenty-five hundred. I have faith in the judge's judgment.

The defendant's lawyer leaves the room to telephone the head of his claims department. He returns a few minutes later.

DEFENDANT'S LAWYER: I spoke to Jim Frisbie, our head man. He says he has great respect for Your Honor's judgment, and against his own better judgment he'll go to two thousand. But if it isn't accepted today the offer is withdrawn.

JUDGE: Is that the most you can get, Joe?

DEFENDANT'S LAWYER: The very limit, Judge. You know I wouldn't hold out on you.

JUDGE: I know that, Joe. (To plaintiff's lawyer) Two thousand appears to be the most you can get.

PLAINTIFF'S LAWYER: What do you think, Judge? You've had so much experience.

JUDGE: It's a fair offer. You might do better on trial—you might do worse. But it's a fair offer.

Plaintiff's Lawyer: All right, then. I'll close it for that figure. I guess I can sell it to my clients.

This case was settled in contemplation of a trial. Gog's case was settled in contemplation of a feud. Some such threat is necessary to spark a settlement.

When the parties are far apart in their offer and demand, the judge will sometimes talk with each side separately, in the absence of the other, but with full knowledge of both. Each lawyer will tell him confidentially and off the record how much he will offer or how much he will accept in settlement. If there is some prospect that the gap can be bridged, the judge will resume negotiations; if not, he will remand the case for trial.

There is little that is esoteric in the role of the judge, and a judge of caliber will not diminish in stature if the veil of mystery is lifted. Certainly there is nothing mysterious about a judge's efforts to settle a case. Like so many other judicial functions, it is something which you yourself have done many times. You have rendered reasonable facsimiles of such efforts in personal and business affairs.

This might be a typical example. Assume that a publisher shipped a hundred copies of a book to a book jobber. The book didn't sell as well as anticipated and the jobber sought to return ninety copies, claiming the shipment had been on "consignment," a commercial term which actually means that the jobber could return any or all of the books. The publisher insisted the books had been sold outright, refused to accept any returns, and demanded payment.

At this juncture it was suggested that the parties submit the dispute to Mr. Smith, a mutual friend and a highly respected figure in the book business. After business hours one day he met with both parties at a cocktail bar and heard their respective versions. By this time there was a tinge of bitterness in the recitals and the face-saving factor had overshadowed the money involved. Mr. Smith heard them out.

Then he said, "Boys, this is a case of mutual misunderstanding.

I think it would be too rough if either of you had to carry the entire freight. Suppose you, Mr. Jobber, pay for fifty and get rid of them somehow, and you, Mr. Publisher, accept the return of fifty. And I'll buy the drinks."

Both sides agreed. The function performed by Mr. Smith was in essence no different from that of a judge in the settlement of a case. His effectiveness was measured by the regard which the parties had for his experience and integrity, and by his personality and skill in conciliation. A judge's effectiveness is measured by the same standards.

For a judge cannot direct a settlement in the same way as he directs judgment. I have indicated the distinction between Mr. John Q. Citizen and a judicial officer in judging a dispute. The judge may command the sheriff to enforce his judgments. Only in rare instances do you enjoy the status to enforce your decisions, whether as employer, parent, or teacher. But in his negotiating capacity, as contrasted with his decision-making capacity, a judge has no more power than you have in settling controversies that arise at home or in business. He must persuade, rather than direct.

It would be naïve to deny that by the very force of his title a judge has certain collateral authority with which he can, if he desires, implement his powers of persuasion. Judges, even those most anxious to reduce their calendars, tread most gingerly in these areas, lest they coerce unwilling litigants to settle cases.

If anything, most judges place rigorous, self-imposed restrictions upon their freedom of action in settlement activities. Because of the disparity in positions inside the courthouse, they avoid scrupulously any attitude resembling remotely the coercing or bullyragging of counsel. Nor, for obvious reasons, will they wheedle or cajole lawyers to settle cases.

A judge will rigidly refrain from attempting to influence a settlement of a case where anything resembling a point of honor or a party's personal privilege is involved. If, for example, a defendant is charged with fraud in a commercial transaction, he cannot be expected to plead guilty in the eyes of his industry by paying the plaintiff a sum of money in settlement, no matter how small. In attempting to compose the differences of parties to a labor dispute, a judge is often confronted with the factors of internal politics, face saving, and public relations.

Sometimes the danger of loss of face, respect, or dignity implicit in the trial of a case outweighs possible monetary loss. Whatever form it takes, the risk involved in law trials is usually the most potent factor influencing settlements. This is a form of settlement with the unpredictable.

The personalities of the actors sometimes dictate the extent of the risk. The most difficult lawyer or client with whom to discuss settlement is the little Napoleon type. Whether he is the client or the lawyer, he will dominate the other. As a boy he was the fighting gamecock of the neighborhood—always boring in with head bloody but unbowed. He'd risk the most frightful punishment rather than be deemed weak or a sissy.

As he grew up he found that in a world of fairly easygoing people these tactics paid dividends. So his watchword became "No compromise." This type of litigant or lawyer often wins stunning, sensational victories; but he also suffers decisive, and sometimes humiliating, defeats. His Achilles' heel is his vanity.

In a recent trial the two lawyers and the plaintiff were normal people—reasonably shrewd, aggressive, but socially pleasant. The defendant was a bristling, dynamic young man who had started a business on an insignificant scale and built it in a short time to sensational dimensions. Abnormal postwar conditions yielded rich returns to the single-minded ferocity of his pyramiding tactics.

A customer was suing him because of the allegedly defective quality of goods he had been sold. During the trial recesses the lawyers fenced with one another about a possible settlement. They asked me what I thought was a fair figure, and I suggested five thousand dollars. The lawyers and plaintiff agreed this was reasonable, but the defendant, I was told, refused to pay anything—as a matter of principle. Some bitterness had developed from the litigation.

I refused to speak with the defendant. Laymen too often misinterpret any judicial intervention. But I did tell his attorney, during a recess, that he could quote me as saying it was a fair settlement. He walked from the bench to the counsel table, where his client was seated, and spoke with him in low tones. The defendant shook his head vigorously. Suddenly he pounded the table and shouted, "I won't give that lying bastard a nickel. But I'll give ten thousand dollars to any charity the judge names."

The plaintiff was pretty overwrought. He shouted back, "I can't afford it, but I'll take you up on that."

The little Napoleon was game and went through with his offer.

The cases which lend themselves most readily to pretrial disposition are those arising out of accidents—also called negligence or personal-injury cases. Almost invariably the defendants are represented by insurance companies. Most lawyers will not invest the filing fees requisite to prosecute an action against a defendant who is not insured. They reason shrewdly that such a defendant will not be good for a judgment. In these days it is rare that a person of property or means will operate an automobile unless he carries liability and property damage insurance.

Most accident cases, unlike breach of contract, equity, or almost any other kind of litigation, fall into fairly conventional patterns. So standardized have the commoner types of accident cases become that they have acquired code names, a form of professional shorthand among the initiate.

If a pedestrian is hit by an automobile, the resulting suit is called a "knockdown" case. If falling plaster hits the lady of the house (or apartment) on the head, she has a "ceiling" case against her landlord. A "stairs" case results from someone's slipping on steps, whether owing to debris or defective tread or otherwise. A "foreign substance" case results from eating food with harmful ingredients. A "sidewalk" case is instituted if a pedestrian trips because of a broken flagstone or a hole in the sidewalk, while a "snow and ice" case is an obvious indication of why the plaintiff fell. A "windshield" case, occurring with greater frequency than generally appreciated, is one in which the impact of a collision or a sudden stop propels an occupant of a car forward so that his head strikes the windshield, or in a taxicab against the intervening glass partition. A "blind" case is one which is not reported within a reasonable time to the agency which undertakes its defense—usually a transportation or insurance company. Sometimes a bus company is served with a summons and complaint reciting an accident which happened months before. The driver never reported it, and vows it never occurred.

Once liability is established, and given the same injuries, juries should apply the same measure of damages in every type of case. The amount should be governed by the kind of injury, the duration of the pain and suffering of the plaintiff, the permanency of any of his injuries, his loss of earnings, medical bills, and the like. Yet a jury will return a larger verdict in a typical "knockdown" case than it will in a typical "snow and ice" case against a municipality. This is because jurors do not become aroused if their city is a day or two late in cleaning its thousands of miles of streets and sidewalks following a snowstorm.

At pretrial conferences almost all of the defendants are represented by claims adjusters or lawyers of insurance companies and large self-insured corporations. The judges presiding in pretrial parts become well acquainted with these defendants' representatives. In the same way, he is familiar with the thirty to forty lawyers who specialize in the trial of negligence cases on behalf of plaintiffs. They are generally hired as specialists by other lawyers who are retained at infrequent intervals in such cases, and who have neither the skill nor the experience to prepare and try them properly.

The conventional bridge between lawyer and judge is never crossed or weakened, and the relative status of each is unchanged; but the evidence is handled quite differently than it will be on trial. It is something like the difference between a rehearsal and the formal opening of a play. The script in rehearsal is substantially similar to that of the ultimate production, but the actors while rehearsing may frankly characterize the lines as putrid or excellent, corny or exquisite.

A similar candor prevails in the pretrial conference room. The judge participating in the conference is disqualified from presiding at the trial. He has no inclination to bludgeon either party into an unwanted settlement. To do so would soon destroy his own effectiveness. His recommendations or suggestions would come to be viewed with distrust as inspired by a desire to settle cases at any cost, instead of being accorded the consideration earned by good faith, experience, and objectivity. No record whatsoever, no minutes are taken of the discussion, which is off the record in every sense. It is not regarded as cricket, although there are no legal prohibitions, for an attorney at some future time, before another judge, to repeat a statement made at a pretrial conference.

Therefore, the shots are called pretty much as they are seen. Most often the characteristics of the participants are known to one another. The judge and defense counsel know who are the bad boys among plaintiffs' counsel. The judge and plaintiffs' counsel know which defendants' representatives will never offer the insurance company's full reserve on a case, who will lie about the amount of reserve, and who will be truthful. And, of course, both lawyers know the strengths and weaknesses of the judges.

Most pretrial conferences are conducted by three experts—the parties' representatives and the judge. There is no jury to be swayed; the discussion is fairly direct and businesslike.

The pretrial part is the market place to which are trundled the serious injuries of the district. The grist that comes to the mill of a pretrial part on an average day will certainly include post-concussion syndromes and sacroiliac sprains, and may include a transverse cervical fracture of the right femur, a fracture of the surgical neck of the right humerus, a transverse fracture of the right olecranon process of the ulna—with displacement—just to select a few at random. In a pretrial conference it is better to know the value of a fractured astragalus (anklebone) than the full import of the legal doctrine of *res ipsa loquitur*. These injuries are raw material in the course of manufacture into a possible plaintiff's verdict. The evidence has been gathered, examined, and polished, and is ready to be placed on the assembly line of a trial by jury. It may emerge as a beautiful, shining, plaintiff's verdict; or it may be destroyed in the process by its own weaknesses, and end in a defendant's verdict.

The three experts appraise their commodities dispassionately and efficiently. A fur merchant, when fingering a skin, gives no thought to the pain, agonies, and writhings of the trapped animal. His thoughts center on the type and quality of the fur, and how much a doting husband will pay for it.

Similarly, pretrial conferees, discussing a fractured leg, think only in terms of how much a jury will pay for it. There is no thought of the frightened blast of horns, the foreboding squeal of brakes, the sickening thud of the impact. There is no sympathy for the plaintiff's dismal ambulance ride, or for his discomfort during an entire midsummer month in the hospital, with his leg in an oppressive cast and suspended in mid-air in traction like a trolley pole.

A good deal of nonmalicious joshing punctuates these conferences. Never at the expense of the judge, who is always deferred to despite the informality of the proceedings. But heavy-handed allusions will be made to insurance companies which will offer as much as a thousand dollars "only if a lawyer walks in with his client's head under his arm." Or to a plaintiff's attorney whose stenographers can type out only one identical set of injuries for all clients when furnishing bills of particulars.

A judge in a pretrial part listens with weary resignation to injury recitals which he is morally, but not factually, sure are fictitious. The following is a typical excerpt from a pretrial conference, recurring each week with discouraging regularity.

The plaintiff's lawyer is one of the handful of bad boys. He has tried many cases before the judge and the judge knows he will not flinch from cutting a corner to strengthen his case. The preliminaries have been dispensed with and the conflicting versions of the manner in which the accident happened have been presented.

JUDGE: (skimming over bill of particulars) Now as to the injuries. Hmm, postconcussion syndrome, headaches, dizzy spells, permanent, et cetera.

DEFENDANT'S LAWYER: Judge, if he didn't lug in that blamed syndrome, all he'd have left would be contusions and abrasions. And he'd have to bring this lawsuit in the Small Claims Court—where it belongs.

PLAINTIFF'S LAWYER: Don't fight with me. I'm only the lawyer. I've got a doctor's certificate which states he has a postconcussion syndrome.

JUDGE: May I see it?

PLAINTIFF'S LAWYER: Certainly, Judge. You may see anything in my file. But not that tightwad! (Indicating defendant's lawyer.)

JUDGE: This is a neurologist's report, dated last month. Almost two years after the accident.

PLAINTIFF'S LAWYER: That's right, Judge. I'll tell you honestly that I myself sent the plaintiff to that neurologist soon after the attorney of record retained me to try the case.

DEFENDANT'S LAWYER: If George sent him to a neurologist I'll bet it's Dr. Blank. From the way he uses that phony I think he pays him an annual retainer.

PLAINTIFF'S LAWYER: Dr. Blank is one of the outstanding neurologists in the city.

DEFENDANT'S LAWYER: Did he ever fail to find something radically wrong with any of your clients?

PLAINTIFF'S LAWYER: Many times.

DEFENDANT'S LAWYER: You can't prove it by me.

JUDGE: That's enough sniping, boys. Was the plaintiff hospitalized?

PLAINTIFF'S LAWYER: Just first aid, Your Honor. You know the kind of once-over they give in Uptown Hospital.

JUDGE: Have you a copy of the hospital record?

PLAINTIFF'S LAWYER: (fumbling among papers) Here it is, Judge. It's very skimpy.

DEFENDANT'S LAWYER: I'll say so! I have a copy, too. Not the slightest hint of a head injury. Just slapped a little iodine on some contusions and abrasions.

JUDGE: There is no mention of a head injury.

PLAINTIFF'S LAWYER: That's because they didn't suspect a head injury at that time.

DEFENDANT'S LAWYER: I don't suspect it now. There's no history of unconsciousness, and everyone knows you can't have a real concussion without unconsciousness.

PLAINTIFF'S LAWYER: My plaintiff was unconscious, all right. He revived just before the ambulance arrived.

DEFENDANT'S LAWYER: Yeah? Who'll testify to that?

PLAINTIFF'S LAWYER: The plaintiff, of course.

DEFENDANT'S LAWYER: Well, my doctor examined him and found absolutely nothing.

PLAINTIFF'S LAWYER: If he did your company would fire him.

The judge will permit enough of these exchanges to enable the parties to feel each other out and to give him some idea of the merits of the case. In piloting a settlement conference he is even more an administrator than when conducting a trial. In charting the course of a conference he does not have the advantages of altitude, formalism, and the deliberative and foreseeable processes of trial procedures. Yet he must never relinquish control of the negotiations.

There are often intrinsic flaws in a plaintiff's case which are patent to defendant's counsel and the judge. For example, there were several features which would cause the defendant's lawyer and the judge to reject the plaintiff's claim of a postconcussion syndrome in the pretrial conference quoted above.

Yet they had only limited trading value in settlement discussions, because such features might not impress jurors as fatal weaknesses. A jury might resolve its uncertainty about the nature of the injuries by bringing in a compromise amount.

Given a responsible defendant, there are two major factors involved in the settlement of an accident case. One is liability. What are the plaintiff's chances of proving his version of the case to the satisfaction of a jury, of proving the defendant guilty of negligence, and thus holding him liable in damages? The second factor is, of course, the nature and extent of the plaintiff's injuries. How much will the damages be in the event of a verdict for the plaintiff?

In theory these two features should be separate and distinct. A jury should not consider the issue of damages until it has first decided whether the plaintiff is entitled to a verdict in the first instance. In practice the lines blur and often fuse.

It is thus apparent that in a pretrial conference, or any settlement conference, the basis of negotiations is not only the intrinsic merit of the case but also the amount of the verdict to which the defendant would be exposed; not what the conferees, with their specialized knowledge, would award if they were jurors, but what they believe a jury would award. In other words, experts subordinate their realistic appraisal. Just as when a critic of the script of a melodrama might complain that in real life only an utter fool would be deceived by the decoy note which lured the hero into peril, the author could point out that inside a theatre an audience does not apply such critical standards. For example, sometimes the most important aspect of a case is the amount of the defendant's insurance policy, information which never comes to the ears of the jurors. A case may be worth twenty thousand dollars in settlement, but the insurance coverage may be limited to five thousand dollars. If, as is usually the case, the defendant has no assets, the case can be settled only on the realistic premise that five thousand dollars is the utmost the plaintiff can recover.

Insurance companies are required by law to set aside a reserve for each pending claim. The Insurance Department inspects the files periodically to make certain that the reserves are adequate. The reserve is released only when the claim is extinguished.

The company cannot use the funds frozen in claims reserves except to pay claims—either before judgment or after judgment. It cannot pay dividends, salaries, or other expenses with such funds. Therefore, an insurance company, unlike other defendants' representatives, is usually disposed to settle claims, whether it be before suit, two years or six months before trial, or during trial. The allocation of its reserves frees it partially from the human tendency of almost all defendants to postpone as long as possible the evil day of potential reckoning. If a company settles a case for a sum below the reserve figure, the difference goes into surplus and is freed for general corporate uses. The ability of a claims adjuster is measured by the savings he can effect out of the claims reserves.

Sometimes a claims representative will make no offer or an insignificant one, although a substantial sum is held in reserve. This will happen when the injuries are serious but the claim is very weak. Although constrained by caution or Insurance Department surveillance to maintain a high reserve, the company is confident it can win the case on trial. It may offer at most what is called "nuisance value" for a case. This varies from one hundred dollars to two hundred and fifty dollars, and represents the cost of defending the lawsuit—legal fees, witnesses' expenses, etc. Rarely, very rarely, does a company offer more than its reserve on a case.

Many injured persons are in dire need of funds. The bread-winner of the family may be on his back for months, out of employment, with the family's slender resources soon exhausted. Many plaintiffs are forced to go on the relief rolls until such time as they have recovered sufficiently to resume gainful employment. The pretrial conference serves a useful purpose by affording a plaintiff an opportunity to settle for a reasonable figure well in advance of the trial date. Otherwise, if in dire need, a plaintiff would be tempted to settle for an inadequate amount. If a judge senses that an insurance company is trying to take advantage of such a situation, as insurance companies sometimes do, he will range himself on the side of the plaintiff.

At times an insurance company, because of long-range policy, will refuse to settle a certain type of case. A judge will recognize and respect such reluctance. Instead of buying peace, a settlement may at times stir up a veritable hornets' nest of lawsuits. For example, some claims men contend that if they settle one claim for "nuisance value" in certain apartment buildings, it will encourage ten or twenty other tenants to make similar claims. If the first tenant making claim charges that she fell from a defective step, the others will likewise assert they tripped over the same step. In self-defense the insurance companies contend they must resist stoutly every such claim.

I have made notes of the offers made by the larger insurance companies in several hundred cases processed through the pretrial parts—offers which were not accepted by the plaintiffs. As a result the cases were remanded for trial. I followed the course of these cases during the ensuing year. Some were settled, some went to verdict. The gross experience would indicate the claims adjusters know their business. Some cases in which small offers had been made went to large verdicts. But some cases in which substantial offers had been made resulted in defendants' verdicts. The total payments made on the cases, including settlements and verdicts after the cases left the pretrial parts, were not much in excess of the total offers made in those parts.

A few companies, notoriously not "early settlers," paid out much more than the amounts at which they could have disposed of cases in pretrial conferences. One traction company, in seven cases, made aggregate offers of only seven thousand dollars. These cases could have been adjusted for about thirty-five thousand dollars, or less. In the various trial parts to which they wended their way the company paid out $113,250 in verdicts or settlements during trial. But this company's experience was unusual, and occasioned by financial difficulties which at certain periods required it to eke out its precarious way on a hand-to-mouth basis.

No defense can be offered on behalf of lawyers who lend themselves to distortion of evidence in negligence cases. The bar is grateful that they are so few in number. In condonation of ambulance chasing it has been urged that if lawyers did not take accident cases on a contingent retainer basis, poor people unable to advance legal fees would be without legal representation. Also, it is argued that most of the so-called respectable areas of law practice are closed to young men without influential or wealthy connections, thus forcing them into unsavory activities. At best, these are causes, and not justification, for the transgressions.

Just as guilty, and more essential to the perpetration of the fraud, is the doctor who certifies or testifies to the fake injuries.

Armed with his medical report or certificate reciting sacroiliac sprains or postconcussion syndromes where properly there should be only bruises and scratches, a lawyer may with impunity bring the case into the court of highest jurisdiction, instead of the court of lowest jurisdiction where it belongs. In the higher court the judgment exposure of the defendant is greater, and so the settlement value is greater. Most cases are settled and the doctor is not required to testify. When the case does go to trial the doctor appears to testify—if paid his fee. The fees for examinations and furnishing reports vary from ten to twenty-five dollars, and for appearance in court from fifty to one hundred and fifty dollars.

The bar is helpless to police and discipline its own transgressors when they are shielded by physicians. The judges must maintain a frustrated silence. Only the medical profession can purge itself of this small band of medical outlaws, representing an infinitesimal percentage of its membership, which casts disrepute on their honored calling.

Co-operation between the two professions might take the following form. In each district the local county medical society could establish panels or boards of specialists in every branch of medicine. These specialists would volunteer their services for a limited number of cases a year. Upon designation by a judge, when the nature of the injuries is in issue, they would examine the plaintiff, report to the judge, and testify at the trial if necessary.

The pretrial parts in New York County dispose of more than four thousand cases annually by settlement and otherwise. The total amount represented by these dispositions aggregates many millions of dollars each year.

Yet the money amount of the settlements does not convey the entire picture in terms of results. There are cases, important cases, in which money damages are only an incidental feature. Many libel actions fall within this category. The plaintiffs seek satisfactions transcending pecuniary recovery. One such case was a libel action brought by a nationally famous figure against a group of magazines.

In several articles the magazines had referred to the plaintiff as a communist. The New York courts and courts of many other jurisdictions have held that to call someone a communist is libelous. In the minds of average people in the United States the label of communist tends to expose someone to hatred and contempt. A magazine article so characterizing a person might well destroy his reputation.

This libel case would have taken two months to try. The result even after trial might be indecisive, so efforts were redoubled to settle it. There was the usual shadowboxing at the outset.

The defendants finally balked only at the use of the nasty word "retraction." They agreed to publish an article extolling the plaintiff as a good and patriotic citizen. He was adamant about the specific inclusion of the word "retraction." He felt that a news release which could not quote that word would have little exculpatory value.

Finally he and his lawyers concluded that at best a retraction only partially repairs the damage done by a libel. Tongues wag very merrily in spreading evil and malicious gossip, but very slowly in passing on the less tasty morsels of refutation. There were grave dangers for both sides in proceeding to trial. The plaintiff was not interested in money damages, only in clearing his reputation. The testimony would be newsworthy in view of his prominence. It would give national circulation to what had thus far reached only a comparatively limited audience. The defendants would attempt to prove either that he was in fact a communist or that his conduct had justified the defendant's assumption in good faith that he was a communist. A verdict for the plaintiff would probably not cure the additional damage done by the trial itself. And there was always danger that a jury might return a verdict in favor of the defendants.

So there was finally evolved an article without the word "retraction," but which was eminently satisfactory to all concerned. The case was marked officially settled, and everyone was happy.

It is easier to settle cases in which plaintiffs seek money damages than equity actions where the court is asked to direct affirmative action or restraint by injunction. In damage suits ordinarily the only question is how much of a money payment will close the claim out. In equity cases many other factors complicate negotiations.

It is difficult, almost impossible, to compose the tightly knotted differences of an estranged couple, once they have gone to law.

It is hard enough to surmount the injuries, real or fancied, which caused the breach. But superimposed are wounds reopened by the litigation and the resultant exchange of accusations. No doubt if caught in time, many a breach could be closed by a skilled social worker. But the parties usually have drifted too far apart by the time they come to court.

A judge can seldom dissolve the maladjustments of a lifetime in a one-hour conference. I'm afraid that after a couple have brewed a bitter cup of tea for years, a judge may not sweeten it to their taste in one afternoon.

The settlement of cases aids immeasurably in the administration of the courts. Great economies are affected. It has been estimated that the upkeep of one part alone in the State Supreme Court costs five hundred dollars a day. This includes salaries of the judge and other personnel, maintenance of the courthouse, supplies, etc.

If most of its cases were not settled, no court in an urban center could function without many times its present personnel and courtroom facilities. In many courts, if all cases were tried to a conclusion, they could not be reached for trial in less than fifteen years.

It is well known that delay defeats justice. Essential witnesses die or disappear. Needy and desperate plaintiffs settle for a pittance. Stale lawsuits, like other stale rights, shrink in value.

In its degenerative effect on the nerves of the parties, pending litigation is sometimes akin to a minor-scale cold war. Sometimes only a settlement can bring about a just result. A trial may end in a judgment that is too stark or extreme. The legal formula to be applied may permit only recovery of all or nothing, whereas a more equitable result would be a verdict somewhere in between. A party to a lawsuit may be required under the law to comply with a harsh edict that may prove ruinous to him, or he may be released from any compliance whatsoever. A sane compromise can avert risking either terminal.

As Shakespeare puts it, in *Henry IV:*

> *A peace is of the nature of a conquest.*
> *For then both parties nobly are subdued,*
> *And neither party loses.*

* XVI *

A Day at Bellevue

BELLEVUE HOSPITAL sprawls over several square blocks in lower Manhattan. If a visitor were to stroll through the halls of the seventh floor, on the Thirtieth Street side of the hospital, he would come upon a small courtroom. It probably appears as incongruous in its setting as a hospital ward would seem in the County Courthouse.

In this courtroom hearings are held upon petition of the superintendent of the hospital to commit allegedly mentally ill persons to state institutions. It is about one-half the size of the courtrooms in the County Courthouse. It has an elevated bench, a railed enclosure beneath the bench, which contains a few chairs and a table, and a desk for the court stenographer. There is no jury box and no elevated witness stand. The proceedings are informal, but a complete record is made by an official court stenographer. Hearings are held every Tuesday and Friday throughout the year.

On an average Tuesday or Friday a judge will sign orders committing over a hundred persons to state hospitals for the mentally ill for limited periods of observation. Most of the commitments will not be contested by the patients, their relatives or friends. A judge will conduct hearings on fifteen to twenty of the petitions to commit. With few exceptions, all of the persons committed are patients in the Psychiatric Division of Bellevue Hospital.

In all other forms of judicial proceedings the parties go to the judge. In these matters it is more expedient for the judge to go to the parties. Many years ago it was the practice to transport the patients to the courthouse, a practice which posed many problems in hospital administration. Then one morning in chambers, a patient heaved a heavy inkwell at the head of the judge and narrowly missed him. Ever since then the hearings have been held in Bellevue. An unverified and probably baseless rumor has persisted to the effect that one of the psychiatrists, haunted by the biweekly responsibility of transporting so many patients, had suggested the pitching exercise to one of them.

The public knows little of the remarkable work done in the Psychiatric Division of Bellevue Hospital. It is a port of short call for the mentally ill population of New York, Bronx, and Richmond Counties. The average period of hospitalization for a patient is eleven days. After diagnosis the Division will file petitions for the commitment and treatment in state or private institutions of the more serious cases. The others will be treated for a time, if treatment is required, and then discharged.

Other hospitals—which are not equipped to observe and diagnose mental cases—social agencies and outside physicians, the police, and occasionally the courts, send patients to Bellevue. There are also many applications for admission made directly by patients or their relatives.

The Division has over one hundred physicians on its staff—interns, assistant residents, residents, junior psychiatrists, senior psychiatrists, and fellows. Upon admission the patient is examined by a qualified psychiatrist, who will assign him to a service suitable for his condition. There are the disturbed, semidisturbed, neuropsychiatric, and alcoholic services, as well as the adolescent and children's wards. Ninety-five per cent of the patients in the alcoholic service are discharged after treatment. If the medical requirements predominate, or are more urgent, the patient will be assigned to a medical or surgical service.

The Division has a case load of one physician to eight patients —reputedly the best ratio in the country. Twenty-three thousand patients are admitted each year. Of this number about nine thousand are committed to institutions for long-range treatment. These figures alone would seem to refute the notion held by some people that psychiatrists are prone to regard all their patients as insane.

The law surrounds the commitment of allegedly mentally ill persons with many protective features. After a Bellevue patient has been assigned to a service, he is closely attended by an intern and resident. They examine him and give him all the required and indicated tests. Then they present the entire case, with their findings, to two senior psychiatrists, who jointly make the determination as to whether or not the patient should be committed.

If they decide that he should be committed, they execute a certificate to that effect, which contains their findings and diagnosis. Upon their certificate the superintendent of the hospital verifies a petition to the Supreme Court, asking for the patient's commitment. The Mental Hygiene Law of the State of New York provides that a mentally ill person may be committed to a public or private institution, for care and treatment, only upon order of a judge of a court of record, following submission of such a petition and certificate.

When a patient has been certified for commitment, he is served personally with notice of the hearing, which he is entitled to have before the judge. His nearest relative, or closest ascertainable friend, will be notified of the date of the hearing by mail, and invited to appear at the hearing or to speak to the doctor in charge in advance of the hearing. Hearings are requested on behalf of fifteen per cent of the patients sought to be committed. For some reason this ratio never varies substantially from year to year. In the remaining eighty-five per cent of the petitions the judge renders his decisions upon the papers, which include the findings of the psychiatrists.

About two years ago a hearing involving a fourteen-year-old girl named Mary was held before a colleague of mine, while he was sitting in Bellevue Hospital. Mary was a product of a broken home. When she was two years old her parents were divorced. Her mother had left Mary's father and had gone to live with another man.

The divorce action brought by the father had been undefended, and custody of Mary had been awarded to him. He was sober and steadily employed, at a moderate salary, as an automobile mechanic.

He had arranged that he and Mary would live with his older married sister and her husband. They were an elderly, benign couple, whose only daughter had married recently. They were happy to have a child to brighten their home again, and to supplement their modest income with the weekly contribution that Mary's father would make toward household expenses.

As it developed, Mary's aunt and uncle were too old and too rigid to adjust satisfactorily to the raising of a small child. Her father saw little of her. During the war he worked in Detroit, and when in New York he left early for work and returned late. By the time Mary was nine years old her aunt had no control over her. A trained social worker, upon visiting the home, would have discerned the danger at this point, and possibly have averted it. But the law had taken leave of Mary, after awarding custody to her father. And twelve years later the law encountered Mary again.

She had been admitted to the Psychiatric Division of Bellevue Hospital for observation. Mary had visual and auditory hallucinations. During the daytime she complained of seeing cats and other animals running around the room. At night she heard voices calling her name. She also had paranoid delusions, of a gang conspiring to stab her. She felt the urge at times to strangle herself, once had tried to choke her aunt, and on another occasion had attacked a girl friend. She had uncontrollable impulses to steal and ring fire alarms.

Most shocking of all, however, had been the record of the sex experiences of this fourteen-year-old girl for the past two years. There is no point in detailing the sordid history of numerous affairs with adults, schoolmates, strangers in automobiles, and others. From age twelve on, her aunt and uncle were unable to keep her home evenings. Her father worked in another city most of the time. Mary's sex escapades with teen-age boys in remote corners of the school building finally came to the attention of the principal, and led to an interview with her aunt.

The principal, apprehensive of the aunt's irresolution, had insisted that she telephone her family physician from his office. She had made an appointment for that morning and taken Mary from the school to the doctor. After a one-hour examination, the doctor had sent Mary and her aunt to Bellevue, the aunt bearing a sealed note to the admitting office. Mary was examined by two physicians and assigned to the Female Adolescent Service of the Psychiatric Division.

The aunt and uncle, suffering from a deep sense of guilt and inadequacy, had written to Mary's father, who was working in Cleveland. They were convinced they could effect Mary's reformation by dedicating themselves to that purpose. Since they did not wish to alarm her father, they had informed him that she was undergoing treatment for some minor nervous disorder and that his presence in New York was not required. They were gentle, impractical people, who could not face up realistically to a situation.

They had visited the hospital regularly. Mary, surly and unresponsive, had rebuffed them at first, but after the first week her attitude had changed. She begged them to get her out of the hospital, and promised to be a good and obedient girl. They also spoke with the psychiatrists in charge of Mary's case, who would not venture any specific opinion until after she had been under their observation for ten days. Then they informed her aunt and uncle that in their opinion the only hope for permanent improvement lay in extended hospitalization in an institution. The doctors were in agreement that she was suffering from schizophrenia, and recommended her commitment to a state hospital which had special facilities for adolescent cases.

The aunt and uncle were panic-stricken by this advice. They pleaded with the psychiatrists to permit them to take Mary home. They promised to handle her with firmness, but also with new understanding. The psychiatrists told them gently that Mary required specialized professional treatment which they were unable to give her. On that day they were also served with notice of the proposed commitment hearing.

In desperate straits, the frightened couple sent a long letter to the father, informing him of the true situation. On the evening before the date fixed in the notice of hearing they received a telegram from him, stating that he was leaving Cleveland and would meet them at the hospital the following morning.

The next morning they had a long talk with Mary in the hospital ward. They told her that her father was expected and that they would oppose her commitment. Unaccountably, Mary was now flat and morose, and unconcerned with the outcome of the hearing. At about 10 A.M. they accompanied her and a hospital attendant to a reception room adjoining the small courtroom. At 10:30 Mary's father stormed in. He was in a towering rage and vented his wrath on his sister and brother-in-law. Mary was moody and abstracted, and did not respond to his tears, his entreaties, or his eventual reproaches.

The senior psychiatrist in charge of Mary's case came in a little later. He guided her father to a corner of the room, where he briefly summarized his findings and repeated the advice he had given her aunt and uncle a few days earlier.

"But, Doctor," the father pleaded, "I'm the guy who's to blame for this whole mess. I've been blind and selfish. I'm the guy you ought to send away."

"You're thinking in terms of punishment," said the doctor, soothingly. "We're not punishing Mary. We want to help her. And, if we're going to help her, we must work together."

"By sending her to an insane asylum?" asked the father.

"It's not an insane asylum. It's a hospital—for sick people. Mary's a sick girl."

"Can't she get the treatments some other way, Doctor?"

"Yes, it's possible," said the doctor. "But you'll have to shoulder a great responsibility."

They had a discussion involving the amount of savings the

father had, his income, and the type of home maintained by his sister. About a half hour later Mary's matter was called for hearing. They filed into the courtroom and the psychiatrist addressed the black-robed judge on the bench.

"This girl's father has offered to engage a private psychiatrist to treat and supervise her. He and his sister have pledged themselves to co-operate. It is possible that a well-regulated course of outside treatment may be adequate. I'll ask Your Honor to adjourn this case for a few days, to give the father an opportunity to make satisfactory arrangements."

Upon the adjourned date the Bellevue psychiatrist informed the judge that he had conferred with a reputable psychiatrist, who had been engaged by the father. This physician had agreed to undertake a program of treatment and supervision of Mary, which met with the approval of the Bellevue staff. The staff psychiatrist withdrew his previous recommendation and recommended her release, in the custody of the private psychiatrist and the care of her father and aunt. The judge followed the recommendation and Mary was discharged from the hospital.

Whenever the circumstances indicate that it will be safe for the public and the patient, Bellevue will release him in the care of an outside psychiatrist. All it asks is that the physician accept responsibility for a course of treatment which promises to be beneficial to the patient. There are a few outside doctors whom the staff views with suspicion. Such physicians assure the distraught relatives that the patient's condition has been grossly exaggerated by the Bellevue psychiatrists. For a fee they will engage to procure the patient's release; and to the Bellevue authorities they agree to furnish the patient with the prescribed care and treatment.

Once the patient is released these doctors leave him to his own resources. They neither treat him nor supervise his activities. They are called "taker-outers" by the members of the Bellevue staff, who, as earnest and sincere doctors, resent their unscrupulous conduct. Fortunately, they represent a very small fringe of the body of devoted men and women who minister to the needs of the mentally ill.

If given certain minimal assurances, the Bellevue staff will extend itself to arrange that a patient be released in the care of an outside psychiatrist or a licensed private institution. Few patients or their families have the financial resources to pay for maintenance in a private institution. Therefore, most patients requiring institutional care must be sent to state hospitals.

Contrary to popular opinion, there is no effort or desire on the part of hospitals to cling to their mentally ill population. In fact, a great many patients released to their near relatives are returned by them to the hospital weeks, months, sometimes years later. The pattern is dismally familiar; there has been a recurrence of the old condition. The family has tried frantically to cope with the situation but must finally admit defeat. The patient is accepted again, without any "I told you so" 's by the hospital. The not unexpected failure has at least obliquely had therapeutic value for the family. The relatives feel they personally have spared no effort and have exhausted every avenue to help the patient.

The tendency of the crowded state hospitals is also to discharge patients, if circumstances permit. They release many patients on what is termed a convalescent status, which is a form of parole supervision.

Six months after her release by Bellevue, Mary was returned to that hospital by the Bureau of Adjustment of the Children's Court. Early one morning a policeman patrolling in a radio car had found her in a dazed condition, wandering alone in the streets. He had taken her to the station house, where she was questioned by detectives.

Mary told a hideous story of having been picked up the evening before by some youths in a car, who drove out of the city to some sort of lovers' lane. There were other cars at this spot. Mary said that she had there had sexual relations with twelve men. A detective took her home to her distracted father, aunt, and uncle. From there they all went to the Children's Court. After extensive questioning the social workers attached to that court decided Mary belonged back in the Bellevue Psychiatric Division.

It was revealed that the psychiatrist employed by her father had made an earnest effort to treat her. He had given her a series of shock treatments which appeared to help her. After a few weeks, however, she failed to keep her appointments with him. By dint of calling her father, and the latter's threats and cajolery, the doctor managed to see her two or three more times. Then Mary flatly refused to go to the psychiatrist's office any longer.

Her father kept stern watch, but at irregular intervals she would steal out of the house and return late at night. She offered no excuses and no explanations, except that she was choking for want of air and had to get out. Her father, helpless in the situation, had decided to ask the advice of the Bellevue psychiatrist. However, he temporized with this decision; at first, because Mary showed flashes of sweetness and normality, and later, because he had a long and exhausting stretch of overtime work. It was while he was on the job one night that Mary had this last escapade which brought her back to Bellevue.

This time the psychiatrists discouraged all overtures by her father to recommend her release. Ten days after her admission her case appeared on my calendar in the Bellevue courtroom. Her father had requested a hearing. When the case was called he and Mary entered and took seats at the table in front of the bench. The father gave his name and address to the stenographer.

The staff psychiatrist briefly reviewed the history of the case and recited his findings. He again made a diagnosis of schizophrenia and recommended her commitment to a state hospital. I asked indulgence while I read through the papers. When I had finished, I looked up.

"Mary," I said, "is there anything you wish to say to me?"

She was a slender, fragile-appearing child, who seemed incapable of the behavior attributed to her in the reports I had just read. She had even, delicate features, with pale eyes that stared abstractedly past me. It was difficult to imagine this diffident creature using the obscene language quoted in the records.

Mary tugged at the cord of her drab, shapeless hospital robe. "No," she said finally. "I got nothing to say."

In view of the history and record, it would have been pointless to press her for a statement. I told the attendant to accompany her out of the courtroom, but asked her father to remain.

After Mary had left the room, I said to him, "You have asked for a hearing, sir. I'll hear anything you wish to tell me."

He started to rise from his chair.

"You may remain seated," I said. "This is very informal. We're all trying to help Mary."

"I know that, Judge. Everybody here's just swell," he agreed. "They warned me last time that something like this might happen if I didn't keep close watch on her. But when she was brought back here nobody bawled me out. Maybe if they did I'd feel better. Because it's all my fault. I never gave the poor kid a decent home. She never had a chance."

"Come now, you mustn't blame yourself," I said. "After all, you couldn't run your home like a prison. She was bound to get out now and then."

"I should've been with her when she was a baby, instead of gallivanting all over the country. I was glad to shut my eyes and pass the buck to a couple of old people who'd forgot how to bring up a baby. And now my sin's caught up to me."

Suddenly his voice rose. He half raised himself out of his chair and hit the table with his fist.

"But it ain't all my fault, Judge. Mary's never had a mother. If I ever lay my hands on that whoring wife of mine I'll choke her to death."

He sank back and ran his hands through his hair.

"You're not going to help Mary or yourself by that kind of talk," I said. "There are almost one hundred thousand patients in mental institutions in this state. I'm told that one person in every twenty past the age of fifteen will at some time become a patient in a mental hospital. I'm sure that in almost every one of those cases the relatives can and do find some reason to blame themselves."

"I never knew there was so many, Judge," he said, perking up momentarily. Then he sagged again. "But they weren't so terribly disgraceful, like Mary's case."

"Mary's sick. Please understand that. It's never disgraceful to be sick. When a child is sick the sensible thing is to face up to it, and try and cure her."

"That's what I want to do, Judge. That's the only thing I want to do in life."

"Fine," I said. "Now, the doctor recommends we send Mary to Kings Park Hospital, where they have special facilities to take care of cases like hers."

"No, please, no hospital," he implored. "She could never take it, Judge. She ain't used to that kind of treatment, and she'd blow her top for sure."

"What do you think of the treatment she gets in this hospital?" I asked.

"Oh, this is fine."

"Well, she'll get the same kind of treatment in the state hospital—the same kind of doctors, nurses, and attendants."

"Judge," he pleaded, "I know my little girl. What she needs is the love and attention of a good woman who'll act like a mother to her."

"How can you give her that?" I asked.

"I've been going with a fine woman, a widow without any kids, for a couple of years. I explained all about Mary to her a few days ago and asked her if she'd marry me and help me bring her up. I even had her over here to see Mary, and they liked each other. She has a nice little apartment, and we can move in. Mary'd have a real home and a mother for the first time in her life. My sister meant well, but she was too old and too easy. I can bring this lady over here, if you'd like to see her, Judge."

He looked up at me, hopefully. I addressed the psychiatrist.

"What do you think, Doctor?"

"It won't work, Judge. In her present condition this patient could never adjust to a normal relationship in her home. Maybe, after some intensive treatment at Kings Park Hospital, a combination of a private psychiatrist and devoted and intelligent family co-operation might be effective. But not at this stage."

"I'll get a psychiatrist to give her all the treatment she needs.

I'll work my fingers to the bone to pay him," cried the father. "We'll watch Mary day and night."

"I think I understand how you feel," I said. "Believe me, if I thought it would do Mary any good, I'd let you work your fingers to the bone. I'd even let you sacrifice the rest of your life for her, because I know you'd get relief and happiness in doing that. But the doctor says it wouldn't help her. In this case I'm sure he's right."

Judges do not always follow the original recommendations of the psychiatrists. They will rarely reject a psychiatrist's report outright. But sometimes facts will be brought out at a hearing which will cause a judge to question a psychiatrist closely—not necessarily on the validity of his diagnosis, but more often on the soundness of his recommended disposition of the patient. On the occasions when I have expressed misgivings to Bellevue psychiatrists they have never bridled or exhibited professional pique; nor have they defended their opinions at all costs. We have, after discussion, usually reached some middle ground satisfactory to both of us.

In Mary's case I had no doubts as to the wisdom of the psychiatrist's recommendations. My only purpose in continuing the hearing or discussion was to furnish some measure of comfort and hope to the father. I daresay more hearings in the Bellevue courtroom become slanted toward reassuring nearest of kin than to resolving the advisability of committing the patient.

Most near relatives, like Mary's father, feel that the patient's affliction is the cross they must bear. They believe that they can manage the patient better than any institution can; whatever crushing sacrifices may be involved, they will not falter in their determination to take the patient home.

When they finally realize that this door is closed to them, they struggle with the possibility of committing the patient to a private institution. Most of the patients' relatives are possessed of an obsessive apprehension of state hospitals. Second, most of them experience some sense of guilt, which they want to expiate by personal enthrallment to the patient.

Of course, once a patient is lodged in a state hospital, there is little scope for such self-enslavement. There are no heavy hospital charges which a relative can scrimp and save to meet, and the visiting periods are restricted.

Mary's father ran true to type.

"I'd like her to get the best treatment possible," he said. "Could you put her in one of them private sanitariums?"

"How much do you earn a week?" I asked.

"From seventy to ninety dollars, depending on overtime."

"You wouldn't have enough to pay for Mary's care in any good private institution," I said.

His face fell.

"Don't feel badly about that," I continued. "Few families can afford to pay the rates of a private hospital for mentally sick people."

"I don't know what else I can say, Judge."

"Let's leave it this way. You're against sending her to a state hospital. You're anxious to bring her home, and ready to devote every minute of your time and every dollar you can earn, beg, or borrow to take care of her. You've done everything you possibly can to take over the care and treatment of Mary. I am assuming the responsibility of overriding you and sending her to a state hospital."

"You're all making a terrible mistake!" he suddenly blazed forth. "I know my little girl. Who do you all think you are anyway—God?"

"No, we're just doing everything we know how to do. I hope she'll come back to you and grow up to lead a useful and happy life."

The resistance suddenly ebbed out of him. "Thank you, Judge," he mumbled.

An attendant tapped him on the shoulder. He rose and shuffled out of the courtroom.

The next patient brought into the courtroom was a frowzy-looking woman in her middle forties. She glared at the psychiatrist, who had stationed himself near the bench, in readiness to render his report.

"Well, Doctor," she fairly spat out at him. "Are you all set to accommodate my husband, and railroad me?" She looked about the courtroom. "Where is that little toad?"

"He's just coming in," said the psychiatrist, mildly.

A short, dark man hurried into the courtroom. He cowered into the farthest corner of the railed enclosure.

"Where's my lawyer?" she demanded. "I have rights. I want my lawyer."

"Who is your lawyer, Madam?" I asked.

"Mr. Proctor," she replied. "He saw me here two days ago, and left this card."

She gave the attendant a business card. He in turn handed it to me. I had never heard of the lawyer.

"Call this lawyer, and find out why he's not here," I directed, handing the card back to the attendant.

While he was making the telephone call I glanced at the petition and report. The patient, who had two grown children, and whose husband was a prosperous merchant, had been in several mental hospitals. Consistently diagnosed as a paranoid schizophrenic, she had at times responded well to shock treatments and had been released from the hospitals. After varying periods of time she had suffered relapses and been returned to the hospital.

The attendant returned to the courtroom and reported that he had spoken with the lawyer.

"He told me he had looked into this lady's case and didn't think he could help her. He isn't going to represent her."

It is seldom that a lawyer appears for a patient at one of these hearings. They are not contested proceedings, in the conventional sense, and there is little scope for a lawyer's talents. When a lawyer launches into an impassioned plea for his client's release, the judge will interrupt and ask him whether he is urging the court to accept his rhetoric in place of the considered opinions of trained psychiatrists. I usually suggest an adjournment of the hearing, to afford the lawyer an opportunity to retain an outside psychiatrist.

In most of these cases the psychiatrist agrees with the recommendation of the Bellevue staff, and the lawyer withdraws his opposition to the commitment. Sometimes an arrangement is worked out by which the patient is released under the supervision of the outside psychiatrist.

As the attendant was reporting his conversation with the lawyer, the patient watched him with narrowed eyes.

"I don't believe it!" she snapped. "You're all in a conspiracy with my husband to railroad me. He wants to get a young wife. But I know my rights. I'm an American citizen. I want a lawyer."

She was entitled to a lawyer, or at least to a reasonable opportunity to retain a lawyer. I adjourned her hearing for one week.

The next patient was a sad-looking little man, who sat throughout the proceeding with a sweet, uncomprehending smile. A burly, roughly dressed man had accompanied him into the courtroom. He introduced himself as the janitor of the tenement house in which the patient had a two-room apartment.

"Joe's lived in my house fifteen years," he told me. "Everybody loves him—the neighbors, my wife, my kids. He always lived by himself, but he was very kind to everybody. He used to work steady and make good pay. Then suddenly, about six months ago, he got very sad. He stopped working, just moped around the house and looked sad. All he says is that he's no use to anyone, he might as well be dead. But he's gotta snap out of it sometime, Judge. The neighbors asked me to tell you that we'll take good care of him, till he gets better. The women'll cook his meals and the men'll keep him company."

"I imagine you're all poor people," I said. "Has Joe any money?"

"No, he's used up the few bucks he had. But the rent ain't much and we'll all chip in for that and food. That's all he needs. He don't leave the house anyway."

I read the report. The diagnosis was involutional melancholia, and the recommendation was commitment to a state hospital.

"The doctors think that Joe needs some treatment in a hospital," I said.

"What we're afraid of is that if he goes to a hospital when he finally comes back he'll have no apartment. The rent is very cheap and I gotta long waiting list for vacancies."

I beckoned to the psychiatrist to come to the bench, where we could talk without being overheard.

"This man impresses me as completely sincere," I said.

"He was in to see me yesterday, Judge. I agree with you," the psychiatrist said.

"These are good people," I said, "and I'd like to recognize their efforts."

"This patient really requires hospitalization, Judge. If there are no complications, he shouldn't be in very long. This type of case responds rapidly and usually permanently to electro-shock treatments, Judge. I'll be happy to send along a special report and check his progress."

"Thanks," I said. I addressed the janitor. "The doctors say that Joe needs some hospital treatment, but that unless something goes wrong he'll be home soon—all cured. I suggest you hold the apartment for Joe for a while. Come here to see the doctor in a month and he'll tell you how Joe's coming along. Meanwhile I'll send him to a hospital where you'll be able to visit him without too much trouble."

There were a dozen more hearings. Several of the patients were women in the sixties, suffering from types of chronic depressions of old age. Grief-stricken children, some with families of their own, husbands, and other relatives, pleaded with the court to be permitted to make crippling personal sacrifices which would be doomed to certain failure—and possible tragedy. Few, all too few, had the facilities and resources to undertake private treatment and supervision. In some cases, under appropriate safeguards, the patients were released in their custody. In the others, I tried to reassure and comfort and reason with the relatives, to the best of my ability.

Finally, the hearings are concluded. A judge leaves the hospital, sobered by the glimpse of the fragile barriers separating soundness from disease, awe-stricken by the glimpses he has been shown of human tragedy and human sacrifice, and disquieted by the sense of his own shortcomings.

Dissatisfaction has been expressed from time to time with the commitment of mental incompetents by judicial process. Judges themselves are conscious of a lack of technical qualifications for dealing with mental ailments. As an alternative for the judicial process, it is often proposed that hearings be conducted by a commission comprised of persons with varied experience and skills in the medical and social sciences.

When I sit at Bellevue I experience a sense of distress which is almost physical in its intensity. I am also aware of my technical inadequacies for this phase of my judicial duties. And yet, for one reason alone, I would counsel caution in displacing the present judicial process for the commitment of incompetents in New York.

My reason is that I have come to appreciate that the black-robed figure of the judge on a bench signifies a great deal to the patients, their friends and relatives. It conveys to them an assurance of a day in court, a priceless psychological reassurance, and for good reason. Legally, the patient or any friend or relative may obtain a rehearing before another judge, with trial by jury of the question of his mental condition. To the average American a day in court, presided over by a fair and experienced judge, is a pledge of the protection of his rights as an individual. It is more familiar, more reassuring, and more comforting than a hearing before a commission. No commission, no matter how qualified by specialized experience, can hold out this mental and emotional security to those whose lives will be touched by its functioning.

* XVII *

The Child in Court

In New York County alone over three thousand marriages are dissolved each year in undefended actions for divorce or annulment. Eighty-five per cent of such matrimonial actions are uncontested. Some minimal evidence must be presented at these one-sided hearings to satisfy the court that there is a basis for granting the decree of dissolution of the marriage. In New York City, since the cases follow a familiar pattern of proof, the evidence in uncontested matrimonial cases is heard by official referees. These referees are all men with many years of judicial experience, who have been retired as judges because of age limitations or other reasons.

The official referee files a report with the judge, setting forth his findings and his recommendations. Rarely does the judge fail to confirm his report. When there are children of the marriage who are under twenty-one years of age, provision must be made for their custody. Such custody is usually given to the presumably blameless plaintiff.

Recall the case of Mary, who, while in her early teens, was twice confined in Bellevue Hospital for psychiatric observation. She was the product of a broken home. Her father asked for custody; there was no opposition and there was some proof of the mother's unworthiness. Therefore, the referee recommended, and the judge directed, that Mary's custody be given to her father. Neither referee nor judge has the time or facilities for the exercise of individual initiative or adequate investigation in each case. Every week a judge must read nearly a hundred official referees' reports with the annexed minutes of the hearings, in addition to disposing of his regular calendar of motions. Where there is surface substantiation of the plaintiff's claims, the judge is seldom in a position or disposed to question the referee's report.

This appears to be an easy acceptance by referee and approval by judge; and yet I know of no class of decisions rendered in our court which have greater importance than those involving the awarding of custody of children. It is not entirely fair to criticize overworked judges and referees for not challenging most uncontested requests for custody of children—especially when there is nothing in the record to excite misgivings. No court of general jurisdiction that I know of is equipped to probe thousands of such situations a year, to investigate homes, reputations, and environments, and to secure a psychiatric examination of every proposed custodian of a child. There have been proposals that a unit of trained social investigators and psychiatrists be attached to every court which has the power directly to chart the lives of children. Another proposal is that in any instance where the custody of a child is sought, whether by out-of-court arrangement or contested or uncontested action, the court appoint a special guardian to protect the best interests of the child.

I do not believe these proposals go far enough. Certainly competent inquiry should be made to place the child where its welfare and happiness will be promoted, and to put an end to the prevailing practice which generally gives the child to the successful party, as a sort of prize of war.

But I believe that anybody who seeks and accepts the custody of a child should do so subject to periodic check and supervision by the court, over a long probation period. A person may impress a judge as a responsible and well-meaning guardian at the time of appointment. But children are complicated little creatures—particularly those who are the frightened, insecure products of broken homes. The best-intentioned person may unwittingly do them irreparable harm. A timely visit from a social worker with trained insights may result in remedial guidance for the guardian. And if he or she cannot or will not follow professional instructions, the child should be taken away and the custody award vacated.

In the case of Mary, no investigation was made of her father's fitness to assume custody. There seemed to be no need for it. Evidence was presented as to the adultery of her mother, proving that she was living with her lover, in his apartment. No one appeared for the defendant, the entire hearing took ten minutes, and the father's lawyer moved for a decree of divorce and custody of the child.

Even a thoroughgoing investigation would probably have resulted in the same initial disposition of the case, although the fact that a woman has been found guilty of adultery does not necessarily render her unfit, in the eyes of the law, to rear her children. The law has a profound, an almost reverent respect for mother love as an ingredient in the sound upbringing of a child.

I have awarded the custody of children to a disillusioned mother whose lover deserted her after a brief and torrid affair, and in another case to a mother who was about to marry the corespondent in her divorce case. In each instance the history of the woman indicated that the single lapse from grace was the result of powerful emotional pressures, and was not likely to be repeated; it was not indicative of promiscuity. Most important, the mother seemed equipped to furnish the child with tenderness and understanding in a wholesome environment.

But Mary's mother did not seek custody of her infant daughter. Even if she had, it is doubtful that a judge would have entrusted her with the child's upbringing. She lived in squalid circumstances with her lover. They both drank heavily, he was not employed steadily, and her status as his mistress was most precarious.

Although investigation would probably have indicated that Mary's custody be given to her father, subsequent professional inquiry might have averted the miserable outcome. A court investigator might have ruled out the aunt and uncle in the first instance, and advised the father to make other arrangements. Or, a trained observer might have later noted their loss of control over their ward, and then stepped in at that point.

Judges also deplore the absence of independent investigating facilities in contested custody proceedings, despite the fact that they have the benefit of evidence presented by both parties, designed to prove their virtues and their adversaries' deficiencies. A judge agonizes more about reaching the right result in a contested custody issue than about any other type of decision he renders.

The lives and personalities of at least two adults and one child are telescoped and presented to him in a few hours. From this capsule presentation he must decide where lie the best interests of the child or, very often, which parent will harm the child least. The judge's verdict is distilled from the hardest kind of fact finding. From sharply disputed evidence, he must predict the future conduct of parents on his appraisal of their past conduct. And his decision is disturbingly final. Since it is based fundamentally on factual findings, an appellate court will rarely disturb it.

In most lawsuits the only concern of the judge is to exert his best efforts to afford both sides a fair trial. In a fight over property and personal rights, the natural tendency of a judge is to inject himself with reluctance and caution.

In a custody proceeding, however, the history of the case, the equities as they affect the parties, everything, is subordinated to the one prime consideration—the welfare of the child. Even before this nation was established, English courts of equity evinced a special concern for the protection of the person and property of infants, and regarded them as wards of their courts. The rights of the parents are fully recognized. They may introduce any material evidence, assert any relevant arguments. But the state has a direct interest, a paramount stake in the subject matter of the proceeding—namely, the child. It is in furtherance of that interest that a judge will intervene to the extent that I did in two cases which carried over suspense and uncertainty from hearing to hearing like the old movie-serial thrillers.

One of these two cases involved the custody of a six-month-old baby girl. The mother was a brilliant young woman who had earned high honors at a Midwestern university. Her husband was a young veteran who had required extensive postwar shock treatment at the Veterans' Hospital. He appeared incapable of holding down a job for any sustained period of time. Shortly after the marriage, his father-in-law, out of his meager resources, had given him sixty-five hundred dollars, which he invested in a tavern and promptly lost.

The couple and child made their unhappy home with the wife's parents. After the loss of the investment in the tavern, home conditions became very trying. The young veteran, jobless and unable emotionally to face up to the situation, escaped from it by leaving his wife and taking the infant to his parents, who lived in poor circumstances in the lower East Side section of New York.

Upon the wife's application, I had signed a writ of habeas corpus, directing the husband to produce the child in court. The writ of habeas corpus may be employed to inquire into the detention of any person when such detention is alleged to be unlawful. In this case the mother claimed the father was detaining their child unlawfully, because, she asserted, she was the proper custodian. The writ which launches such an inquiry is known among lawyers as a custody writ and the resulting proceeding is called a custody proceeding. It is customary to try these proceedings in a judge's chambers, so as to shield the parties as much as possible from public intrusion into their family privacy.

The parents, the Johnsons, appeared on the stated day, and I had a preliminary informal discussion with their attorneys, who assured me that a reconciliation was impossible.

However, shortly after the hearing commenced, the husband blurted out that if his wife would leave her family and set up a home with him he was sure they could make a go of it. This statement tempted me, despite the forebodings of counsel, to attempt to effect a reconciliation. I received some flutterings of encouragement from Mrs. Johnson.

Preliminary explorations involved finding an apartment for the

Johnsons, a job for him, and procuring some limited financial assistance from relatives. This presaged lengthy negotiations. Mrs. Johnson was distressed at what she termed the cramped and unhealthy conditions under which little Anna was being accommodated by her paternal grandparents, and her complaint seemed justified. Both parents consented to placing the child in neutral territory, in an accredited orphanage and kindergarten home. Johnson agreed to pay the institution six dollars a week toward the child's maintenance.

In a few weeks it became evident that any hope of an adjustment had to be abandoned. The hearings were resumed. I referred the matter to an official referee, who recommended, after holding hearings of his own, that Mrs. Johnson be given custody. Exhaustive examinations of Mrs. Johnson were conducted by both lawyers and the referee. He also inquired into her family background. Upon reviewing the referee's report I had an uneasy impression that she was somewhat flighty and impulsive, but attributed such failings to her youth. Finally, after representations by her parents which gave me some assurance of family depth as a reserve asset, I awarded custody of Anna to Mrs. Johnson. She promised to take the child from the orphanage to the home of her parents.

One morning a few months later I received a letter from Mr. Johnson's attorney. He wrote that he had been informed that Mrs. Johnson had been committed to a state hospital as a mental case, and asked that I reopen the custody proceeding.

My secretary arranged a conference with both attorneys in my chambers that afternoon. From the welter of charges and countercharges I gathered that little Anna was still in the orphanage; her mother had never taken the child to her parents' home. I also learned that Johnson had not done a lick of work since the decision had been rendered. I told the lawyers I would read Mrs. Johnson's hospital record, and confer with them again.

When I read the record it became shockingly, depressingly clear that she was unquestionably unfit to rear the child. No point could be served by recounting the sordid medical and psychiatric details which made such a conclusion inescapable. She had been an inmate at this hospital for three months, and then was provisionally discharged.

There had not been a hint of mental illness, at least a hint discernible to a layman, during the hearings—before either the referee or myself. That was one of the few deficiencies with which Johnson's lawyer had not charged her. Had such an issue been raised I would have insisted that Mrs. Johnson submit to a psychiatric examination, since she was the relator seeking relief in the proceeding.

The lawyers came to chambers for another conference. I told them that the hospital record indicated strongly that Mrs. Johnson was not a proper custodian for the child, but that if she desired the proceeding would be reopened so as to give her an opportunity to prove her fitness.

Whereupon Mrs. Johnson's attorney advised me of a recent and surprising development. She had recently, upon her discharge from the hospital, taken a position as a domestic for a family living in Florida, although she was trained for secretarial work. Her mistress had charged her with stealing jewelry and had her arrested. Mrs. Johnson had written her attorney from the jail in Florida, seeking to enlist his help in both the Florida and New York proceedings. He told me he would advise Mrs. Johnson to relinquish any custody rights but asked for time to communicate with his client.

I told the lawyers that, if desired, either party would be afforded the traditional day in court. However, I urged them to regard the matter more in the light of a social problem than a partisan proceeding, and sought their co-operation in the best interests of the child.

For the first time in the proceeding they evinced a disposition to co-operate. We then reasoned as follows. Johnson could not assume custody of the child. Both sets of grandparents, aside from the financial considerations, were too old to undertake direct charge of so young an infant. I asked each lawyer to undertake a survey of his client's family, in an endeavor to find some suitable couple who would accept immediate custody of Anna, with a view to ultimate adoption.

I was not too optimistic about finding a solution for the problem within the families. If necessary, I was prepared to invoke the almost limitless powers the Supreme Court may muster on behalf of a child, and place Anna in the permanent custody of an appropriate agency.

Next week Mrs. Johnson's lawyer informed me that her parents, exhausted and defeated, wished to wash their hands of the entire matter. She had no other relatives interested in the proposal I had made.

We had better luck on the father's side of the family. His sister and her husband appeared. They made a very favorable impression. They were in their early thirties, had been married four years, and had no children. They were neat, sober, and industrious in appearance, and soft in demeanor.

I questioned them at great length, both on and off the record. He was employed steadily as a men's clothing operator, earning at least sixty-five dollars a week. They were thrifty, putting something aside each week. They lived in a three-room walk-up apartment on the lower East Side.

When I asked them whether they were prepared to adopt Anna, if it proved feasible, they fairly glowed at the prospect. I tried to foresee and forewarn them of every contingency and explained that, with appropriate precautions, Mrs. Johnson might at some future time be given visitation privileges. They showed an intelligent appreciation of this possibility, and agreed it would be only fair.

I was heartened by a conviction—or judicial "hunch"—that this couple would provide a good home for Anna. I informed Mrs. Johnson's lawyer that he would be given an opportunity to examine into their qualifications; and second, I proposed, in view of my own court's lack of facilities, to enlist the services of a trained social-service investigator from the Court of Domestic Relations to investigate them immediately and then report to me.

The Johnson proceeding was adjourned for another week. It was my intention, if the reports proved favorable, to turn the child over to Johnson's sister and brother-in-law then and there and mark the case closed. With this in mind I asked my secretary to call the orphanage and direct it to produce Anna in court the following week. A few minutes later he reported that the director had advised him that Anna was no longer in the institution! After a number of telephone calls to the attorney for the orphanage, he promised to appear in court and place the story on the record.

At the hearing the following week, he produced a receipt for the child, signed by Mrs. Johnson and dated about two months previously. This document was unquestionably genuine and was received in evidence. Then he stated that simultaneously with the furnishing of the receipt and with Mrs. Johnson's consent, Anna had been turned over to two foster parents. The lawyer said that they were a devoted couple, cultured, pleasant, and in affluent circumstances. They were presently in Florida with Anna, on a winter vacation. They loved her very much, wished to adopt her, and had informed the institution that they intended to fight with every means at their disposal to keep her.

The proceeding was adjourned for another two weeks, upon the lawyer's assurance that the foster parents would appear in court with Anna on that date. A hearing would then be held to determine which couple had most to offer for the welfare of the child. Wealth alone would not be decisive.

Next week the foster parents appeared, with the baby, in my chambers. They were evidently passionately devoted to the child. They had retained a lawyer and were prepared to fight for custody.

In the course of his opening statement their lawyer stated that they had understood that both parents had consented to their first taking custody of, and eventually adopting, the child. The father blurted out a vigorous denial—evidently a sincere one. I suggested that in view of the father's opposition, and the unpredictable conduct of the mother, it was very unlikely the foster parents would ever be able to adopt the baby. The consent of both parents would be required to validate an adoption and, without such consent, the status of the child would always be uncertain.

I further suggested that in the light of the newly revealed circumstances perhaps all of the parties and their lawyers had better confer separately or together. They left my chambers. About an hour later the foster mother and Johnson's sister re-entered, with their arms about one another. From their ravaged faces it was evident both had had a good cry.

The foster mother, on the advice of her lawyer and husband, had decided to relinquish the child. In the agony of her renunciation she exhibited a nobility of spirit I have seldom seen equaled. She wanted the child from the depth of her soul. But she felt there was just as much love offered by the sister, with a better chance for adoption. She had worked out with the sister a complete program for transferring the baby, to avoid any trauma or inconvenience to the child.

The mother's lawyer stated for the record that his client was still in jail. She had instructed him to join in the foster parents' application for custody. He, therefore, did not consider himself authorized to consent to the sister's application.

I had received a report from the social-service investigator bearing out completely the favorable impression the young couple had made upon me. I marked it in evidence. At this point Mrs. Johnson's attorney asked leave to make a statement for the record. He had received additional communications and instructions from his client, which he was to disclose only if it appeared likely that I would award custody to any member of her husband's family.

She now claimed that her husband was not the father of her child!

In her letters, one of which was addressed to me in care of her lawyer, she named the man she claimed as the real father. Her story had surface possibilities—and even a measure of plausibility.

Her husband was not in my chambers when the lawyer exploded this bombshell. We discussed the new development, and decided that the husband's lawyer had to inform his client of this new claim. I adjourned the hearing for another week.

The following week the husband disparaged his wife's charges as absurd, and inspired by bitterness and pique. He begged me to approve his sister's application for custody. All of us—including the wife's lawyer—were inclined to agree with him. But in the child's interest I could not risk the hazard that the father's certainty might not always be so unwavering—particularly if in some future legal proceeding a blood-grouping test might prove that he was not Anna's father.

I had learned that the wife was about to be released from jail. Because of her mental condition, the charges were to be dropped. I ordered blood-grouping tests to be made of the child, husband, and wife.

Such tests will not establish affirmatively the parentage of a person. They can, however, definitely exclude such parentage.

The tests were made. To the great relief of everyone but the wife, the tests proved that the father's group and type of blood corresponded to the child's. Under the circumstances of the case, his paternity could not be disproved.

I awarded custody to the father's sister and brother-in-law and closed the proceeding.

There were minor complications and climaxes I have not touched upon. I have never had a comparable proceeding—and trust I never shall, although the ending was a happy one. The husband's attorney has appeared before me a few times in the several years elapsed since my decision, and he assures me that the child is being raised under very happy and wholesome circumstances.

Another custody case rivaled the Johnson proceeding in presenting strange and unexpected developments at each hearing. I was not only confronted with the vexing problem of a child's welfare, but I was also called upon to defend the integrity and dignity of the court. While sensitive to affronts, a court does not go about picking fights, with a chip-on-shoulder attitude. But the law is a living, pulsing organism, and on occasion, rare occasions, a court must strike in self-defense. The Hansen case presented one of those rare occasions.

About fifteen years ago, when he was a young man of twenty-five, Dr. Halsdan Hansen left his native Denmark and came to the United States. He was a scion of an old Danish family, fairly dripping with distinction and tradition. He established himself as a consulting chemical engineer here. Four years later he married an

American girl, an actress. One child, Lisabeth, was born of the marriage. Hansen lived continuously in the United States on a Danish passport. He took no steps toward acquiring American citizenship.

Several years later the marital relations of the Hansens began to deteriorate. He claimed his wife was high-strung and inattentive to her household and parental obligations. She claimed she was a good and devoted mother and wife, particularly since she had to bear the greater part of the household expenses out of her modest earnings as a radio and television actress. She also charged him with cruelty.

Finally, her attorney wrote to Dr. Hansen, advising him that she intended to bring suit for separation. At that time Lisabeth, who was ten years old, was attending school in Virginia. After he received the lawyer's letter, Dr. Hansen visited the school, collected the child and her belongings, and whisked her over to Denmark by airplane. There he left her with one of his sisters and returned to this country, after spending a weekend with his child and relatives.

Mrs. Hansen commenced a habeas corpus proceeding for the custody of Lisabeth, which came on before me in the fall of 1949. Since then, there have been many, many hearings on this matter.

Dr. Hansen blandly denied that the threatened separation suit had anything to do with his decision to take his daughter to Denmark. It was merely coincidental that at the time he received the lawyer's letter he had decided Lisabeth was ailing and maladjusted and required the salubrious climate of Denmark; also, he thought it was high time she met her aunts and cousins on his side of the family. I made no issue of his taking the child out of the country, but limited the hearings to the conventional custody question: namely, which parent was better qualified to raise the child.

The first three hearings were devoted to the usual gross accusations and recriminations which seem to feature all matrimonial litigation, calculated to prove, of course, that the other spouse is not fit to be entrusted with the custody of the child.

At the close of the third hearing I informed Dr. Hansen and his counsel that I desired them to make arrangements to return Lisabeth to this country. A considered and informed decision could not be rendered unless and until I interviewed the child, either formally on the record or preferably informally and off the record.

A child is seldom sworn as a witness in a custody proceeding. Even hate-blinded parents realize the traumatic possibilities inherent in introducing a child of tender years to the tense, bitter atmosphere of a court session, or in subjecting a child to formal examination by opposing counsel. But a judge can often gain a shrewd notion of the true home conditions and the personalities of the parents by having a cozy little chat with the child, with parents and counsel excluded.

It would have been pointless, obviously, to have had such a talk with an infant of the tender years of Anna Johnson. But I believed a talk with ten-year-old Lisabeth Hansen would be informative and was therefore imperative.

When I made my wishes known, Dr. Hansen and his lawyer held a whispered conference in a corner of the room. Then Dr. Hansen pressed me to conclude the hearings and render my decision first. I explained to him that I could not properly make a decision without interviewing Lisabeth. He finally acquiesced and pledged cooperation.

He then raised the question as to who should have custody of the child during her stay in this country prior to final decision on the writ. He was opposed to his wife or her mother having her and "poisoning his child's mind" against him. I suggested some neutral, mutual friend, and finally they agreed on a distant cousin of Mrs. Hansen's. I promised to brief this temporary custodian upon his status as a neutral.

Then Dr. Hansen said he was without funds to bring his daughter back. In fact, his company was in the bankruptcy courts at the time. Mrs. Hansen agreed to advance the cost of air transportation and of the special services of a stewardess. She turned the funds for such a purpose over to her husband's attorney the next day.

There then followed one or two conferences a week. Several revolved about our immigration authorities' requirement of vaccination, since Lisabeth had not been vaccinated for several years. Dr. Hansen solemnly stated that his family's physician in Denmark did not believe in vaccination. I, just as solemnly, directed him to instruct his sister to get another physician. This second physician refused to vaccinate, it transpired, because there was a polio epidemic in Denmark, which ruled out vaccinations for a long period of time. This difficulty was finally resolved by arranging for Lisabeth's vaccination at the port of entry in the United States.

The vaccination hurdle and several similar technical admittance difficulties required a month to overcome. Then we learned that through some mix-up Dr. Hansen's attorney had not purchased the airline transportation. He was directed to do so immediately. Whereupon Dr. Hansen, who had himself flown his daughter to Denmark, suddenly expressed a fatherly solicitude about the hazards of a transatlantic flight. This posed a nice problem; I ordered that the child be brought over by steamship. Mrs. Hansen provided the extra funds required for an adult companion.

Then followed a series of what might be termed delaying actions, too petty to recount here, but requiring a number of conferences. Finally we were assured the way had been cleared, and that Lisabeth was on the *Stockholm,* sailing from Denmark. A cablegram Mrs. Hansen sent to the ship, however, elicited the answer that the child was not on board.

A number of the difficulties previously reported had been resolved through the co-operation of the Department of State and the American Embassy in Denmark. Through these sources Mrs. Hansen now learned that her husband's sisters refused to relinquish the child. They asserted a variety of reasons for this refusal; among them, the physical and mental health of the child and misgivings as to the fitness of either parent. But most significant, they expressed a determination to keep the child pending a determination as to her custody by a Danish court in a proceeding brought there by Dr. Hansen for a divorce. This was the first intimation Mrs. Hansen or the court had of the pendency of a divorce proceeding, or that Dr. Hansen was seeking custody of Lisabeth by parallel suit in Denmark.

Dr. Hansen admitted he had instructed the family counselor in Denmark to commence the divorce action. He shrugged off his sisters' actions by reiterating that he had requested them to co-operate in the transportation of the child to America. He could not account for their flouting his instructions; but he bore his cross with Christian forbearance, and forgave their insurgence with a "girls will be girls" complacency.

The hearings were adjourned once more. In the interim Mrs. Hansen's lawyer submitted to me a warrant for the arrest of her husband, which I signed. The warrant was sought on two grounds: first, that Dr. Hansen had disobeyed the writ of habeas corpus—a species of contempt of court; and second, that he was about to leave the country. On the morning of the next hearing a deputy sheriff served Dr. Hansen with the warrant and brought him before me. I afforded him an immediate hearing on the charges contained in the warrant.

His lawyer introduced a chronological series of carbon copies of letters sent to the sisters in Denmark, giving carefully detailed instructions to co-operate with my directions. The picture presented was too flawless, particularly since the record of the proceeding already contained numerous letters sent by Dr. Hansen to various people, always written in longhand. Two of his acquaintances testified to recent conversations with him, the substance of which was that he had no intention of bringing the child back at this time. He told one of them he had no such intentions "even though it might mean his being thrown in jail." He proved a good prophet. At the end of the hearing he was committed to the county jail without bail. This was the first time in my judicial career that I had taken such drastic action.

I filed an opinion—furnishing the relevant facts, law, and reasoning underlying my decision—from which I quote:

"I am convinced that the child is within the control of the respondent [Dr. Hansen]. . . . I am satisfied . . . that he has made a studied effort to portray a pattern of purported compliance with the court's directions, a pattern which was sham from beginning to end.

"So far as I can ascertain, he has no roots nor ties in this country which would even momentarily detain him here should the decision upon this proceeding be adverse to him. . . . The respondent's [Hansen's] anchorage in this country is quite provisional and may be slipped with a minimum of inconvenience. . . .

"But more is involved here than placing statutes in juxtaposition and distilling power to act. The child whose best interests are to be determined and the parties to this proceeding have the fundamental right to ask that the court act with vigor to protect its mandate against willful, contemptuous conduct. This duty the court unquestionably owes to the persons involved in the litigation. If it is to function properly it owes a correlative duty also to society and itself of retaining and maintaining public respect and self-respect for its mandates. When confronted with a situation such as this, a court may not lift its hands in despair and condemn itself to ineffectuality."

It will be noted that in addition to protecting the rights of Mrs. Hansen and Lisabeth, I was upholding the arm of the court. As much as nature abhors a vacuum, a judge abhors issuing a directive which has become a futile gesture because of the judge's previous acts or omissions.

Dr. Hansen remained in the county jail for a year and a half. Finally, through the good offices of the Danish Ambassador to the United States, he agreed to discontinue the divorce proceeding in Denmark and to bring about the child's return to America. I then signed an order directing his release. Lisabeth was returned to this country. I have just learned, as I write this chapter, that she has been reunited with her mother, and that they have spent a happy summer together.

In these two cases I could at least direct my efforts along lines which I believed to be in the best interests of the child. Recently I held a custody conference which presented a situation defying judicial correction.

The father, a man in his late thirties, was a shipping clerk earning forty dollars a week. In his early youth he had been convicted of a felony, a circumstance which did not enhance his prospects for financial betterment. His wife was a full-blown young woman with dyed blond hair.

An informal conference in chambers with the lawyers developed the pertinent facts. The couple had been married seven years, and had a six-year-old daughter. They had lived on the husband's meager earnings in a squalid tenement apartment. The wife's indolence made conditions at home even more miserable than they had to be.

She met a prosperous man in his fifties, who was separated, but not divorced, from his wife. Soon after and about six months before the date of the hearing, she left her husband, took their child, and went to live with her middle-aged lover. He set her up in an apartment which was luxurious by her previous living standards and bedecked her with finery.

A few weeks later he refused to permit the child to remain in the apartment any longer. So she was shipped off to an expensive boarding school in Westchester County, for which, of course, the lover paid. The school authorities permitted parents to visit the children on weekends; and the husband and wife had agreed that each should visit the child, separately, on alternate weekends.

After some months of these arrangements, the husband had hired a lawyer and brought on this custody proceeding. He claimed the child was very unhappy in her present surroundings.

"Can he offer any kind of adequate home for the child?" I asked the husband's lawyer.

"No, Judge," he answered. "He goes to work and couldn't take care of the child. And all of his relatives barely manage to get by."

"Then what do you hope to accomplish by this proceeding?" I asked. "I can't force his wife's paramour to take the child back into their apartment. I might arrange to place her in a public institution, but it's unlikely she'd be any happier."

"I've told him that," said the lawyer, "but he insisted on coming to court. I suspect he's hopeful that you can persuade his wife to return to him."

"Is he willing to take her back?"

"Only for the sake of the child. He's simply crazy about that kid, Judge."

The husband and wife joined us. She soon made it clear that under no circumstances would she go back to live with him.

"What will happen to your child?" I asked. "Is she to spend all her young lifetime in schools—with no home influence whatsoever?"

"Oh, Gus is going to marry me as soon as he gets a divorce from his wife," she said. "He says once we're married, he'll have no objection to Helen being with us. But he don't think it looks right at this time."

"I've been in touch with his wife," said her husband. "She'll let him rot in hell before she'll give him a divorce. What's more, he knows he can't get no divorce. He's made his wife all kinds of propositions, he's offered to give her a lot of money, and she turned him down every time."

"Oh, Gus'll get a divorce," said the wife, smugly. "He's no sap, like you. He knows how to get things done."

Her composure appeared to desert her when her husband said, "Yeah, and if he ever does get a divorce do you think he'll marry you? He's just giving you a line. But where does my kid come off in all this?"

With some show of sharpness I put an end to these exchanges. I questioned the wife further. She continued to profess no doubts about Gus getting a divorce, or about his marrying her. Besides, she averred she loved Gus and loathed her husband. Finally, I turned to him.

"Your lawyer tells me you are in no position to take care of Helen," I said. "I agree with you that the present arrangements are very bad. But can you tell me how we can give her anything better?"

"I don't know, Judge," he groaned. "I hoped you could work something out."

"I'm afraid not," I said.

"Then I'll go mad, I tell you," he suddenly burst out. "I can't take these visits any more. I bring her back Saturday, that ain't so bad. We know we'll be together Sunday. Then on Sunday we go to Playland, or the beach. We have lunch and a lotta laughs. And then I take her back to that—that prison.

"I kiss her good-by, and she just holds on to me—very tight. She don't cry, she don't make a fuss, Judge. I'd feel better if she did. She just says, 'Let me hold you, Daddy, till that funny feeling goes away.' And then she suddenly lets go and runs down the hall and upstairs. I take a train back to a hall bedroom, and she goes to a bedroom with seven other kids. Is that any way to raise a kid, Judge?"

"What do you think?" I asked his wife, who seemed bored with the whole procedure.

"That's an act she puts on for him, 'cause she knows he's a softy," she answered. "Helen would never pull it on me, 'cause she knows she'd never get away with it. She's doing fine there. She's healthy and getting a good education. We pay sixty dollars a week to keep her there, 'cause I only wanted her to have the best. That ain't hay, Judge. There were places that would take her for thirty-five dollars, but I'd have no part of them. I want only the best for my daughter."

Every approach failed to dent her complacency with the situation. Finally, I had no alternative but to dismiss the writ.

Only too often separated and estranged parents attempt to assert their legal rights to children in the same way that they would assert their legal rights to the household furniture, or any other property.

The obduracy of such a parent resulted in an unexpected aftermath to a custody proceeding. The parents of a six-year-old girl had been divorced two years before the case came on before me. The divorce decree contained a provision giving custody of the child to each parent for six months of the year. Incidentally, this is a form of divided custody which few judges approve but which occasionally seems to offer the only solution. After failing to assert his custody rights for two years, the father took the child from camp to his home on Labor Day, and told his former wife he proposed to start his six-month custody period. She sued out a writ.

Both parents were young. They had both remarried and seemed well adjusted to their second spouses and new homes.

When they appeared I tried unsuccessfully to persuade the father that his position was unsound and harmful for the child. An uprooting of school, home, and social ties was involved. He was adamant. I told him that my opinion was entitled to no greater weight than his, but suggested that as laymen we secure the opinion of either a child psychologist or pediatrician. He said he would abide by such an opinion. Both parents agreed upon one of the leading pediatricians of the country, and an appointment was made for the following day.

The pediatrician reported that after studying and interviewing parents and child, he was of the opinion that in this instance the proposed split custody was desirable. He based his opinion largely upon the child's high degree of intelligence and adaptability, and her great affection and devotion for her father. Small wonder! Daddy and his new wife had been plying her with gifts and attention.

While I attached great weight to the specialist's report, I was still far from satisfied that such an arrangement was in the best interest of the child. Hearings were held. The father finally prevailed, not because of the opinion of the famous doctor but because of the testimony of the child's own pediatrician. He was a weary-looking, middle-aged man of modest bearing and as modest a reputation. He testified impressively on behalf of the father that the divided custody was desirable. He based his opinion upon the consuming possessiveness of the mother, and said that periodic respites would benefit the child. I decreed that the child spend six months with each parent.

Two months later the husband's lawyer told me the aftermath to this decision. It seems the little girl became keenly aware that she was the center of all this legal fuss and excitement, that she was the leading lady in the courtroom drama. She had become badly spoiled by the poorly concealed overtures each parent made for her favor. Both parents trembled for a favorable word in court from so influential a witness, and had wooed the child assiduously.

Quite understandably, she reacted badly to the courthouse courtship. She threw a tantrum whenever her father and his wife went out, and demanded constant attention. Within a month the father's second wife informed him that either she or the child had to leave the house—that she could not endure her intolerable demands any longer. He shipped the little girl back to her mother.

I can grin at this frustration of my decision. Unfortunately, there is little humor in court proceedings affecting young children; and such as there is will be on the grim side. The savagery with which estranged and embittered husbands and wives assail each other is dismal enough, but the lasting scars which they inflict upon their innocent children are appalling. And there is so little that the best-intentioned, most skillful, most sensitive judge can do about it.

No judge, no law, can step in and repair the damage already done to a child by the two people who dominate his little world. He stands, frightened and impotent and uncomprehending, in the widening breach between those two people. The erosion of the familiar and comfortable home ways eats away at his happiness and security. Often the final rupture is the kindliest surgery. It at least gives the child a fighting chance to grow roots in another and more stable environment; and it replaces the muddled and emotional decisions of his parents with a mature and selfless advocate and arbiter—the court.

* XVIII *

Influence and the Courts

IMPARTIALITY and honesty are the attributes which, above all others, the community expects of a judge. In much the same manner it expects morality of a minister. Somehow, these qualities are regarded as indigenous to the respective callings. Of course, impartiality and honesty are looked for in every decent person; but they are demanded more insistently of judges, as being among the basic working tools of their occupation.

It is expected that judges, with different talents, education, and experience, will vary in ability and that their decisions will reflect these varying qualities. But there is no such tolerance or recognition of degrees of judicial honesty; upon that the conventions are rigid and inflexible.

Community expectations, his legal training, and the traditions of bench and bar condition a judge powerfully to exercise honesty of judgment. Bernard L. Shientag has said: "As a man is affected by a change in physical climate, so is he affected by a change in intellectual climate." These considerations also make a judge most sensitive to the standards of integrity demanded of him; and therefore he is keenly aware that his reputation rests upon his success in fulfilling those standards.

Judges realize that once lawyers begin to distrust their strength of character and sense of fairness, their usefulness is impaired.

When a lawyer looks up at a judge, that judge wants to read in his eyes the unspoken expression: "You may rule for me or against me, you may get the point of my argument or miss it: I know my client's cause will receive earnest, honest consideration in your hands."

Consequently, and apart from the prickings of his own well-developed conscience, a judge resents overtures for favoritism because they impute a belief that he lacks the attributes of judicial fitness. The very request implies an existing tarnish. Judges are aware, too, that they function under the scrutiny of expert and critical eyes; their activities are observed by alert lawyers loyal to the interests of their clients.

There are more tangible bulwarks of judicial independence and rectitude. Most judges can serve for their useful lifetimes, subject to good behavior. If not appointed for life, as in the federal courts, they enjoy the practical equivalent of life tenure by political protocol. The founding fathers and their contemporaries in the states extended themselves to make the judiciary the most independent of the three arms of government; they sought to make it immune from legislative, executive, political, or any other type of influence.

Judges, on the average, are the highest paid of all civil servants. In many states federal and the higher state court judges receive larger salaries than governors, commissioners, and U.S. senators. Of course, most public officials are underpaid by the standards of our economy.

The inconsiderable amount of improper influence actually exerted in the courts scarcely warrants the devotion of an entire chapter to such a subject. Prevalent and pervasive misconceptions, however, make it advisable to include this chapter—and to mark it as one of the most important in the book.

I do not say that judges are not subjected to a variety of corrupting temptations from time to time—or that some few do not succumb. There are some black pages in the otherwise glorious history of the Anglo-American bench. Beamont, the Master of the

Rolls in King Edward VI's reign, confessed that he purchased the interest of a defendant in a case before him, and caused a deed to be forged in order to support his decision. Lord Bacon, writing of the corruptions of Empson and Dudley in the time of Henry VII, described the dual activities through which they enriched their king and themselves, "preying," he said, "like tame hawks for their master, and like wild hawks for themselves."

Among other expedients for raising money, they would cause indictments to be returned against wealthy persons. After their arrest and imprisonment, these hapless victims could win liberation only through the payment of large sums of money—termed "compensations" and "mitigations."

Empson and Dudley were also rumored to have acted as liaisons in the procurement of royal pardons, for valuable considerations. Lord Bacon wrote: "I do remember to have seen not long since a book of Empson's, that had the king's hand to almost every leaf, by way of signing, and was pastilled in the margin with the king's hand likewise, where was this remembrance: 'Item, received of such a one five marks for a pardon to be procured; and if the pardon do not pass, the money to be repaid, except the party be some other way satisfied!' And over against this memorandum (of the king's own hand) 'otherwise satisfied.' "

The gifted Lord Bacon himself, Lord Keeper and High Chancellor in Elizabeth's time, was removed because of corruption and favoritism. He was not above accepting gifts from successful litigants in his court; nor did he turn a deaf ear to any intervention on behalf of litigants by his patron, the Duke of Buckingham.

Of course, these judges did not attain office through the democratic process. Perforce they reflected the venality or the morality of the kings to whom they owed their appointments. No true analogies can therefore be drawn between judges designated under such auspices, particularly by certain of the Stuart monarchs, and judges either elected by the people or appointed by an official elected by the people.

It is heartening, therefore, to read of the incorruptible Sir Matthew Hale, who held court in the days of Charles II. Roger North relates this story of Sir Matthew: "A courtier who had a cause to be tried before him, got one to go to him, as from the king, to speak for favor to his adversary, and so carried his point, for the chief justice could not think any person to be in the right that came so unduly recommended."

There have been instances of judicial corruption and improprieties in modern times. The present generation of lawyers remembers the trial and conviction, a little over a decade ago, of Martin T. Manton, Presiding Judge of the Federal Court of Appeals in the New York area. This is one of the most important courts in the country. It was with consternation and heavy hearts that the bar followed the sordid revelations of the many judicial favors sold by Manton, as though they were vendible commodities of the market place.

The bar's distress and disappointment were not relieved by the realization that this was a rare lapse from grace, or by the fact that on the very bench presided over by Manton were some of the most revered and noble figures of the contemporary judiciary.

In 1939, shortly after Manton's highly publicized conviction, Dr. Gallup conducted a nation-wide poll of American voters, addressed to their faith in the honesty of the judicial system. The questions and answers were as follows:

"In general, do you think judges in the federal courts of this country are honest?"

Yes 86%
No 14

"In general, do you think judges in the state courts are honest?"

Yes 76%
No 24

"In general, do you think judges in the municipal or local courts are honest?"

Yes 72%
No 28

Nearly one-third of voters reached in cities said they felt there was dishonesty among their local judges, and one-fourth questioned the honesty of state judges. Among small-town and rural voters, however, the ratio of skepticism was much lower; only about one voter in every five questioned the honesty of the courts. In explaining the reasons for their opinions, the voters stated that they thought local judges were less in the public eye and more subject to political pressures than state or federal judges.

Dr. Gallup hailed this poll as an indication of the faith of "the overwhelming majority of American voters . . . in the honesty of the judicial system." But I find it very disturbing that so substantial a minority distrusts the integrity of its judges. It may be that the then recent Manton disclosures had a marked influence on the answers. It may be that the answers did not represent deep and considered convictions on the subject, but vague misgivings. This is understandable. The isolated scandals have been newsworthy, whereas proper, painstaking performance of duty does not make headlines.

I am certain very few people really have an abiding belief that our court system is ridden with corruption. The best proof of this assertion is that virtually no efforts are made directly to influence a judge improperly; relatively few efforts are made to influence him indirectly, and these few are stupid and inept. Most Americans have an inbred, and completely justified, reverence for the integrity of their judicial processes, which shines through their occasional grousing about the courts.

Since I have become a judge, people no longer are prone to discuss judicial deficiencies in my presence. But as a practicing lawyer I heard a good deal of such talk—mostly from lawyers, at luncheon tables or lawyers' gatherings. Lawyers, like members of any profession or trade, talk shop almost exclusively when they congregate, and this shop talk must embrace judges—their faults and virtues, their strengths and failings. An attorney on the losing side of a case can expect good-natured chaffing from his fellows at the bar. He may engage in rueful, even good-humored griping at the judge—his lack of erudition, his inattention, or some other fault to which defeat might be attributed.

Rarely, very rarely, does a lawyer hint at judicial corruption. And then his innuendoes will be dismissed by lawyers as a poorly advised effort to shift his own shortcomings or those of his case. Lawyers know with conviction bred out of years of intimate association with the courts that the overwhelming majority of judges are honest and upright men.

It is infinitely more dangerous when a lawyer passes on that kind of an insinuation to his client, and equally dangerous when he credits his client's victory to an "in" with the judge. Laymen are not conditioned, like lawyers, to reject such unfounded aspersions. So another little eddy of vile gossip is launched onto the body of public opinion.

I remember, in the days before I became a judge, hearing loose talk by laymen about the judiciary, in the living rooms of friends. When challenged, there always was cited the experience of a friend in the courts. The evidence of corruption, to a trained legal mind, was never very persuasive. The friend, of course, had always lost his case.

But these laymen did narrate many personal experiences in getting what many people are inclined to regard as small or unimportant court favors, such as taking care of jury notices, traffic tickets, or municipal ordinance violations. There is no doubt that just because these favors are regarded by the careless or unthinking as insignificant and not *really* obstructive of justice, that they are granted prodigally in many communities. To a layman, however, a court is a court, whether a traffic, justice of the peace, or superior court.

A few years ago, two old friends came to my chambers. They were partners in a flourishing textile business.

"We were in the building," one of them announced, "and didn't want to leave without paying you a visit. But we hope we never have to set foot in this den of ignorance and stupidity again!"

"What's eating you?" I asked.

They related a sad, sad story of suing a customer for the purchase price of some fabrics. The defendant contended that the weave was defective and evidently persuaded the jury, which returned a verdict in his favor. My friends reviled the jurors as simpletons, who did not know the difference between an invoice and a promissory note.

"By the way, and not really changing the subject," I asked, "when did either of you fellows last serve on a jury?"

They did not remember. From their attitude, they also did not think this question germane to their plight.

"Think hard," I urged.

"Well," one of them said, "I'd say at least fifteen to twenty years ago. You know, business was so bad before the war that we had really to hump ourselves to keep afloat. And business has been so good since the war that we need every possible minute to take care of it."

"Those happen to be stock excuses offered by most businessmen," I said. "How can you expect a trial by a jury of your business peers, or to get a fair ratio of businessmen on a panel, when by one device or another most of you manage to duck jury duty? If your analysis of the verdict is correct, there's an element of poetic justice in it."

They protested that they had no desire to shirk any civic responsibility. They pointed to an imposing record of communal activities—participation in charity drives, industry associations, membership on church and hospital boards, to all of which they devoted considerable time, effort, and worry.

"That still does not excuse your getting out of jury duty," I said.

"Well, you know how it is," one of them said lamely. "The blamed jury notices always seem to come at our busiest seasons. So we give them to one of our salesmen, who belongs to some political club, and we never hear any more about them."

"Every time your salesman fixes a jury notice—for that is what he does, in effect—doesn't that diminish your respect for this court just a little?"

They hastened to assure me that such was not the case. After all, everyone knew the courts had adopted a very lenient policy toward enforcing jury duty. The influence required to obtain a jury excusal was so negligible that it should not be termed a "fix," with all the ugly and corrupt connotations of that word.

"Put that way it sounds horrible!" protested one of my friends. "But nobody ever thinks it through that far. It's such a minor court favor."

"But it's a beginning," I said. "I wonder to what extent it subconsciously affects thinking about judicial integrity. It's just not healthy. And what about the fellow who does serve? He either has no friends in court or he thinks it's his duty to serve. There is a stubborn notion in this community that one is a sucker to serve on a jury—a dolt who doesn't know anyone with enough influence to get him off."

"That's the kind of jury we had," murmured one of my friends. "They sure scraped the community barrel for that one."

"I'm sure the jury was not as bad as you paint it," I said. "But it may have contained some people who wanted to be excused and didn't know how to go about it. What kind of opinion can those people hold of our courts when they learn that fellows like you get excused regularly, even though it may work less of a hardship on you than on them to serve for two weeks?"

Perhaps one of the reasons that these shoddy practices have excited no general public condemnation is that they do not involve or apply to private litigation, nor do they usually find any direct human victims. Who is harmed if a friend is excused from jury duty, or a traffic violation killed, reason those who do not think the results through to their impact upon the community or body politic. Aside from other substantial evils, there is encouraged a disrespect for law enforcement generally.

Judges are not recluses. Their conduct responds in some degree, consciously or unconsciously, to the moral notions of the community. If their neighbors countenance or lightly accept judicial favoritism in so-called minor matters, a mighty bulwark against such practices is razed.

I recall the glee with which attorneys recounted a story current when I was a practicing lawyer—possibly apocryphal in origin—

about a justice of the peace. It seems, so the tale went, that this justice dispensed favors readily and profusely. In political parlance, such a favor from a public official is called a "contract."

This justice of the peace had evolved an uncomplicated method to keep track of his contracts. Before ascending the bench he sent for the court papers, stuffed those papers in which he had promised to help the defendant in his right-hand pocket, and those in which he proposed to favor the complainant in his left-hand pocket. One morning he inadvertently switched pockets, and dispensed an unexpectedly high order of justice.

I contrast the chuckles with which we lawyers greeted this story with the heaviness of heart with which we discussed the resignation under fire of a federal district court judge, and the conviction for judicial corruption of Judge Manton. The latter, we felt, undermined the very foundation of the administration of justice. I wonder whether these so-called minor judicial peccadilloes do not, over a period of time, weaken the structure just as effectively.

The fellow who can fix a jury notice or a traffic court ticket—and those within the orbit of his boasting—may wonder uneasily at times whether civil litigation or criminal indictments can be disposed of in the same manner.

It's not smart to serve on a jury. It's not smart to pay a traffic fine. A logical extension of such thinking on these levels might lead to the dangerous conclusion that it's not smart to lose a case in court—in any court. Fortunately, I believe, few have reached this conclusion.

But some judicial activities in so-called higher courts cast judges in a poor light and are difficult to defend. The most widely criticized phase of the work in our court relates to our handling of undefended matrimonial matters; i.e., divorce and annulment actions. There is no doubt that few judges or referees submit the evidence in these matters to the same rigid scrutiny as in other forms of litigation. We share this dubious distinction with many other courts throughout the country.

I cannot discuss the social implications of this problem, if only because of limitations of space. It is no excuse that both parties to the undefended lawsuit ardently desire the severance of their marriage ties. The law requires that the judicial officer be satisfied as to certain facts, and he should not accept incredible evidence of those facts. To alleviate the conditions discussed in this chapter, to preserve the dignity of judicial officers, for these reasons alone an end must be put to these stultifying practices.

Involved here is the major court function of making decisions and entering judgments in a most important area of litigation. Judges handling these matters do not emerge as paragons of consistency or staunchness.

But here again no human being is victimized. The judge is permitting estranged spouses to do what their wealthier neighbors may accomplish by a trip to Nevada or Florida. Still, one wonders whether even the party who seeks the end result does not experience a certain disrespect for laws so easily circumvented.

Why have the court ceremonials, the judge's robe and many other trappings, survived the centuries and our own cynical age? They may fill a special psychological need. They symbolize; they are the external manifestations of the court's impersonality, anonymity, and rectitude in administering justice. They translate the ideal into a tangible setting.

Sometimes people exhibit a surface irreverence toward institutions they revere most profoundly. The more dignified the institution, the more irresistible the impulse to lampoon it. The ponderous dignity of court processes makes them vulnerable to caricature. A sure-fire formula for laughs in the old Keystone Comedies was to splatter a custard pie in the startled face of a high-hatted dignitary. All this is healthy and democratic, provided the laughter does not trail off into overtones of suspicion and distrust.

Some of the low fixing activity has a high psychological content. It involves convincing oneself that one is a "big shot." The ordinary rules and laws are fine and necessary for the next fellow—but not for me. We all know some man who will exert one hundred dollars' worth of time, energy, and reciprocal favors to avoid paying a possible five-dollar fine for a traffic violation, or to help a friend avoid a fine or jury notice. These efforts are often ludicrous to behold. They would be more amusing than important if they did not contribute to whittling down respect for the integrity of courts everywhere.

In the ten years I have been on the bench only three direct attempts have been made to influence my decision in a pending lawsuit. They were pretty feeble.

The first one occurred during the first year I was a judge. A man representing himself to my secretary as a personal friend was ushered into my chambers. I could not place this friend, even after he informed me we were members of the same fraternal lodge. He was an insurance broker, he told me.

"Judge," he said, "I know you wouldn't do anything wrong, and I'm not asking you to. But a customer and a friend of mine has a case coming up before you—"

"You'd better stop right there!" I snapped. "If you tell me the name of your friend I'll disqualify myself from hearing his matter and take harsh measures with you."

"But I didn't want to discuss the merits of the case," he whined. "I just thought I'd tell you what a swell fellow he was—the soul of honor. I thought you'd be interested as a judge in knowing that. I didn't think there was anything wrong."

I made short shrift of this intermediary. He was a busybody trying to impress a customer with his "connections."

The second attempt, several years later, was made by a mortgage broker I knew very slightly. The scene and dialogue were almost identical with the first one.

The third attempt was made by a minor politician. One of the clerks of the court escorted him into my chambers and introduced him to me as a captain in his political district.

"I won't take up much of your time, Judge," he said. "You got a motion on tomorrow—Jones against Smith. Jones is one of the neighbor's children, good boy, active in our club. He asked me to talk to you and I couldn't refuse him. I know you'll call the shots as you see 'em and I'm not asking you to give him any breaks. Whatever you do is okay with me, for him or against him, only I didn't want to break my promise to Jack Jones. So I spoke to you."

The clerk, who had remained in the room, looked so distressed that it was evident he had not known the purpose of this peanut politician's visit. I reassured him.

"I'm sure you knew nothing of this, Jim." Then I turned to the politician.

"You're going back to Jones," I said. "What are you going to tell him?"

He fumbled with his hat. "Oh, the truth. That you'd make no promise."

"A half truth," I said. "But never mind that. Suppose I decide in favor of Jones. All his life he's going to think he won because you spoke to me—not that he won on the merits."

"Oh, I don't know, Judge. He thinks he's on the right side."

"But he wanted to make doubly sure," I added. "I'm going to disqualify myself and adjourn the motion over to the next judge."

And then I told this gentleman what would happen to him if I ever found him in the vicinity of my chambers again.

When a judge is aware of venal overtures, he is at least in a position to take measures to protect his reputation. But there is one mean, vile practice against which a judge, or for that matter any public official, is helpless to defend himself. It is similar in pattern to touting a horse at the race track.

A tout will approach a likely-looking victim at the race track and whisper to him that he has inside information that arrangements have been made for a certain horse to win the next race. The tout wants no money in advance for his tip. He assures the sucker that he is so sure of the horse's winning that he does not want to be rewarded for his information until the race is over. This sounds reasonable to the race-track novice, who agrees to place a bet and share his winnings with the tout after the horse wins. The tout repeats this process with as many victims as he can find, giving each one the name of a different horse in the race. If one of the touted horses wins, he seeks out the bettor to whom he gave that name, collects his share, and shuns his other customers.

There are touts who infest courthouses, and who are much

lower than their counterparts at the race track. They batten on the fears and despairs of litigants. These gentry ply their conscienceless calling almost exclusively in the criminal courts. The bewilderment, ignorance, and agitation of defendants and their friends and relatives render them easy prey.

The judge, like the horse, is not aware that the contest has been supposedly fixed.

The task of the race-track tout is more difficult than that of the courthouse one. The former is paid off only when one out of six or eight horses wins. A court tout selects one in a two-party contest.

When I first entered the district attorney's office many years ago, I was assigned to a magistrate's court. Nobody paid much attention to me, except a bondsman who plied his trade in that court. He was very smooth and personable. Every morning he would walk to the counsel table in front of the bench, where I would be examining the complaints on that day's calendar. He would greet me cordially and engage me in conversation for a few minutes, discussing the weather, last night's prize fight, or any other subject that came to mind. I would respond politely.

Finally, after a week of this ritual, a lawyer took pity on my innocence. He informed me that this bondsman, for as much money as the traffic would bear, had no doubt told a defendant or someone interested in a defendant that he was going to fix the case with the district attorney. Then, as earnest for his promise, in full view of his client, he would walk up to me and engage me in what appeared from the rear of the courtroom to be a most confidential conversation. If the complaint were dismissed, the defendant would never believe it had been accomplished upon the merits, and another person would go out into the world to spread talk of official corruption.

This procedure is known as "selling out" a public official. It usually takes the form of the fixer assuring a party or his distraught relative that he has an "in" with the judge, district attorney, commissioner, immigration-service official, or whoever has charge of the matter. For a specific sum of money, the party can be helped. Most of the money, it is represented, must be given to the official. If a favorable result eventuates, it is attributed to the deal. Otherwise, the fixer invents an unexpected break to which he ascribes the unfortunate result. If the victim complains too volubly, part of his money will be returned to silence him. The official, of course, is unaware of the transaction.

This represents the sale of "influence" in its crudest form. In this stark fashion human vultures can victimize only ignorant and unworldly people, rendered desperate and frantic by forces they can comprehend only dimly.

Fortunately, the range of this type of trickery, even in the criminal courts, is very narrow. It is circumscribed by the caution which the tout—usually a bondsman—must exercise. Any slip would be devastating.

Do you marvel that people can be so gullible and simple as to accept such assurances at face value? At higher levels of intelligence, education, and worldliness, people are likewise duped, and also by implausible representations which should sound incredible to persons of their experience.

When I was practicing law a young attorney in my employ brought his uncle into my office. This man, of long and varied business experience, had been indicted in the federal court for a mail fraud, and his nephew had recommended that he engage me as trial counsel.

I tried to question him about the facts of the case. I could not make much progress, because every few minutes he would ask a question like this: "Do you know John Law, the assistant district attorney in charge of my case?"

"Yes," I would answer. "A very fine fellow."

A little later: "Can you do anything with Law?"

"What do you mean?"

"Well, will he listen to reason from you?"

"Listen," I said, "John Law is a very fair, honorable man. Whoever your lawyer may be, you will get fair treatment at his hands—nothing more, nothing less."

A few minutes later: "How do you stand with the judges in the federal court?"

By that time it was evident that I would not represent this defendant. I suggested to my young lawyer that he take his uncle elsewhere. The next day he took him to a well-known criminal lawyer.

He asked the same questions about the assistant district attorney.

"Well," said the lawyer, "John's a very dear friend of mine. Thoroughly honest, you know—good public servant and all that, but a regular fellow. I don't think a client of mine ever got the worst of it from John."

The nephew told me that after they had conferred a little while, the telephone bell rang. The lawyer picked up the phone.

"Yes," he said. "Oh yes, Judge. Would you and the missus care to join me for dinner and the opening of that new musical next Thursday night? Some of your colleagues will be in my party. Fine, fine, I'll hold two tickets for you."

A little later the phone rang again.

"How are you, Mr. District Attorney? I've looked into that matter and I think I can help your brother-in-law. Have him drop in here at—let's say three o'clock tomorrow. Don't mention it. Glad to be of help."

He turned to his visitors.

"One of the assistant D.A.'s. Relative's in a little jam. They all come to me for legal advice and help. I never charge them—all on the cuff. But it promotes good will."

The young lawyer, who was fresh out of law school, was somewhat shocked at this aspect of the practice of law. But to my surprise, he was impressed by the official connections which he believed the criminal lawyer enjoyed. He entertained no suspicions that the telephone calls were spurious or planted to impress a prospective client.

I knew, from my previous experience as a prosecutor, that this lawyer's clients did get the worst of it, in one sense. His reputation was so bad, his word so worthless, that district attorneys and judges were especially wary of any cases in which he appeared.

An associate on the district attorney's staff told me of how he had stumbled onto the fact that he was being "sold out" in an important case.

A notorious confidence man had been indicted for swindling an old woman out of a large sum of money. Before the case came on for trial the elderly complainant died. The defendant's lawyer learned of her death and arranged a conference with the assistant district attorney in charge of the case. The lawyer, at the conference, stated that in view of the complainant's death, he was certain the state could not prove the false representations alleged in the indictment. Therefore, he concluded, the case must fall, and he asked the assistant district attorney to recommend dismissal of the indictment. The latter had to agree, and said he would file such a recommendation within a few days. More experienced prosecutors have learned caution in giving such advance notice.

Those were the days of free and untrammeled wire-tapping. It seems that the police were tapping the private, unlisted telephone of this defendant on suspicion that he was the ringleader of a band of bond thieves. These activities had no connection with the subject matter of the indictment. The day following the conference with the defendant's lawyer, a lieutenant of police entered the office of the assistant district attorney.

"We're on the wire of Dan Osborne," he said with a broad grin. "I thought you might be interested in this part of the transcript of yesterday's tap." Dan Osborne was the defendant.

The lieutenant handed him a sheaf of typewritten papers, and pointed out a particular conversation. As I recall it, it read substantially as follows:

DAN: Hello.
VOICE: Dan, this is Joe (the lawyer).
DAN: Yep.
LAWYER: Dan, I've got good news for you.
DAN: Yeah?
LAWYER: I can get that indictment dismissed.

DAN: Now that the old lady is dead, any kid out of law school could do that.

LAWYER: If that's the way you feel about it, I'll step out and you get some kid out of law school to handle it.

DAN: What'd I pay you a fee for?

LAWYER: To defend you. If you want to stand trial, I'm ready to defend you without any additional charge.

DAN: Isn't it part of your job to get the D.A. to kick it out without any additional charge?

LAWYER: Sure. Only it can't be done that way.

DAN: Why not?

LAWYER: Oh, a few thousand reasons they don't teach kids in law school. With those reasons the case can be dismissed in a few days.

DAN: How many thousand?

LAWYER: Five.

DAN: What d'you need all that dough for?

LAWYER: Let's call it expenses. I'm not going to discuss it over the phone any more. If you're interested, come to my office at four o'clock.

DAN: If you and that D.A. think you can put the bee on me for five grand, you're crazy.

LAWYER: Who said anything about the D.A.? I said expenses.

DAN: Don't kid me. Listen, Joe. I know they can't convict me any longer in this case. It's worth a few bucks to me at this time for the convenience of booting it out right away and discharging bail. But nothing like five grand. I'll be up at four.

Here a shrewd swindler, accustomed to living on his wits, had been partially duped by a variation of his own confidence games.

The undeserved smear resulting from a "sellout" is an occupational hazard from which no public official is immune. Fortunately for the official's state of mind, he rarely even suspects that he has been sold out. There is only one way in which a judge or any other public official can be protected against these stealthy stabs at his reputation. That is by bringing home to a gullible public the fact that the odds are overwhelmingly against the courthouse hanger-on, petty politician, or renegade lawyer performing what he promises.

Some laymen, particularly businessmen, have no compunctions against participating in what they regard as a permissive zone of influence. They regard the exertion of influence to shape the course of litigation as a component of the competitive pattern. They don't want an unjust decision or verdict. Justice lies irresistibly on their side, so they are not employing corrupt means to effectuate such justice.

The process is not essentially different, to their minds, from selling their product. Their machines or materials are clearly superior to those of their competitors. But, nevertheless, it is desirable to wine, dine, and lavish gifts upon buyers so that their eyes will not be closed to that superiority. And similarly, they wish to assure themselves that the judge's eyes will not be closed to the superior merits of their side of the case.

When businessmen have a salesman, they try to choose one who enjoys the good will of the trade. When they hire a lawyer, they sometimes try to choose one who enjoys the good will of the judge. They will then try to retain a friend, a former colleague on the bench, or a politician to whom they think the judge is beholden for past favors, or to whom he will be gracious in anticipation of future favors. These efforts are almost always wasted and wasteful, and they probably cost gullible litigants millions of dollars yearly.

In the New York County Supreme Court, it is practically impossible to foretell before what judge a case will be tried. About twenty trial parts are in operation continuously for the trial of law and equity cases. Until a case has been assigned to one of those parts, on the eve of trial, there is no way of identifying the trial judge. This will not hold true in certain communities, particularly rural ones where only one judge sits in a courthouse at a given term.

It also does not apply to motion parts. Although the judges rotate in assignments to the motion term, only one judge sits at any one time. The assignments of judges for the entire year are published before the New Year. Thus a motion may be made returnable on a date when a particular judge is sitting in the motion part.

It also does not apply to special terms, handling specialized matters, which are presided over continually by one judge. I, for example, have exclusive jurisdiction of the reorganization of large trust mortgage bond issues. Other judges have exclusive jurisdiction of condemnation, tax certiorari, and other matters.

I have had gratifying and distressing experiences with friends in court. In some my policy was difficult to define. In others, as in the case of George Feasor, my course was clear.

George was an intimate friend of a former law partner of mine. I knew him and liked him. He was an able, moderately successful, and fairly obscure lawyer.

Several years ago this former partner telephoned me. I was sitting in a part for the trial of cases at the time.

"You've got a case entitled White against Black in your part?" he inquired.

"Yes," I answered. "It's due to go to trial tomorrow. I think it's a nonjury goods sold and delivered case. Why?"

"Well, George Feasor has just been offered a retainer by the plaintiff's lawyer to try the case before you. He called me to ask whether it was ethical for him to come in at this late stage."

"What did you tell him?"

"I told him it could be very embarrassing for you, particularly if he was retained because the plaintiff's lawyer thought he was a friend of yours. He maintains that it's clearly understood that he's to go in and try it on the merits. I asked him if he'd ever acted as trial counsel for the plaintiff's lawyer before and he said no. I then asked him why in heaven's name they were retaining him."

"Particularly since he's not a trial specialist."

"Right. I advised him not to touch it, but he asked me to sound you out about it. That's the only reason I'm calling."

This situation presented no difficulties.

"I don't want to deprive George of a fee he would otherwise earn," I said. "If he has any reservations about the bad faith of the plaintiff, tell him he may give him the following proposition, with my blessing. Let the plaintiff retain him, and tomorrow morning I'll transfer the case to some other judge, who I'll make sure does not know George. By this offer George will know whether they want him for his exceptional talents."

The following morning George did not appear in my courtroom. But I did not try the case anyway. I sent it to another judge.

It is not always easy for a judge to exercise neutral judgment when a friend appears before him. Contrary to the popular notion, a weak judge may be tempted to lean over backwards. He may be tempted to rule against a friend and figuratively thump his chest, saying, "How noble and upright I am! Friendship cuts no ice in my courtroom."

One has, of course, several circles of friends, of varying degrees of intimacy. Most of my closest friends are lawyers. I have never been embarrassed by the conduct of any of these intimates. I have been astonished, however, to learn, since I ascended the bench, that certain lawyers with whom I have a bare nodding acquaintance are now bosom companions. Some lawyers, fortunately very few, will chat briefly with a judge at some meeting or at the home of a mutual friend. For weeks afterward they will narrate to everyone they meet a version of this talk, which gets cozier and more intimate with every recounting.

The same hazards and the same advantages which obtain when a friend appears in court apply to the retention of a former associate on the bench. These former comrades in arms are friends of most of the sitting judges. It is wise to retain them on the basis of the character and of the experience, know-how, and erudition they have gained while on the bench. It is unwise to expect anything else by reason of the former associations. This problem is minimized by the fact that most judges remain in office until retirement for age limitations or death.

Therefore, judges, unlike many other officeholders, are not "on the make" politically. There is nothing a politician can give them. They have tenure by a well-rooted custom which transcends partisan politics.

True, politicians expect judges to be grateful to the party which lifted them onto the bench. But only the shoddiest politician would expect that gratitude to pervert a just decision. The only form in which a politician of any stature looks to a judge for an expression of his gratitude is in the dispensing of patronage. This term embraces the remunerative appointments which a judge makes occasionally, such as receiverships, references, committees, and guardianships. The politicians expect a judge to strengthen the political organization by giving a substantial portion of these appointments to worthy party members.

A receiver is a person appointed by the court to act as a sort of trust officer for the court—to collect and receive money or property which is the subject of litigation pending the outcome of the lawsuit. A referee, usually an attorney, is appointed to act on behalf of the court in determining or reporting back to the court on an issue referred to him in a pending legal proceeding. A committee is appointed to manage the person or property or both of a person incapable of managing his own affairs; a guardian performs similar functions for an infant.

In making many of these appointments most judges I know, including myself, accept and recognize recommendations from the party of their affiliation. They require that the person to be designated be honest and competent. Judges will also appoint friends on the same basis, and encourage deserving young lawyers by thus recognizing them.

If the job to be done requires specialized abilities, or has unusual dimensions, a judge may go outside the circle of his friends or his party, and ask an outstanding member of the bar to serve. It must not be inferred from this that political leaders do not submit the names of distinguished lawyers. But sometimes a particular lawyer is peculiarly qualified to handle a certain matter—and a judge will appoint him without regard to ties of politics or friendship. I recently appointed a former judge of the highest court in our state—and not a member of my party—to the most important and remunerative reference I have had in years. He didn't need the fee involved, as he is one of the busiest lawyers in the state. But the court needed his talents, experience, and prestige to clear up a very involved lawsuit that had been on our calendars for years.

I believe judges drift away from their political organizations because the nature of their duties affords so few contacts with political leaders. By general acceptance the duties of a governmental executive or legislator embrace constant policy consultation with political leaders. Under the system of party responsibility for elected officials, a form of interdependence has evolved between party policy and the official acts of the party's elected legislators and executives.

There is no such relationship between the permissible province of the politician and the official functioning of a judge. The state chairman of a dominant political party will openly express his position on, let us say, emergency rent legislation, to a caucus of his party's legislators. His avowed and accepted purpose is to influence their voting, in what he considers the best interests of the party. But when that legislation is enacted and tested in the courts, he would not and dares not make any such representations to the judge or judges handling the case.

When a newspaper mentions a legislator it almost invariably affixes an *R* or a *D* to his name, to indicate his party affiliation. Have you ever seen a judge's name tagged in this fashion?

Furthermore, politicians do not expect or exact the fealty from judges, high or low, which they command from certain nonjudicial officeholders. Strict party co-operation is not a *sine qua non* for promotion within the judicial framework. For example, in selecting a candidate for district attorney, assemblyman, mayor, and the like, the political leaders are greatly concerned about his record of party loyalty, his emotional stability, and other factors. An inconstant district attorney or mayor can ruin his political sponsors, by refusing to recognize their recommendations for the jobs which are the sinews of their organization, or by running afoul the party on good-government issues. These are not dangers inherent in any judicial post.

Political tradition, bred out of bitter experience, has stamped any interference with the judicial dispensation of justice, or with the functioning of the district attorney's office, as political "dynamite"—highly dangerous.

Nothing will rock a party in power to its foundations so much as revelations of corruption in courts or in the prosecutor's office. This speaks volumes for the deep desire of the average citizen for the integrity of those institutions. Equivalent proof of corruption in other governmental agencies will be received with some equanimity, often with amused resignation.

In New York City all political parties concede, from a sense of realism, that a judge in a high court who has served capably for one term is deserving, irrespective of party affiliation, of unanimous endorsement for re-election. There have been rare occasions when the dominant party has deviated from this code. Invariably an aroused electorate has caused it to regret such action. The last time this was attempted, in 1919, the rejected candidate was re-elected by a fusion movement. Incidentally, the public was so aroused that many minority party candidates for other offices who had been given little chance were elected. One of these unexpected beneficiaries of the voters' indignation was Fiorello H. La Guardia, running on the Republican ticket for President of the Board of Aldermen.

In 1898 Richard Croker, then leader of Tammany Hall, refused a renomination to Judge Daly. Daly had rejected Croker's recommendation in the appointment of a court clerk. Theodore Roosevelt was the Republican candidate for Governor that year. He made a major issue of the Judge Daly incident and was elected in a poor Republican year.

Politicians are quite content to subscribe to a "hands off the courts" policy. It means so many less political errands to run. Like most other people, they do not care to engage in unnecessary work. So long as all political parties frown on asking favors in the courts, a politician is not at a political disadvantage in declining to intervene. There is a distinction, of course, between a politician trying to please a constituent and a "fixer" trying to tout himself into a fee. The politician will seize upon any reasonable excuse to avoid undertaking the unpleasant and burdensome task of procuring a favor from any officeholder.

Politicians of any consequence are completely unimpressed by titles. They have no desire to preen themselves on their friendships with officeholders, as do others whose vanity drives them to seek the procurement of favors. Favors are just chores to politicians.

One politician had a favorite formula for shunting off a constituent who sought political intervention in the civil courts. A constituent would visit the district clubhouse and ask the leader to speak to a judge about his case.

LEADER: Do you know Assemblyman Ryan over there?

CONSTITUENT: Yes, sir.

LEADER: What would you think if I went over and snatched his wallet out of his pocket?

CONSTITUENT: (uncertainly) Why, er—that would be stealing.

LEADER: Well, that's just what you're asking me to do. To take money out of the other party's pocket and put it into yours. You can believe me, if the fellow on the other side came to me or any other political leader in this city, he would get the same answer.

Judges are subject to a form of influence. A lawyer with an established reputation for competency and integrity will always gain respectful attention. If he presents seriously a point which a judge at first thinks has no merit, the judge will examine and re-examine it, because of the respect which he has for the lawyer's erudition and intellectual honesty.

Laymen, even lawyers, may be surprised to learn that judges regularly compare notes on lawyers who appear before them. There is also astonishing unanimity in conclusions as to who may be trusted and who must be watched closely. During my first month on the bench I mentioned at the judges' luncheon table that a certain lawyer represented the plaintiff in a case on trial before me, and that I was impressed very favorably by him.

"Oh, he's one of the best in the profession," said an older judge.

"Yes, and he's a thorough gentleman," volunteered another

senior judge. "Never takes advantage of his opponent or the court."

"You can go to sleep when he's questioning a witness," said another judge. "He always protects the record."

By "protecting the record" this judge meant that the lawyer did not try by hook or crook to win a verdict and take his chances on appeal. He was careful to ask only proper questions and introduce proper evidence, so that the verdict would be sustained in the event of appeal.

I doubt that many of the judges know this lawyer's political affiliations, or have ever met him socially. He has earned our regard solely on his performance in court.

And why not? Attorneys are officers of the court. While retaining their status as advocates, they may not obstruct a trial judge in his major function of searching for the truth. A judge is justified in reposing more confidence in an agent he has found to be trustworthy than in one he has found wanting, even though one may be unobtrusive or obscure and the other renowned. A judge can apply the same standards in placing his trust as does a businessman in his dealings.

* XIX *

Judge's Diary

A September Day

I LEFT MY HOUSE this morning at the usual hour of 8:15 A.M. and walked three blocks to the Third Avenue Elevated Railway station at Eighty-fourth Street. For years I have traveled by "El" to the Chatham Square station, which is two blocks from the courthouse. At one time I took the subway, as it is five to ten minutes faster. But the subway cars are wretchedly overcrowded at that hour, and I decided to sacrifice some time for comfort and a few shreds of personal dignity. On most mornings the El cars begin to discharge more passengers than they take on at the Fifty-ninth Street station, and below that point a passenger can hope to exchange his strap for a seat.

On this morning I clutched a strap, poised my newspaper at eye level, and started to read as I swayed. Out of the corner of my eye I saw the face of a man a few feet away light into recognition. He rolled toward me and said, "Good morning, Judge."

"Good morning," I answered cordially.

His face was vaguely familiar, but I could not place him. Since I have a poor recollection of faces and names, I am often placed in such a dilemma. To cover my confusion I usually greet such strangers with added heartiness. Each year hundreds of jurors, witnesses, parties, and lawyers stream through a judge's courtrooms. While some will stamp the impress of their personalities upon him, most attract only casual attention.

This man lurched for the strap alongside mine. We exchanged the usual inanities about the weather. Then he commented that one of my associate judges looked poorly. I wondered whether he was one of the courthouse personnel. There are hundreds of clerks, attendants, secretaries, law assistants, stenographers, and other employees in the building.

"Say, Judge," he went on, "did you believe that plaintiff yesterday when he said the defendant promised to take back the goods?"

A horrible suspicion was beginning to dawn on me.

"What makes you ask that question?" I said, cautiously.

"Oh, I was discussing it with a couple of other jurors. They thought the plaintiff was telling the truth. I think he was lying his head off."

My suspicions were confirmed. My fellow passenger was a juror in the case then on trial before me. It was highly improper to discuss a case still on trial with the judge, particularly to elicit his views on evidence.

"When we recessed yesterday I cautioned all the jurors against discussing the case with anyone," I told him sternly. "That means me, your fellow jurors, your wife, anyone."

And I fled to the other end of the car.

It is seldom that a judge is thus accosted while a case is in progress, but it is not unusual for former jurors to open up conversations about old and forgotten cases. And lawyers who corner a judge in a car or a living room are particularly disappointed when he cannot recall the fine subtleties of cases they tried so brilliantly before him years ago.

I generally arrive at my chambers a few minutes before 9 A.M. They are entered through an outer office, which contains the desk of my personal attendant. This room has a door opening on the corridor, which is always open during court hours. All inquiries and business are initially screened through the outer office. My attendant routes all telephone calls through to my secretary or myself. He keeps a diary of my appointments, and, when all persons appearing for a conference have arrived, conducts them into my room. He maintains my records and attends to the innumerable errands that must be run every day—delivery of files, opinions, lawbooks and many other courthouse chores.

Another door leads into my private office, a larger room containing my desk, a conference table, a couch, and a number of chairs. On the other side of my room is my secretary's room, so that I am flanked by my secretary and attendant. My secretary, who is a lawyer, acts as my buffer and arranges most of my appointments. He holds preliminary discussions with lawyers who wish to see me, to ascertain whether he can dispose of their matters satisfactorily and obviate the necessity of my seeing them. He does some legal research for me and I consult with him frequently on court matters.

The various courtrooms start to do business at 10 A.M. In the hour or so I spend in chambers before the opening of court, I endeavor to dispose at least of my correspondence and to skim through the *Law Journal*. Sometimes I also hold a morning conference.

The correspondence relates almost exclusively to court matters. The mail is heavy only during four months of the year—the two months or terms I sit in motion parts and the month following each such motion term. During those months I am deluged with requests for reargument, for extensions of time to submit papers, and with letters which are in reality briefs, and should not be submitted in letter form.

In this month of September I was sitting in a trial term—a part in which I preside at the trial of lawsuits. Since I had not been in a motion part for some months, my correspondence was light. A lawyer wished to reject a settlement and place the case back on the calendar, because his client, on reflection, was not satisfied with the offer made by the defendant. A wife wrote that her husband had stopped paying the temporary alimony I had ordered him to pay. Her lawyer was tired of working without compensation, and she had no resources to hire another lawyer. How should she go about compelling her husband to pay? The Bar Association invited me to participate in a round-table discussion of a legal subject.

I discussed these communications with my secretary and instructed him to answer them on my behalf; then I picked up the *New York Law Journal*. This is the bar's trade paper, published five days a week. Every practicing lawyer and every judge in New York reads it as though it were part of the mail. It publishes court notices, announcements of events of interest to the profession, recent significant decisions of all courts, and all decisions and opinions of the State Supreme Court filed the preceding day.

I find I require a half hour to an hour to read the portions of the *Law Journal* of interest to me. Sometimes I finish it at home or strap-hanging on the way home.

This morning I put the *Law Journal* aside at 9:30. My attendant ushered in several lawyers, to keep an appointment made the afternoon before. A brokerage commission case was on trial before me. When court had adjourned at 4:30 P.M. the preceding day, I had invited the lawyers to join me in the robing room to the rear of the courtroom. We had there resumed a prior discussion of the possibilities of settling the case.

I had finally suggested the figure of five thousand dollars as fair to both sides. The lawyers agreed, but the plaintiff's lawyer pointed out a snag. The plaintiff had worked in conjunction with a cobroker, who was entitled to share in any recovery, but who was not in court.

We had adjourned the settlement conference to the next morning at 9:30, in my chambers. The plaintiff's lawyer had promised to speak with the cobroker that evening. The parties, the cobroker, and the lawyers all appeared in chambers this morning. A feeble effort was made to secure a higher offer, but the defendant stood firm. After a few exchanges the cobroker capitulated and the case was settled. I had taken no part in this morning's negotiation, as I seldom attempt to influence the lay parties to an action.

We all went down to the courtroom. The necessary stipulations were entered upon the minutes, the jury discharged with the thanks of the court, and another jury was selected for the case to follow the one just settled.

The plaintiff in this case, a manufacturer of television sets, sued the defendant for failure to manufacture certain essential parts in accordance with their agreement. About half an hour was consumed in selecting a jury. At 12:45, after opposing counsel had made their opening statements to the jury, and some evidence had been taken, I recessed until two o'clock.

Most judges believe that to limit the luncheon recess to the conventional one hour would work a great hardship on the trial lawyers. Before leaving the courtroom a lawyer must put away his papers, placate impatient witnesses, sometimes make arrangements for the afternoon testimony. Then he must call his office, find out what happened during the morning and give instructions to his secretary. Very often he must telephone clients who are awaiting his calls. By the time he has performed these midday chores he usually has just enough time left of the hour-and-a-quarter period to bolt down his lunch.

Many jurors also require the extra time to communicate with their offices. The judges too put the time to good use. There is usually some small accumulation of judicial business in chambers after a judge has been on the bench for a morning. When he returns to chambers attorneys may be waiting for him, to discuss some situation which has come up unexpectedly. His secretary will have a list of telephone messages, official and personal. Some may be put over to the late afternoon; others require immediate response.

Where and with whom to lunch also poses a problem for judges. Until a few years ago the justices of our court had a private lunchroom in the building. Mounting food costs and diminishing patronage forced the caterer to abandon so unprofitable a venture. Now the judges lunch in neighboring restaurants or in their chambers.

A judge is sometimes embarrassed when he enters a public restaurant without a luncheon companion. Someone is bound to sing out, "Are you alone, Judge? Why don't you join us?"

"Us" may include some persons unknown to the judge. He may be asked to sit with a person of dubious repute. On several occasions I have entered a restaurant with another judge, and while waiting for a table we have been invited to join people who were already seated.

"Who is your friend?" my colleague would ask, after we had declined politely. "His face looks familiar."

"I don't know," I would answer. "He looks familiar to me, too; but I thought he was your friend."

A judge is especially sensitive to certain externals. He is animated only partly by a desire to shield his own reputation; he also strives constantly to sustain public confidence in the court system, of which he is a prominent representative.

Many judges lunch in chambers when they have no appointments. They send out for a sandwich and coffee, or make coffee or tea in chambers on a hot plate. This is not the most restful way to spend the luncheon recess. No sooner has a judge washed down his sandwich than he commences to consult the lawbooks to resolve that elusive question which arose during the morning.

On this day I had arranged to meet two of my associate justices in a near-by restaurant. Because of the small chores awaiting us in chambers none of us arrived before ten minutes after one. I had made several telephone calls on personal and court business. My secretary had conferred with me concerning some pending matters. It was nearly two o'clock before we had finished our meal and chatted a bit about our respective cases. We hurried back and went directly to our courtrooms, just in time to open court at two o'clock.

I generally sit in trial term until about 4:30 P.M. This means that about five and a half hours a day are devoted to actual trial. Trial work is grueling and exacting, for the lawyers particularly, but also for judges and jurors. After five hours or so lawyers become tired and irritated and jurors inattentive.

On this day, after I adjourned court, I held a conference in chambers with the referee and lawyers who were endeavoring to reorganize a nine-million-dollar trust mortgage on a large office building in mid-Manhattan. We were at it until six o'clock. We made some progress.

I then repaired to the courthouse library for a quick review of a few cases on questions of damages which had arisen during the course of the case on trial. I wished to consult some textbooks and federal reports which were not to be found in my modest private law library at home.

At about twenty minutes of seven I left the courthouse and took the subway home. At that hour the subway trains are not crowded, and they are faster than the El trains.

After dinner, and a short report from my wife on household affairs, I spent about an hour preparing a rough draft of a charge for the case on trial. While it was unlikely that the case would be concluded the next day, I wished to be prepared in case the defense was brief. I laid the charge aside when two old and cherished friends visited us. When a court is in session, my wife and I try to restrict our more formal social engagements to Friday and Saturday evenings.

Then to bed, where I read a few pages of an erudite article in a current law school review. As usual, this was an irresistible soporific, so I soon turned off the bed lamp and went to sleep.

An October Day

This month I was assigned to Trial Term Part II, which is known as the calendar part. In this part the day calendars, which comprise several hundred cases, are called daily. A case is placed on the calendar by filing a paper called a note of issue with the court clerk. Within a short time, either party may demand a jury trial and pay the jury fee; most cases on the calendars are jury cases. The case is then placed upon the reserve calendar, and grad ually works its way toward the head of the list.

When it is reached in regular order, the case will be added to the day calendar. It will then be a matter of weeks until it is assigned for actual trial. There are four day calendars: Contract Jury, Tort Jury, Contract Nonjury, and Tort Nonjury Calendars. The day calendars, as their titles imply, are called daily. Cases marked "Ready" are sent to the various trial parts for trial.

These are the calendars on the so-called law side of the court. All litigation stemming from contract obligations is placed on the contract calendars; tort actions, such as negligence, assault, defamation, etc., are placed on the tort calendars.

A tort jury action will be reached in our court about three years after the requisite notice has been filed. A contract jury action will require about nine months, and the nonjury cases can be tried within three months. In most other courts the waiting periods are considerably less—dependent upon the number and the caliber of the cases in each court.

The judges appreciate that justice delayed may be justice denied, and that the delay in reaching tort actions for trial is dangerous and unhealthy. Tort cases constitute about two-thirds of our calendars. In other counties in the state the proportion is higher. The calendar is always uppermost in the judges' minds. It is discussed at every judges' meeting. It has almost assumed nightmare proportions.

Some idea of the dimensions of the calendar challenge may be gained from a simple statistic. The twenty-nine judges in our court dispose of fifteen thousand cases annually, by settlement, trial, and discontinuance. This figure is more impressive in view of the fact that in any given month only two-thirds of the judges are engaged in trial work. The remainder are sitting in the appellate term, which hears appeals from the city courts and municipal courts, in the motion parts, calendar parts, or they have special assignments. Furthermore, somewhere in the courthouse, one or more judges are always busy with the trial of a case or cases requiring weeks or months of court time. Equity cases in particular, such as derivative stockholders' actions, actions in specific performance and for accountings, are often very long. Statistics may be misleading as to the work of any one judge. But they must be valid when applied to the composite efforts of an entire court.

As the calendar judge this month, I had to keep fifteen parts continuously supplied with cases. There was a plentiful supply of ready contract cases, but I had to increase somehow the flow of tort cases to the trial parts, lest that calendar fall even further behind.

This involved the unpalatable job of forcing plaintiffs' attorneys to try weak cases which they had felt obliged to accept from lawyers who sometimes referred good cases to them, but which they feared would result in defendants' verdicts and a consequent loss of prestige. So they sought to avert the evil day by repeatedly adjourning these cases. I also had to force defendants' lawyers to proceed to trial in strong cases which would probably result in large verdicts for the plaintiffs. This required keeping a chart of other court engagements of those plaintiffs' and defendants' attorneys who appeared in most of the negligence actions.

No profundity is required of a calendar judge. But he must be practical, firm, and resourceful, or he will find himself in the distressing position of hearing several judges clamoring for cases to try, while he has no ready cases to send them. He must know the lawyers who appear before him—their reliability, honesty, and office resources. He must be able to recognize and pierce their wiles and stratagems.

The calling of the four calendars, what with passing on excuses and applications, consumes an hour. The disposition of the cases marked for "second call" takes the remainder of the morning. Cases are so marked when one of the parties wishes to enlist the court's aid in a final effort to settle the case before going to trial. Or a judge will hold a case for the second call when he is trying to pin down elusive counsel to get ready for trial, and does not wish to delay the call of the remainder of the calendar for so protracted a discussion. The eternal tussling with reluctant lawyers becomes wearying.

And all through the day the jury clerk brings in contingents of jurors who wish to be excused or have their date of service deferred. Judges are very lenient in granting deferments the first and even the second time they are sought. When a businessman advances the usual excuse of having been summoned at the height of his season, we invite him to select a date which will fall within his slowest season. We then defer his service to that date. We are patient when he returns a second time and states that business is unexpectedly active and he cannot be spared. We may even be tolerant a third time, if he has a fair record of jury service in the past. But if he has an unbroken record of excusals and evasions, we then stiffen and require him to serve.

This morning was busier than usual. The county clerk had brought contempt proceedings against a score of persons summoned for jury duty, who had failed to respond to, and disregarded completely, at least two notices. The petitions to punish for contempt were all returnable this morning.

Most of the respondents admitted receiving the notices, but advanced a variety of reasons for failing to appear. One offered the excuse that he had turned the notices over to an influential friend, and had been assured the matter had been "taken care of." A few denied receiving any notice, and in their matters I conducted short hearings and took testimony, and was convinced in most of the cases that they had received at least some of the many notices sent them. I fined those who had never served previously from twenty to one hundred dollars each. Those who had some record of service were fined lesser amounts.

After the clerk had made the noon hour call to fifteen parts and ascertained that they all had cases in various stages of trial, I directed four of the ready cases to return at 2 P.M., and passed the remainder of the calendar to the following morning. I estimated that four cases would be a safe reserve to take care of the afternoon demands. Often a judge who reports in the morning that he cannot take another case calls frantically for one in the afternoon. The case on trial is settled or dismissed; the next case is settled; a third one he is holding in the part is not ready because a witness left town on a business trip.

During this afternoon the judge in only one part asked for a case, at about half-past two. When the clerk's 3 P.M. calls disclosed that all of the parts were busy, I released the three remaining cases until the following morning. The lawyers would return then with their witnesses, and would in all probability be assigned to parts during the morning. After the three o'clock call all jurors being held in readiness were also dismissed for the day.

All through the day, whenever there was a lull, I would call counsel in the various cases to the bench and explore the possibilities of settling their cases. In this fashion I managed to settle fourteen cases.

During the course of the month I conducted the trial of a few cases. I selected only nonjury cases, since they are usually short, and can be accommodated to the many interruptions in a calendar part much more easily than jury cases. I was about to start the trial of a nonjury case late this morning when I learned that a friend and former client of mine was a key witness. I disqualified myself and sent the case to another part.

There is no need for concern when a friend is a party or an important witness in a case tried before a jury. It is another matter if the case is a nonjury one, and the judge must decide the facts as well as the law. In such a case the judge must pass upon the credibility of the witness and decide whether or not his friend is telling the truth.

Every judge fashions his own formula for handling such situations. There are no fixed rules or law which govern. A judge in a rural district is confronted constantly with neighbors and friends who appear as lawyers, litigants, and witnesses. There are no facilities for transferring any case to another judge, so he must dispose of it himself. In an urban district there are generally several judges of identical jurisdiction and a judge has a wider area of discretion.

At four o'clock I performed a wedding ceremony in chambers. This is a power I exercise very sparingly, since I regard it as essentially in the province of the clergy. But I have no hesitancy in officiating when one or both of the couple are friends. I feel that the warmth of our relationship compensates for the inadequacy of my performance. Whenever possible, I try to conduct such ceremonies in my own home, in the belief that it affords a more agreeable scene to review in later years than my bustling chambers. Besides, I can serve drinks after the ceremony—something I would not do in chambers.

I performed this marriage at the request of a colleague. The ceremony had been scheduled for his chambers, but he had been taken ill and had asked me to substitute for him. For the couple's book of memories I tried to muster all the eloquence and graciousness at my command, but I fear I made a poor job of it. It was nonetheless legal.

I am reminded of a former judge, now gone to his just reward, whose marriage ritual consisted of the following:

"Do you want to marry him?"

"Do you want to marry her?"

"Okay, you're married."

His marriages were just as legal and binding as those performed by the most courtly of jurists, in the most flowing and felicitous prose. And I have no reason to doubt they were just as happy and successful.

I also held an informal hearing this afternoon on a matter stemming from the special trust mortgage term over which I preside. The management of a large midtown office building, owned indirectly by several thousand bondholders, sought approval of an expenditure of eighty thousand dollars to convert three floors of the building from D.C. to A.C. current. It contended that in order to meet competition from the better-class buildings in that area it was necessary to supply tenants with air-cooled rooms, or at the least to furnish an electric supply system upon which they could construct their own air-cooling units. Under the provisions of the trust mortgage indenture, management had to procure court approval for a capital expenditure in that amount.

I knew very little of the mechanics or economics of the proposed change. I therefore heard expert testimony, both of an engineering and real estate nature. The board of directors of the bondholders' corporation and the managing agent of the building unanimously favored the expenditure. My job was to protect the bondholders. Because of my confidence in the management, and the supporting opinions of the experts, I signified my approval of the proposed outlay.

Upon the conclusion of this conference, and after sundry telephone calls and discussions with my secretary, it was time to leave for home and dinner. I took with me a dozen motions for preferences in the trials of accident cases. These are motions to advance a case to the ready day calendar, so that it will be a matter of weeks instead of years before it will be reached for trial. Judges are quite chary of granting these applications, and have evolved rigid and well-settled rules, which are sometimes harsh in application.

There are scores of such motions every month, returnable before the calendar judge. If he acted in accordance with the dictates of his heart, and without deeper reflection, he would grant almost all of them. Many present pitiful situations, with the long, dreary intervals before trial looming up as unendurable. Most of them fall into one of two categories. Either the plaintiff is unable to work because of the injuries sustained and is destitute, or the plaintiff is aged and in such physical condition that he or she is not likely to live until the trial is reached.

But a judge must bear in mind that every case so preferred over others displaces or retards a case that has wended its way tortuously to the day calendar for over three years. And so judges have held fairly consistently that the competent proof of destitution is evidence that the plaintiff is on the public relief rolls. In the other category a doctor's affidavit is generally required, setting forth the plaintiff's condition and asserting that he will not live until the trial can be reached in regular order.

After dinner I disposed of the preference motions I had brought home. With one exception I adhered to the rules in general use. That exception involved an elderly woman, who, it was clear from the papers, had seen better times. She was without funds and had no recourse for financial aid to friends or relatives. She was eligible for relief, but would not apply for it. Her situation was desperate. A judge develops hunches about the good faith of litigants. Even from so unsatisfactory a medium as affidavits I was convinced that this application was made in good faith and out of desperation. It was unlikely that any judgment or settlement three years later would benefit her much, if at all. An early recovery, however, could ease her declining years. I granted her motion and placed her case on the ready day calendar for the following week.

By the time I had disposed of these motions I was ready for bed. Although I was tired, my brain was spinning too rapidly to augur well for a restful night. So I dipped into a *Law Review* article, which soon produced the usual and desired effect.

A December Day

This morning began the perennial, uncomfortable task of returning Christmas presents and of returning them with a minimum of offense to the givers. Ever since I became a judge I have accepted gifts only from persons with whom I would exchange presents before I went on the bench. I have returned presents from lawyers, real estate firms, and others having business with the courts; returned them as pleasantly, but as firmly, as I know how.

As a result of this practice the flow of Christmas gifts has declined perceptibly from year to year. But this morning I had to refuse two handsome packages which had arrived at my home the day before. One contained a dozen Sulka ties, sent by the president of a large real estate management firm; the other was a case of liquor, sent by a very successful and eminent lawyer.

I knew both these men well enough to address them by their first names. I had occasionally appointed a vice-president of the real estate man's company as an appraiser, simply because he was the best-qualified expert I knew on values in a certain Manhattan area. I had twice appointed the lawyer as a referee, without political recommendation, because he was an honest and competent man.

Neither man was deviating appreciably from general commercial usage in sending the gifts. I know as a practical matter that their Christmas lists were made up not only to express appreciation for past favors, but perhaps also in anticipation of favors to come. However, in both of these instances the men knew that the appointments had been made and merited on the basis of exceptional qualifications for the job.

But the reason I returned the gifts was that we enjoyed no social relationship, either before or after I went on the bench, to warrant an exchange. The giving was to be one-sided. I am sure that had I accepted the gifts and responded with equally expensive ones, both gentlemen would have been astounded.

So I wrote each of them a letter, explaining that only my unvarying practice over the years caused me to return their thoughtful holiday remembrances; that I was very appreciative, but could not breach my rule even once, etc., etc. My wife, I informed one, would return the ties to Sulka and have his account credited. I asked the other to instruct his dealer to pick up the liquor.

These letters dictated, I turned to court business. I was sitting in a motion part, Special Term Part III. Here are heard motions for summary judgment, temporary injunctions, motions addressed to the pleadings, and other types generally regarded as more difficult and involved.

Most motions are submitted by both sides without argument. The judge decides them upon the papers submitted with the motion. At least, this holds true in New York County, where the calendars are so long that it would be impossible to hear arguments on all motions.

Of those motions that are argued, I find the argument helpful in most instances. It helps eliminate from consideration the points which lawyers will raise in their briefs from an excess of caution, but which they do not believe in themselves. When pressed during argument they will often abandon these points.

An oral exposition of the alleged facts often gives the judge a better "feel" of the issues in the case than he can acquire from reading the papers. In oral argument lawyers will discuss the conduct and relationship of the parties more readily and bluntly than they do in affidavit and brief. A judge will grasp quickly underlying motivations and concealed situations which he could at best only suspect after a close reading of the motion papers. For example, while hearing arguments later this morning on a motion for summary judgment in a case involving the alleged purchase of a large shipment of textiles, I noticed that both lawyers skirted gingerly around the second of two conferences which their clients had held. Since this latter conference had taken place after the terms had been arranged at a previous meeting of the principals, and after the order had been given and the invoice had been issued, I could not understand its purpose. The manner in which counsel veered away from any discussion of this conference aroused my suspicions. A few questions from the bench gave me reason to suspect that this had been a black-market transaction, and that the second conference had been called for a clandestine payment—in cash.

If a lawyer has the ability to preface his discussion of the law with a simple and lucid statement of the facts and issues, his argument will be very helpful to the judge. But very often lawyers are so immersed in their cases that they lack the perspective to outline the facts and issues with sufficient clarity. They discuss them either very sketchily or at great length, but in such disorderly and disorganized fashion that a judge cannot understand them. The argument upon the law then becomes a discussion of familiar legal principles in a vacuum, because the judge has no factual structure in which to house them.

A judge can seldom extricate a lawyer who has thus become mired in his own argument. If he asks questions, the lawyer flounders and struggles, but sinks still deeper. If the judge is polite, he will give up and hear an unintelligible argument through to its conclusion. If he grows impatient, he will cut the lawyer short and tell him to submit his papers.

There are certain issues which cannot be presented swiftly, clearly, and succinctly, particularly if the motion involves the study and interpretation of contracts or documents. Disputed clauses are more intelligible when read in context than when quoted in the course of oral argument. Since I receive impressions much better through reading the written word than through oral communication, I thought that perhaps my experience was unique. I therefore discussed this problem with many of my colleagues. Each has assured me that he has often permitted lawyers to finish completely unintelligible arguments. And several expressed relief upon learning I had encountered similar difficulties.

I suspect that some of the insistence of lawyers upon oral argument stems from a fear that judges will not read their briefs. I hasten to assure them that we do, and that we are grateful for scholarly and enlightening briefs. As with any other document, the more compact and less discursive the brief, the greater the concentration and sustained interest with which it will be read.

All through this month of December I would be reminded that the year was drawing to a close. Of course, late in the month the court, like all other enterprises, succumbs to the holiday mood. But a good deal of the court's business also bears the impress of the year's end. Corporations seek to effectuate certain changes within the calendar year. Litigants and lawyers rush papers to receive certain payments within the tax year.

So another year has passed—another year of fulfillment in the public service. As in any other occupation, a year filled with successes and failures, with satisfactions and frustrations. I can imagine no other calling in which the successes are so satisfying, or the failures so frustrating.

THE JUDGMENT OF THE COURT

[illegible]

THE JUDGMENT OF THE COURT

As the years march on there forms an ever-growing library of my decisions on all common legal subjects and on many uncommon ones. This process was illustrated graphically in the recent play based upon the life of Justice Holmes, *The Magnificent Yankee.* All the scenes were laid in Justice Holmes' study and only one change was made in the set. Each time the curtain dropped between scenes, denoting the lapse of years, more shelves were added to the bookcases which housed the United States Supreme Court reports. Law reports are the indestructible and incorruptible evidence of a judge's growth or decline.

As I reflect back upon the last ten years, I realize that in many of its aspects the position is not what I had envisaged before I ascended the bench. I thought it would afford me leisure to do some of the things—such as varied reading—which had been foreclosed by lack of time and energy when I was a busy practicing lawyer. If anything, I do less reading, outside of the domain of legal literature, than I did before. As a judicial craftsman of the law I must keep my tools sharpened for a far greater variety of tasks than was required of me as a lawyer. This involves unending reading of law journals, advance sheets, reports, law review articles and texts, aside from the reading and study of briefs and the research required in the disposition of specific court business.

I am still unable to order certain mechanics of my life in much better fashion than before. I am, however, subject to fewer strains and stresses. There are occasions when a judge works under pressure. Sometimes a decision must be made speedily; sometimes a novel problem must be studied far into the night for a charge to the jury the following morning. The strains, however, are more akin to those of the campus than of the market place. There are no client-lawyer relationships, with demands often impossible of fulfillment. There are no clients, judges, bureau heads, or jurors whose kindly nods must be courted, and upon which success and reputation hang.

The standards of success in the judiciary are largely self-imposed, dependent upon the conscience and capability of the individual judge. And it offers a complete culture in itself, an assimilation of life, in a contemplative atmosphere not often attainable by moderns. A judge's sphere would seem to cover the widest range of knowledge—knowledge and learning prepared by experts and seldom served to persons in other callings.

Judges, of course, have economic problems, but they too differ from those of lawyers. Judges' salaries are fixed and certain. A lawyer can make a fee in a single matter that will carry his office for a year; but he is constantly ground between the uncertainty of continuance of income and the eternal fixity of overhead.

So, few judges ever leave the bench, unless compelled to by operation of age limitation or the will of the electorate. It is much more often interesting than dull, sometimes exciting, and affords continuous contact with people and ideas. And, at least to me, it seems vitally important in its continuing contributions to the functioning of our structure of living.

John Dewey has said:

"As an individual passes from one situation to another, his world, his environment, expands or contracts. . . . What he has learned in the way of knowledge and skill in one situation becomes an instrument of understanding and dealing effectively with the situations which follow. The process goes on as long as life and learning continue . . . every experience should do something to prepare a person for later experiences of a deeper and more expansive quality. That is the very meaning of growth, continuity, reconstruction of experience."

My boyhood and later experiences prepared me for my work as a judge; but growth and development continued after I had become a judge and must of necessity continue unless I wither on the vine. I realize finally that every judicial experience does not drive a stake bounding further growth, but rather pierces another cloud which had hitherto hidden the illimitable skies.

ABOUT THE AUTHOR

Bernard Botein *was born in New York in 1900, and was educated in the schools and colleges of that city. In 1941, when he was appointed a Justice of the New York State Supreme Court, he was practicing law actively as a senior member of a prominent law firm. He had also earned a distinguished record in public service. As Governor Lehman's trouble-shooter, he had investigated the State Insurance Fund and state printing frauds. On behalf of the Bar Associations of New York he had headed an accident fraud inquiry, which, in 1938, earned the American Bar Association award to the local bar association rendering the activity most beneficial to the bar and the public. He is the co-author of a book entitled* The Slum and Crime, *which was quoted repeatedly by Senator Wagner in his fight for remedial housing legislation. He has contributed frequently to law journals and insurance periodicals. Justice Botein is married and has two children.*